Outstanding Studies in
Early American History

EDITED BY
John Murrin
Princeton University

A Garland Series

The Anglican Clergy in Maryland, 1692–1776

Carol van Voorst

Garland Publishing, Inc.
NEW YORK & LONDON   1989

Library of Congress Cataloging-in-Publication Data

van Voorst, Carol.
       The Anglican clergy in Maryland, 1692–1776 / Carol van Voorst.
      p. cm. — (Outstanding studies in early American history)
   Thesis (Ph.D.)—Princeton, 1978.
        Bibliography: p.
        ISBN 0-8240-6293-0 (alk. paper)
        1. Church of England—Maryland—Clergy—History. 2. Church of
England—Maryland—History. 3. Church and state—Maryland—History.
4. Anglican Communion—Maryland—Clergy—History. 5. Anglican
Communion—Maryland—History. 6. Maryland—Church history.
I. Title. II. Series.
BX5917.M3V36   1989
283'.752'09033—dc20   89–7792

Printed on acid-free, 250-year-life paper

MANUFACTURED IN THE UNITED STATES OF AMERICA

Table of Contents

Page

Acknowledgments   iii
List of Tables   vi
Abbreviations   vii

Introduction   4

Part One: **The "Body Without a Head": The Anglican Church in Maryland**

    Chapter I: The Church in Maryland, 1692 - 1750   8

    Chapter II: The Church in Maryland, 1750 - 1776   60

Part Two: **The Anglican Clergy in Maryland**

    Chapter III: Recruitment   98

      The Inflow of Ministers   108
      Ethnic Origins   122
      Social Origins   130
      Education   137

    Chapter IV: Professional Careers   147

      Tenure   181
      Clerical Conduct and Reputation   204

    Chapter V: Wealth   219

    Chapter VI: The Clergy in Society   267

      Families   267
      Parochial Relations   274
      Social Life   288

Epilogue   298

Appendix A: The Church and State in England   301
Appendix B: Ministers Officiating in Maryland,
              1692 - 1775   310
Appendix C: Ministers Accused of Irregular Conduct   311
Select Bibliography   313

Acknowledgments

I am very grateful to those who have helped me complete this thesis.
I cannot thank them all here, but I would like to mention my appreciation
of several people who have been particularly helpful. I thank F. Garner
Ranney, historiographer of the Maryland Diocesan Library in Baltimore,
for his aid, suggestions, and the keys to out-of-the-way collections.
The staffs of the manuscript division of the Maryland Historical Society
and the Maryland Hall of Records were very kind, and pointed out sources
I would otherwise have missed. Edward C. Papenfuse, director of the
Legislative History Project in Annapolis, gave me permission to use the
Project's files, an invaluable collection of officeholding and genealogical
material, and I am grateful to Carol Tolles and Maurine Pyle, members of
the LHP, for discussing them with me. Lois Green Carr and Lorena Walsh
of the St. Mary's City Commission, housed in the Hall of Records, were
very free with information concerning the use of probate materials. I
owe special thanks to both of them. Allan Kulikoff and Russell Menard
also contributed advice. In the final stages of the thesis, Marilyn van
Voorst worked as the proverbial navvy, typing the manuscript to meet the
deadline. Above all, I would like to thank John M. Murrin, my advisor,
who for the past three years has dispensed information, criticism, and
cheer as needed. Studying with a man who so gladly teaches has been a
privilege and pleasure.

All errors and misinterpretations are, of course, my own.

Tables

	Page
Maryland Parishes, 1694–1776	101
Annual Inflow of Ministers into Maryland, 1692–1776	110
Total Arrivals per Decade	111
Influx of Ministers into Maryland from Other Colonial Livings	118
Ethnic Origins of Maryland Ministers	123
The Education of Maryland Clergy by Arrival Date (Inclusive Degrees)	139
The Education of Maryland Clergy by Arrival Date (Terminal Degrees)	140
The Education of Maryland Ministers by Ethnic Background	142
Degree Holding Incumbents in Maryland and Leicestershire, by Terminal Degrees	144
Proportion of Ministers to Population	157
Proportion of Ministers to White Population	157
Parish Vacancies in Cumulative Years per Parish, 1692–1776	186
Parish Vacancies in Percentage of Period of Parish Existence	186
Number of Parishes Successively Held as Incumbent, by Decade of Arrival	193
Parish Incomes, c. 1698, in Tobacco	226
Parish Incomes, c. 1698, at 1.0 Pence Sterling per Pound of Tobacco	228
Parish Incomes, c. 1698, at 5 shillings per Hundredweight of Tobacco	228
Salaries According to "List of the Parishes in Maryland and Their Annual Values, as Returned in the Year 1767"	249
Landownership at Death, Removal Out of Maryland, or the Revolution	260
Landownership at Death, Removal Out of Maryland, or the Revolution, by Decade of Arrival in the Province	260
Inventoried Estates by Decade of Death	264

Abbreviations

Repositories

DLC   Library of Congress, Washington, D.C.

MdA   Maryland Hall of Records, Annapolis, Maryland

MdDL   Maryland Diocesan Library, in the Maryland
                      Historical Society, Baltimore, Maryland

MdHi   Maryland Historical Society, Baltimore, Maryland

Periodicals and Series

Arch. Md.   Archives of Maryland

HMPEC   Historical Magazine of the Protestant Episcopal
                      Church

Md. Hist. Mag.   Maryland Historical Magazine

WMQ   William and Mary Quarterly

Introduction

In 1692 the Maryland legislature passed an act "for the Service of
Almighty God and the Establishment of the Protestant Religion within this
Province." This was the first of four laws enacted within a ten-year
period to settle the Church of England in the colony. Three of them,
passed by the legislature in 1692, 1696, and 1700, were disallowed by the
Crown for constitutional and political reasons, but in 1702 the legislature
approved an establishment bill which received the assent of Queen Anne the
following year. From March 1702 until November 1776, when the Maryland
Convention adopted a Declaration of Rights, the Anglican Church was the
premier religious institution in the province.

The ministers who served in the Maryland Church were members of a
unique organization. Although the Church claimed to be episcopalian, it
was so only in doctrine, not in polity. Like the other colonial Anglican
institutions, the Maryland Church lacked a diocesan, a consecrated super-
visor. The bishops of London, nominally the superiors of the American
clergy, were situated at too great a distance to exercise any real authority.
Their legal claim to any colonial jurisdiction, moreover, was questionable
for most of the seventeenth and eighteenth centuries. A commissary supplied
needed ecclesiastical leadership in some of the American colonies, but in

Maryland such an officer presided over the clergy for no more than fifteen years out of the entire establishment period. Most of the time, the Maryland Church was, as two ministers described it in 1753, "a Body without a head."[1]

However, only in a canonical sense did the Church lack a superior. The effective head of the Maryland establishment was the provincial executive, who wielded extensive ecclesiastical powers. He presented and inducted ministers to livings, and, for most of the period, he was the only authority to claim successfully the power to suspend and deprive irregular clergy. Indeed, the religious prerogatives of the Maryland executive extended into areas the Church regarded, jealously, as its proper sphere. The executive was not the only secular agency to invade traditionally ecclesiastical privileges. The colonial legislature attempted several times to bring the Church more completely under the control of the state by instituting lay supervision over clerical morals. Relations between the Church and the state were strained for most of the period of the establishment.

The Maryland clergy did not, as did their British colleagues, function in a permanent and secure establishment. Sanctioned by the Crown, the Establishment Act of 1702 was considered sacred and inviolable by the clergy, but the legislature amended provisions in the Act practically from the moment it was signed by the queen. The alterations which most perturbed the clergy were ones which changed the financial settlement of the Church. Originally, clerical stipends were based on a tobacco poll tax imposed on parishioners. During the course of the establishment, the legislature

---

[1] Hugh Jones and Henry Addison to Bishop Thomas Sherlock, August 27, 1753, in William Stevens Perry, Historical Collections Relating to the American Colonial Church (Hartford, Conn., 1870-1878), IV, 332.

altered the amount and the medium of payment.

The complex history of the Maryland Church is best studied by combining an examination of the Church as an institution with a prosopographical study of the men who staffed the provincial livings. Approximately two hundred ministers officiated in Anglican pulpits in the colony between 1692 and 1776. Scoundrels and prodigies, poets and near-illiterates, adventurers and visionaries, they shared a profession, a location, and a peculiar occupational situation. The organization they served changed considerably over time, both in response to events occurring outside of the institution and to developments taking place within the ministry itself. Without consideration of the Church as a collection of individuals, the history of the Church as a unified institution makes little sense.

This study is divided roughly into two parts. Chapters I and II provide a brief chronological and institutional history of the Church. They deal with the establishment, the legal structure of the Church, Church-state relations, and the problems encountered by those who wished to replicate the parent Church in a colonial setting. The following chapter focuses on the clergy themselves, discussing their ethnic, educational, and social background. Patterns in recruitment are traced. Chapter IV describes the professional lives of the provincial clergy, explaining changes in the employment market, the types of tenure available to the ministers, and their relations with their congregations. The performance of the ministers as pastors and spiritual leaders is assessed here. The chapter on wealth is really the pivot of the thesis, for the economic changes which occurred in the Church had extraordinarily important ramifications on almost every facet of clerical life. The concluding chapter examines the clergy as members of society rather than members of a profession, as family men and citizens instead of priests.

The sources for the Maryland Church are to be found primarily in three Maryland repositories. The Maryland Diocesan Library in Baltimore houses a large manuscript collection pertaining to the episcopalian colonial clergy. The collection includes sermons, ordination records, family and business papers, and parish records. Copies of published sermons generally thought lost are actually available here. The Maryland Historical Society, also in Baltimore, contains a large store of colonial documents and papers useful to the topic. The Hall of Records in Annapolis contains the probate, land, and legal records of the ministers, besides state papers, parish records, and miscellaneous papers pertaining to the Church. I have also used the S.P.G. and Fulham Library papers in the Library of Congress.

All dates given here prior to 1752 are in Old Style, except that the date of the New Year has been changed to accord with modern usage.

Part One

THE "BODY WITHOUT A HEAD": THE ANGLICAN CHURCH IN MARYLAND

Chapter I

The Church in Maryland, 1692 - 1750

Determined and persistent men tried and failed to erect a miniature replica of the English Established Church in Maryland. Most of the British protestant churches could transplant themselves quite easily to the New World. The sects practicing congregational autonomy, for example, simply formed new independent congregations. The churches with presbyterian-type structures delegated authority to overseas chapters which then supervised the formation of local cells. The Anglican Church, however, was not a self-contained, independent religious institution. It was a complex temporal organization buttressed by and subjugated to a state. Church and state were almost inseparable, even in theory. Anglicanism, the faith, defined and demanded the establishment of episcopalism, the church polity, which was impossible to maintain without the consent and the aid of the state. In England this Erastian[1] relationship sustained the preeminence of the Church relative to other denominations. The very tightness of the bond, however, was largely to blame for the Church's problems in the colonies. It incapacitated the Anglican Church from replicating itself in America without the approval and support of the state, and this project, unfortunately for the Church, did not much interest the English governments of the seventeenth and eighteenth centuries.

An extreme dependence on the cooperation of the state was not the only handicap plaguing those who desired a united Church in the colonies. The Anglican Church was an established institution which had developed in close conjunction with the social, political, legal, and economic structures

---

[1] So called after Thomas Erastus (1524-1583), a Swiss theologian who preached the dominance of state over church.

in England. It had been tailored to suit a particular environment. In
the colonies the Church was confronted with a variety of governments,
societies, and judicial establishments, and despite the efforts of Churchmen to replicate its traditional English internal constitution, the
Church was forced to adapt to new external conditions. It changed a great
deal in the process. Everywhere the Anglican Church was established its
structure was altered to fit the local setting,[1] with the result that it
splintered into a series of provincial churches so mutated from the parent
body that in form they were not episcopalian at all.

***

Church and Crown arrived together in Maryland, the products of the
Glorious Revolution of 1688-1689. Prompted by news of the deposition of
James II of England, a number of Marylanders with political and religious
grievances against Charles Calvert, the third Lord Baltimore, overthrew the
government of the Catholic proprietor in the summer of 1689. A convention
of county delegates subsequently petitioned the Crown to revoke Baltimore's
charter and to place Maryland under a royal government. The request was
favorably received in England. Although efforts to invalidate the charter
failed, King William III effectively removed Baltimore from political power
when he commissioned Lionel Copley as royal governor in June 1691. The new
chief executive arrived in Maryland in April 1692. Two months later Copley
signed an act establishing the Anglican Church in the colony.[2]

---

[1] The Church was established in Virginia in 1607, in Barbados in 1650,
in Maryland in 1692, in six counties in New York in 1693, in South Carolina
in 1704-1706, in North Carolina in 1701-1703, and in Georgia in 1758.

[2] For a full account of the Revolution in the colony, see Lois Green
Carr and David William Jordan, Maryland's Revolution of Government, 1689-
1692 (Ithaca, N.Y., 1974).

Laymen conceived and carried out the initial establishment of the Maryland Church. Henry Compton, who as Bishop of London was nominally the diocesan of the colonies, was the only cleric involved in the settlement. His participation was due less to his ecclesiastical position than it was to his membership in the Lords of Trade. Created in 1675, the Lords were a standing committee of the Privy Council, charged with advising the king on matters regarding trade and colonial affairs. Before the Revolution concerned Anglican Lords had been blocked from interfering in religious affairs in Maryland because the charter of 1632 guaranteed the proprietors the right to govern the colony as a private religious palatine.[1] In their September 1689 address to William III, however, the convention delegates asked the king to appoint a government which would secure the protestant religion as well as the civil rights and liberties of the colonists.[2] Though the petitioners did not request the establishment of the Church, the Crown chose to interpret this and later communications as an invitation to promote such an action. The Lords of Trade sent Governor Copley to Maryland with instructions roughly outlining the structure of the colonial Church, and with an obligation to press the legislature for a formal act of establishment.

Copley's instructions concerning ecclesiastical affairs in Maryland were not unusual for that time. Bishop Compton, anxious to strengthen the

---

[1] The charter (reprinted in Newton D. Mereness, Maryland as a Proprietary Province [New York, 1901], 507-520) permitted the Calverts to rule Maryland as the medieval bishops had ruled the Palatine of Durham. Though the early proprietors were Catholics, they signed a toleration act in 1649 which allowed all Christians in Maryland to worship peacefully. Anglicans were not, however, granted the legal privileges they enjoyed in England. During the 1670s Charles Calvert had been obliged repeatedly to answer queries of the Lords regarding religion in Maryland. Some of the queries and answers are conveniently reprinted in Percy G. Skirven, The First Parishes of the Province of Maryland (Baltimore, 1923), 23-34.

[2] William Hand Browne et al., eds., Archives of Maryland, 72 volumes, (Baltimore, 1883--   ), XIII, 239; hereafter cited as Arch. Md.

Church in the royal colonies, was largely responsible for the routine inclusion of religious instructions in the orders sent to royal governors by the Lords of Trade.[1] Copley was ordered to see that God was "devoutly and duly served" in Maryland and that "the Book of Common Prayer as it is now established [be] Read each Sunday and holiday and the blessed Sacrament [be] administred according to the Rites of the Church of England." He was forbidden to prefer ministers to benefices without a certificate from the bishop of London that they had conformed to the Church of England. The governor was also instructed to issue orders making ministers members of the parish vestries. The Lords of Trade concluded Copley's instructions with their usual summation of gubernatorial and diocesan ecclesiastical authority in the colonies:

> And to the end the Ecclesiasticall Iurisdiction of
> the said Bishop of London may take place in that our
> Province as far as conveniently may be We do think
> fit that you give all countenance and Encouragement
> in the exercise of the same excepting only the
> Colating to Benefices, Granting Licenses for Marriage
> and Probate of Wills, which we have reserved to You
> our Governor or the Commander in Chief for the time
> being.[2]

The orders given to Copley demonstrated the subordination of the colonial Church to secular authorities. For reasons of efficiency or necessity, laymen in London granted colonial officers of state temporal rights customarily reserved for ranking churchmen. The absence of Church courts and legal departments in the colonies led unavoidably to secular control of probate and testamentary proceedings. The lack of a prelate with unquestioned authority over colonial ministers and benefices resulted in lay intervention

---

[1] A discussion of religious instructions to governors during this period may be found in Arthur L. Cross, The Anglican Episcopate and the American Colonies (New York, 1902), 26-27, 29-30, 32. Cross describes Compton's concern for the colonial churches as a member of the Lords of Trade on pp. 25-32.

[2] Governor Copley's instructions regarding ecclesiastical affairs are in Arch. Md., VIII, 276-277.

in matters of ecclesiastical management and discipline. In Maryland, for
instance, Copley was authorized to present and to induct ministers, i.e.,
he could choose ministers to fill vacant livings and then he could legally
invest them with freehold rights to the livings. By English law various lay
and ecclesiastical agencies could present ministers, but only bishops could
induct them. In another departure from English law, Copley was given the
right to remove a minister from his living if the incumbent appeared to the
governor "to give scandall either by his doctrine or manners."[1] Ordinarily
the removal of an incumbent required an episcopal command. Bishop Compton
surely thought the concessions deplorable, but as a pragmatic man he
realized that a fundamental reason for the losses was that the Church in
America had no responsible, accredited superior. Since before the English
Civil War the bishops of London had assumed supervision over the colonial
Church. Their claim to ecclesiastical supremacy, however, was not certified
by any statutes or legal ordinances. Bishop Compton knew that there was
no hope of reversing or ending the usurpations in America unless he obtained
an official acknowledgment of his colonial authority. By 1691 the only
legal recognition the bishop had managed to secure was the rather vaguely
worded concluding paragraph in the instructions sent by the Lords of Trade
to royal governors.[2]

Lionel Copley could have fulfilled most of his ecclesiastical
instructions by simple executive order. The exceptions were the commands
to provide a "competent maintenance" and a house for every Anglican minister
in the province.[3] These orders involved the allocation of colonial revenues,
and Copley had to ask the legislature to grant them.

---

[1] Arch. Md., VIII, 276.
[2] Cross, Anglican Episcopate, 29-30.
[3] Arch. Md., VIII, 276.

Because the legislative journals for this period record action rather than debate, they reveal little about support for and nothing about opposition to the bill "To Lay the Province into Parishes and that care be taken for provision for the Clergy" ordered drawn up on May 16, 1692.[1] The most important decision was reached on May 27, when the lower house debated whether to provide the clergy with stipends of twenty or forty pounds of tobacco per parish taxable and voted to allow the ministers forty.[2] Although pressured by the council,[3] the delegates declined to rubberstamp all of Copley's instructions. They refused for the moment to furnish glebes[4] or houses for the clergy and they did not admit ministers into the parish vestries.[5] Apparently neither the council nor the governor pressed the issues. Copley signed Maryland's first establishment act on June 9, 1692.[6]

The "Act for the Service of Almighty God and the Establishment of the Protestant Religion within this Province" began with a preamble which neatly summarized the reason for the act from the point of view of the government:

> Foreasmuch as in a well Governed Commonwealth Matters of Religion and the Honour of God ought in the first place to be taken in serious consideration, and nothing being more acceptable to Almighty God than the true and Sincere worship and Service of him according to his Holy Word.

It proceeded to enact

That the Church of England within this Province

---

[1] Arch. Md., XIII, 369.

[2] Arch. Md., XIII, 396. Given the population density of the province, twenty pounds of tobacco per poll was an insultingly meager stipend.

[3] Carefully selected by the Lords of Trade, eleven of the twelve members of the council were Anglicans. Carr and Jordan, Maryland's Revolution, 170.

[4] A glebe was a plot of land held as a freehold by the incumbent of an ecclesiastical living.

[5] Arch. Md., XIII, 306, 309.

[6] The act is printed in Arch. Md., XIII, 425-430.

> shall have and Enjoy all her Rights Liberties and
> Franchises wholly inviolable as is now or shall be
> hereafter Established by Law, and also that the
> Great Charter of England be kept and observed in
> all points.[1]

These declarations were ambitious, nicely deferential to the dignity
of the Church, and totally impossible to put into effect. The powers
granted to the governor by the Lords of Trade already violated the Church's
rights and liberties. Moreover, the judicial structure in Maryland was
completely secular and had been constructed without regard to English
conventions of ecclesiastical jurisdiction.[2]

The act authorized commissioners and justices to divide the province
into parishes. Following this, the parish freeholders were to choose six
of their "most able men" to form a vestry. A closed corporate body, the
vestry could sue, accept donations to the church, and fill its own vacancies. Its chief duty was to control the parish's tobacco. The county
sheriff was responsible for collecting forty pounds of tobacco from each
taxable (defined as all males and all slaves over sixteen) and delivering
the tobacco to the vestrymen after deducting five percent as his
commission. The vestry was to use the tobacco to build a conveniently-
located church or chapel. Once the building was completed, the forty per
poll would become the stipend of the parish incumbent.[3]

---

[1] Arch. Md., XIII, 425-426. This odd conjunction of Magna Charta and
Church liberties was an effort by the assembly to obtain from the Crown a
guarantee that the colonists would enjoy all the rights of Englishmen. A
more direct approach would have certainly failed. The Crown, however, did
not miss the significance of the rider and vetoed the establishment bill
because of its inclusion. See David S. Lovejoy, The Glorious Revolution
in America (New York, 1972), 368-370.

[2] Lois Green Carr, "County Government in Maryland, 1689-1709" (Ph.D.
diss., Harvard University, 1968), 13. Indeed, immediately following this
broad declaration of Church rights the act listed a series of moral
offenses which were punishable solely by the civil courts.

[3] Arch. Md., XIII, 429.

The enactment of the establishment bill did not result in a great deal
of local activity. Within two years after it passed thirty parishes were
laid out and most of these had vestries, but the construction of churches
proceeded very slowly and the poll tax was haphazardly collected. Since
there were only about eight Anglican ministers in the entire province in
1694, the colonists probably felt little inclination to exert themselves.[1]

Governor Copley died in September 1693 and was succeeded by Francis
Nicholson, who arrived in Maryland in July 1694.[2] This former lieutenant
governor of Virginia was a dynamic Anglican, passionately determined to put
the Church on a sound footing in the New World. A friend of Bishop Compton,
Nicholson had experienced in Virginia the problems of the colonial
Church and was familiar with its immediate needs: more ministers, more
churches, houses, and glebes, and an ecclesiastical superior to the clergy
to ensure their good behavior.

Before the year was out Nicholson coaxed the legislature into passing
an additional act of religion. This measure rectified the failure of the
Establishment Act to include ministers in the vestry, and it also authorized
each vestry to select two churchwardens every year.[3] The following spring
the additional act of 1694 was repealed by a more forceful one. The act
of 1695 ordered that ministers were not only to be part of the vestry, they
were to serve as principal vestrymen. In addition, churchwardens (selected

---

[1] Arch Md., XX, 106-111; Skirven, First Parishes, passim. The figure
for ministers in the province is my own.

[2] David William Jordan, "The Royal Period of Colonial Maryland 1689-
1715" (Ph.D. diss., Princeton University, 1966), 114, 130. Jordan's thesis
includes a first-rate account of Nicholson's tenure in Maryland.

[3] Arch. Md., XXXVIII, 1-2. The practice of selecting two churchwardens
a year was a Virginian one. George MacLaren Bryden, Virginia's Mother
Church (Richmond, 1947), I, 454.

in the manner stipulated by the 1694 act) and vestrymen were all required to take oaths of allegiance.[1]

Through the council, meanwhile, Nicholson issued a stream of injunctions commanding the vestries to act as the law directed.[2] He was quite willing to sue negligent vestries for ignoring any aspect of their duties, and he inquired constantly into the conditions of vestries, churches, and ministers in the parishes.[3] As an example of public philanthropy, he volunteered to pay the full costs for surveying glebes and offered to donate ₤5 towards every parsonage built while he was governor.[4]

Nicholson was extremely perturbed to learn in the spring of 1696 that on January 4, 1696, the Crown had vetoed the Establishment Act of 1692 and the additional act of 1694.[5] No reason was given for the disallowance of the second act,[6] but the Establishment Act itself was vetoed because the Attorney General, Thomas Trevor, warned that the phrase "and also that the Great Charter of England be kept and observed in all points" violated the Maryland constitution and touched the king's prerogative. Thinking it politic to conceal the news, Nicholson called a session of the assembly and craftily recommended that the lower house draw up another, briefer act of religion.[7] The delegates obligingly rewrote the act of 1692 and added to it the post-1692 provisions regarding churchwardens and the vestry.[8] To

---

[1] Arch. Md., XXXVIII, 37-41. The vestrymen and churchwardens could be punished for failure to take the oaths or to fulfill their duties.

[2] Arch. Md., XX, 283, 284, 388, 523, 524, 584.

[3] Arch. Md., XX, 579-581.

[4] Arch. Md., XIX, 35.

[5] Jordan, "Royal Period," 172-173.

[6] The second act, though, was dependent on the first and was probably disallowed for that reason.

[7] Jordan, "Royal Period," 171-174.

[8] The 1696 act is in Arch. Md., XIX, 426-430.

Nicholson's dismay, the new bill included another guarantee that Marylanders
would "enjoy all their Rights and Libertys according to the Laws and
Statutes of the Kingdom of England."[1] Foreseeing another disallowance,
Nicholson cajoled, bargained, and lectured, but to no avail.[2] When the
lower house threatened to refer the bill to the next session, Nicholson
gave in and signed it.[3] By doing so he gave the ministers legal justification for demanding their salaries at least until the act was disallowed
in England.

Shortly before Nicholson had become lieutenant governor of Virginia
Bishop Compton, in a gesture which emphasized his uneasiness with the
diminution of Church self-government in the colonies, had appointed a
commissary to Virginia.[4] A commissary was an ecclesiastical officer who
held a commission from a bishop to fulfill certain stated duties. The
commissaries appointed by the bishops of London to the colonies were
usually charged with maintaining some measure of ecclesiastical discipline
over Church personnel.[5] Nicholson heartily wanted such an officer in
Maryland. No doubt under his prompting, the upper house recommended in
September 1694 that a fitting competency be arranged for a commissary who
would "Supervise the Lives & Conversations of the Clergy of this Province."[6]
The lower house agreed that a "Suffragan Bishop would be most requisite &
Necessary," but did not think it would be convenient to invite one to
Maryland until the province was able "to make suiteable provisions for his

[1] Arch. Md., XIX, 426.

[2] Arch. Md., XIX, 389, 390, 392-397.

[3] Arch. Md., XIX, 390, 418. Nicholson signed the bill on July 10, 1696.
The act is in Arch. Md., XIX, 426-430.

[4] James Blair's commission was dated 15 December 1689; Brydon,
Virginia's Mother Church, I, 280.

[5] Cross, Anglican Episcopate, 3.

[6] Arch. Md., XIX. 36.

reception and Residence here."[1] The assembly referred the question to the next session of the legislature. Not to be put off, the upper house immediately sent the delegates a letter stressing that "for the Better setling & Regulateing all matters Relateing to Churches and Churchmen" it was most necessary for Maryland to have a suffragan bishop or a commissary "invested with such Ecclesiasticall Authority & power" as Bishop Compton thought wise. The council suggested that the provincial commissary general's office would be a suitable post to bestow on a suffragan bishop or a commissary and would cost the taxpayers nothing.[2] In Maryland the commissary generalship was the office in charge of probate and testamentary causes. What the upper house was suggesting was that, exactly as in England, an ecclesiastical officer would fill the post.[3] The upper house eventually gained the concurrence of the assembly in a representation to the bishop of London which asked him to petition the king to confirm the civil office on a clergyman of the bishop's choosing.[4] Bishop Compton may not have taken the matter to the king, but he did agree to send a representative to Maryland. In October 1695 the legislature prepared a letter to the bishop thanking him for the "suffragan bishop" he had promised them.[5]

The interchangeable use of the terms "commissary" and "suffragan bishop" in the legislative journals is intriguing. A commissary is essentially a deputy of the bishop whose powers are limited by his commis-

---

[1] Arch. Md., XIX, 92.

[2] Arch. Md., XIX, 92.

[3] Arch. Md., XIX, 92-93. The upper house noted that the commissary generalship was a "Judiciall office of an Ecclesiasticall nature." Arch. Md., XIX, 92.

[4] Arch. Md., XIX, 93. The assembly warned, however, that they would not raise any further means of support.

[5] Arch. Md., XIX, 230.

sion. A suffragan bishop is a consecrated bishop with full spiritual authority. His temporal powers, however, are only those which his superior, a regular bishop, may choose to delegate to him. Perhaps the legislature did not fully understand the distinction.[1] In requesting a commissary the legislature was simply asking for a church disciplinary officer equivalent to James Blair in Virginia. In requesting a suffragan bishop, they were asking for a high-ranking prince of the church, one whose presence in the colonies would be politically and symbolically very significant. The Crown would have found it difficult to justify the ecclesiastical power of the royal governors were an anointed bishop sent to the continent.

Bishop Compton must have realized the king was not likely to approve the consecration of a suffragan bishop for the colonies, and in April 1696 he appointed Dr. Thomas Bray commissary to Maryland.[2] Occupied in England with several projects, such as finding clergymen to send to the colony and collecting books to form parish libraries, Bray did not sail for Maryland until 1700. During his absence, Nicholson functioned as a bishop surrogate in the matter of discipline. He disliked the responsibility. Until October 1698, when the council was informed that an Anglican minister was suspected of bigamy, Nicholson avoided exercising his legal right to try and to deprive ministers.[3] The charge of bigamy against George Tubman, however, was too serious to ignore or postpone. After upbraiding Tubman at a council hearing the governor, showing a great deal of tact, asked nearby clergymen to examine the case and to advise the council on what to

---

[1] This would hardly have been surprising. No suffragan bishop had been appointed by the Crown since 1592. Norman Sykes, Church and State in England in the XVIIIth Century (Cambridge, 1934), 141.

[2] Henry Paget Thompson, Thomas Bray (London, 1954), 14.

[3] To deprive a minister is to remove him from his living.

do. The ministers found Tubman innocent of bigamy but guilty of fornication, excessive drinking, and other crimes. The council followed their recommendation to suspend Tubman.[1] By securing an ecclesiastical condemnation before endorsing a civil punishment, Nicholson neatly side-stepped the issue of whether laymen could really regulate ordained ministers. Few future governors showed such a spirit of compromise when their delegated authority to do so clashed with English canon law and the clergy's touchy sensibilities.

The first recorded meeting of Anglican clergymen took place in Annapolis in May 1698. Eight ministers (out of about eighteen in the province) signed an address to the bishop of London which summarized the state of the Church in Maryland.[2] They asked the bishop for help in dealing with a number of problems and external threats. The ministers were very worried that the Quakers, then petitioning the Crown to disallow the Establishment Act of 1696, would be successful.[3] They begged the bishop to intercede with the king on their behalf. In Maryland itself, the clergymen perceived the proselytizing Quakers and Catholics as the most disturbing dangers. What was needed to deal with local enemies and to speak for the Church, the petitioners concluded, was a superior ecclesiastical

---

[1] Arch. Md., XXV, 13, 22, 23, 24, 42. Tubman's suspension was lifted three months later.

[2] The letter may be found in William Stevens Perry, Historical Collections Relating to the American Colonial Church (Hartford, Conn., 1870-1878), IV, 8-13. Perry's books contain transcripts of documents taken mainly from the papers of the Society for the Propagation of the Gospel (S.P.G.) and the Fulham Papers in Lambeth Palace, London. I have compared his copies against the Library of Congress transcripts of the British originals and have made corrections when necessary. However, for reasons of convenience I have cited Perry instead of the DLC transcripts whenever possible. It should be noted that Perry incorrectly dates this letter May 18, 1696; it was actually dated May 18, 1698.

[3] For the attempts by domestic and English Quakers to force the disallowance of the establishment acts, see Kenneth L. Carroll, "Quaker Opposition to the Establishment of a State Church in Maryland," Maryland Historical Magazine, LXV (1970), 149-170.

agent endowed with sufficient power and authority to "capacitate him to redress what is amiss, and to supply what is wanting in the Church."[1] The ministers knew that Bray had been appointed commissary. The context of the letter suggests, however, that they hoped for an officer with larger jurisdiction and more legal clout. Governor Nicholson wanted a commissary to regulate the clergy; these ministers wanted a superior who could contain their religious adversaries.

Nicholson was succeeded as governor on January 2, 1699, by Nathaniel Blakiston, who held the post until July 30, 1702. During his administration several important religious events occurred: the Crown disallowed the Establishment Act of 1696, Commissary Bray arrived and held the first Maryland visitation, and a final religion bill received the assent of the Crown.

An order in council disallowed the religion act of 1696 on November 30, 1699, for the reason Nicholson had anticipated.[2] In early January 1700 Bray sailed for Maryland. The commissary mistakenly assumed that the disallowed act would remain in force in the colony until the legislature could pass a new act of establishment.[3] Bray was in Annapolis with Nicholson and Blakiston on March 25 when, to their complete surprise, they learned that the operation of the 1696 act had ceased from the day of the disallowance.[4] The order stripped the clergy of any legal right to demand

---

[1] Perry, Collections, IV, 12.

[2] The English attorney general filed a report in the summer of 1697 which noted, disapprovingly, the statement in the preamble concerning the extension of English liberties to Maryland. The Board of Trade (the successor to the Lords of Trade) did not, however, advise disallowance until November 29, 1699. Jordan, "Royal Period," 268.

[3] Thompson, Bray, 48.

[4] Francis Nicholson to the Archbishop of Canterbury, May 27, 1700, in Perry, Collections, I, 118.

payment of back salaries. Hoping that the opposition (most notably the

Quakers) would not have time to concert their actions, Governor Blakiston

prepared to ask the next assembly, scheduled for April, for a new bill.

Thomas Bray was the linchpin in the campaign to persuade the

delegates to endorse another establishment bill. Furnished by Nicholson

with an assessment of the disposition of the individual assemblymen, he

lobbied fiercely to win over the dubious and the uncommitted.[1]

When the assembly convened on April 26, Blakiston reminded the

delegates "how useful Religion is in the Good Government of a Nation or

Province, it's the Uniting the People, the keeping men Good and Deterring

them from comitting of Rapines of all Degrees upon each other." He warned

that "fatall Consequences" would result without an establishment. The

reason the Crown had disallowed the 1696 act was, he explained, the inclu-

sion of the rights and liberties clause.[2] To the delight of the anxious

promoters a new religion bill, drafted by Thomas Bray and the Maryland

attorney general, passed both houses quickly and without major opposition.

Blakiston signed it on May 9. In most particulars the act was a duplicate

of its predecessor, except that it did not include any statement concerning

the extension of English liberties to the colony. At the behest of the

Anglican clergy, Bray rushed back to England to steer the act through the

Board of Trade.[3]

---

[1] Thompson, Bray, 50-52. Nicholson's list and comments--he thought
that nineteen delegates were for the establishment, seven were against it,
twelve were uncommitted but rather negatively inclined, and that the
Quakers had "a great Ascendancy on many in the House"--is printed in
Bernard C. Steiner, ed., Rev. Thomas Bray: His Life and Selected Works
Relating to Maryland (Baltimore, 1901), 230-233.

[2] Arch. Md., XXIV, 7.

[3] Arch. Md., XXIV, 7, 9, 10, 20, 23, 32; the bill is on pp. 91-98.
For the request of the clergy to Bray, see The Acts of Dr. Bray's Visita-
tion (London, 1700), reprinted in Francis L. Hawks, Contributions to the
Eccesiastical History of the United States (New York, 1839), II, 499-523.

He was soon engaged in a lively public debate with the Quakers. Well-funded and superbly prepared, the Friends drew on their previous experience in fighting the establishment acts to mount a powerful campaign against the new one.[1] Although the Board of Trade had advised the disallowance of the 1696 act specifically because of the liberties clause, they had listened sympathetically to Quaker objections to other provisions in the act. The Friends objected most vehemently to the forty per poll, the powers granted to the corporate vestries, and the command that the Book of Common Prayer be read "in every Church or other place of Publick Worship."[2] In December 1700 the English attorney general agreed that this final clause could be construed to apply to the dissenter churches as well as the Anglican. He recommended a revision.[3] On January 31, 1701, the Board of Trade decided to overrule the entire act. It agreed, however, to supervise the drafting of a new bill which could then be sent to Maryland for enactment by the legislature. Fortunately for the Anglican clergy in the colony, on February 13 an order from the Crown in council decreed that the 1700 act, though formally disallowed, would remain in effect for the time being.[4]

Bray painstakingly drafted another bill. He worked for months, all the while debating the Quakers and consulting with the Board, before he had a measure which was acceptable to the Crown. In June 1701 his bill received the royal assent and was sent to Maryland in the fall.[5] Although Bray expected a good deal of opposition to the bill apparently little

---

[1] Thompson, Bray, 56, 58, 59.

[2] See Jordan, "Royal Period," 273–277, for an extended treatment of Quaker efforts against the Establishment Act.

[3] A transcript of Attorney General Thomas Trevor's memorandum is in Perry, Collections, IV, 40–41, dated January 11, 1701; Jordan, "Royal Period," 274–275, says it was dated December.

[4] Jordan, "Royal Period," 276.

[5] Thompson, Bray, 60; Jordan, "Royal Period," 276–277.

actually ensued. On March 16, 1702, Governor Blakiston introduced the bill to the assembly, remarking that the changes introduced were good ones and the delegates should have no objections to enacting the bill. A few amendments were indeed proposed, but on March 19 the lower house voted to accept the bill just as it was. On March 23 the council did the same.[1]

Later that year the Quakers tried unsuccessfully to induce the Board of Trade to recommend a disallowance of the act. What became known as the "constitution" of the Church in Maryland was finally secured when Queen Anne approved the act on January 18, 1703.[2]

The Establishment Act of 1702 reflected the impact of the Quaker objections to the previous measures. It carefully stipulated that the Book of Common Prayer and other Anglican rubrics were obligatory only in the established churches. Dissenters were granted the full benefits of the English Toleration Act. The most striking change between this and earlier acts was in the structure of the vestry. The new vestry was not a corporate body and its membership was no longer self-perpetuating. All future vacancies were to be filled by vote of the parish freeholders, who also were empowered to discharge two vestrymen and elect replacements every year. Churchwardens as well were to be chosen by the freeholders. From the point of view of the clergy, though, the central provisions of the establishment had not been altered: ministers were entitled to receive forty pounds of tobacco per taxable in their parishes, and they were still the principal vestrymen.

---

[1] Arch. Md., XXIV, 207, 218, 219, 223, 247.

[2] Jordan, "Royal Period," 279-280. Bray reported that fighting the bills had, according to rumor, cost the Quakers ₤20,000. Thompson, Bray, 60. The 1701-1702 Act is in Arch. Md., XXIV, 265-273.

Dr. Bray seems to have been the only clergyman to help frame the final establishment act. The bishop of London was not a voting member of the Board of Trade, which replaced the Lords of Trade in 1696. Archbishop Thomas Tenison, a member of the Privy Council, probably helped to defend the 1700 act, but whether he advised Bray in 1701 is uncertain.[1] In any case the secular bias of the act is unmistakable. Little in the act indicates that the framers thought constructively about the real problems of establishing a religious institution in a very alien environment a great distance away. Bray knew that the act was badly flawed, but he stifled his qualms in the imperative drive to see the ministers statutorily supported. Considering that the act purported to establish the Church of England, it was a very curious document. It dealt at length with the minutiae of vestry elections and oathtaking and the registration of vital statistics, but about the ministers it stipulated only that they were to be paid; that the governor had the right to induct and present them; that they were the chief vestrymen and were not subject to fines for non-attendance; that they had to hire a clerk and must obey the marriage laws; and that they could not hold pluralities without the consent of the two vestries.[2] The act said nothing about the structure of the provincial church, how it was to be disciplined, organized, or ruled. This was scarcely a detailed framework for so important an institution.

Between 1696 and 1700 the Maryland legislators substantially reduced the jurisdiction they were willing to give the Church. The act of 1692 guaranteed that the Church would "have and Enjoy all her Rights Liberties

---

[1] Thompson, Bray, 59, says that Tenison supported Bray. Nicholson's letters to the archbishop (see, for instance, the communication of May 27, 1700, in Perry, Collections, I, 117-121) suggest that Tenison was interested in colonial affairs.

[2] Arch. Md., XXIV, 265, 266, 268, 269, 271.

and Franchises wholly inviolable as is now or shall be hereafter Established by Law." The 1696 act decreed that the Church would enjoy "her Rights Priviledges & ffreedoms as it is now or shall be att any time hereafter Established by Law in the Kingdom of England."[1] These sweeping pronouncements are not part of the later acts. Perhaps the legislators realized that these clauses gave the Church grounds to challenge the civil legal system in Maryland, and that the Church conceivably could have demanded that the governor give up his induction rights, or that ecclesiastics take over offices (such as probate and the issuing of marriage licenses) which in Maryland, contrary to English practice, were held by laymen.

The primary internal problem of the Church during the colonial era was discipline. Traditionally self-disciplined, the Church was inhibited from regulating its servants in Maryland by two conditions. First, the governor, not a prelate, inducted the clergy.[2] Second, with the exception of the period between 1728 and 1748, the colonial clergy lacked a legal diocesan. The first condition denied the Church a means of screening applicants for Maryland livings, and the second meant that, in practice, none of the colonial churches was really episcopalian.

Discipline was very much on Bray's mind when he summoned the Maryland clergy to Annapolis from May 23 to 25, 1700, for the first provincial visitation.[3] All seventeen clergymen in Maryland attended. Bray examined

---

[1] Arch. Md., XIII, 425-426; XIX, 426.

[2] The royal governors inducted the ministers in their own right. When proprietary government was restored in 1715, the governors inducted by authority delegated to them by the proprietors.

[3] In England bishops conducted visitations by progressing through their dioceses and meeting with the local clergy (Sykes, Church and State, 115-117, 137-138). Bray probably felt it was more practical to summon all the clergy to meet him in one place.

their credentials and lectured them on the necessity for irreproachable behavior. Scandalous clergy were not only a blot against the honor of God, he said, but injured the Church because "the Miscarriages of one unhappy Clergy-Man shall be more taken Notice of, to our Disparagement, than the most Exemplary and most laborious Lives of Ten [of] the best Men."[1] The commissary then re-opened the case of George Tubman, the accused bigamist whom Nicholson had suspended a year and a half before. Although Bray ordered the details of the matter read to the clergy, and though he angrily denounced Tubman's behavior, he did not convene an ecclesiastical court at the visitation. The commissary did, however, order Tubman to produce a defense at the next visitation, scheduled for November. Had Bray remained in the colony to preside over that meeting, Tubman would presumably have been tried then.

Bray fully realized that the clergy in Maryland needed a superior to live among them in the province. Initially, he intended to continue acting in that capacity himself. During his visitation he scheduled a series of meetings for the following year and implied that he would hold ecclesiastical courts when necessary.[2] Shortly after he sailed back to England in 1700, however, Bray decided not to return to Maryland. He discussed the appointment of a new commissary with the bishop of London. For some unexplained reason Compton did not want Bray to step down, but told Bray to deputize a subordinate.[3] In the summer of 1701 Bray accordingly appointed a deputy commissary for Maryland, only to have the man lose his

---

[1] Bray, The Acts of Bray's Visitation, reprinted in Hawks, Contributions, II, 510-511. The entire Acts covers pp. 499-523 in Hawks.

[2] Bray, The Acts of Bray's Visitation, in Hawks, Contributions. II, 514, 523.

[3] Thomas Bray, "A Memorial, giving a true and Just account of the affair of the Commissary of Maryland....", n.d. but c. 1704, in Perry, Collections, IV, 57.

nerve while waiting for a ship in Plymouth.[1] Later that year Bray sent

commissions to three of the "gravest and prudentest Divines" he knew in

Maryland.[2] He was bitterly disappointed to learn that none of them ever

conducted any commissarial business. Bray was very slow to appreciate the

difference between his standing as commissary—a scholar, a friend of the

governors of Virginia and Maryland, a personal appointee of the bishop of

London—and that of the people he chose to commission, who were twice

removed from the real source of authority and lacked his connections with

those in power.[3] By the summer of 1703, though, he had convinced the

bishop of the urgency of sending a full commissary to Maryland. They

introduced their choice, Michael Huitson, the Archdeacon of Armagh, to

John Seymour, the governor-designate of Maryland, as Seymour was preparing

to sail for the colony. Seymour, a hot-tempered, opinionated man, took an

immediate dislike to Huitson and the prospect of having a commissary in

Maryland and managed to scotch the appointment.[4]

Obtaining a suitable maintenance for a resident commissary was a

problem which preoccupied Bray and other well-wishers for many years.

Hearing of Bray's appointment as commissary, the Maryland legislature passed

a supplicatory act in 1696 asking the king to grant him and his

successors the civil post of commissary general.[5] The office went to a

---

[1] Thompson, Bray, 63

[2] Bray, "A Memorial," in Perry, Collections, IV, 58.

[3] Ibid. In his memorial Bray guessed that the three men in Maryland
never acted because "they found that their Brethren on the same level with
themselves would not easily submit to anything like superiority in them,"
which was probably an accurate assessment of the situation.

[4] Bray recounted the affair with Seymour in his "Memorial," in Perry,
Collections, IV, 58-63. Bray and the governor almost came to blows on the
subject. Exactly why Seymour opposed Huitson or the appointment of a
commissary so vehemently is not precisely clear. Compton did, however,
suggest to him that Huitson could be granted the office of judge of testamentary causes in Maryland, and Seymour may have thought such episcopal
interference dangerous.

[5] Arch. Md., XXXVIII, 91-92.

layman when Bray failed to make an appearance in Maryland. During his

short visit to the colony in 1700 Bray did not step into the post, and

neither did any of his successors.[1] Bray's three-year delay, and the

failure of the bishop of London to send a replacement expeditiously, was

responsible for the loss of an appointment which would have meant a secure

income, a permanent role in the government, and much personal prestige

for Maryland commissaries. Bray himself promoted several schemes to

bolster the authority and the maintenance of the commissary but he

succeeded in none of them.[2] When it existed at all the Maryland commis-

sariate was an office without civil sanctions or special funding.

After Bray's departure the clergy in the colony occasionally met and

acted in concert. In June 1702 fifteen ministers (out of a total of about

twenty-three) presented Governor Blakiston with a farewell address. They

thanked him for his help in passing the Establishment Act and his support

for the "Sacred Institution."[3] The date of the address suggests that the

clergy were meeting according to the visitation instructions left by

Commissary Bray. It is possible, though, that this gathering was simply

one of the self-willed meetings the clergy organized throughout the colonial

---

[1] Bray expected to receive the post (worth ₤300 sterling a year) when
he went to the colony. He claimed that an intrigue stripped him of the
profits of the office, but what probably happened was that he was not in
Maryland long enough to secure the appointment (Thompson, Bray, 50). In
June 1700 Blakiston announced his willingness to settle the office on an
ecclesiastical officer, but conferred it on a layman when Bray left for
England (Nathaniel Blakiston to "Your Grace" [probably the Archbishop of
Canterbury], June 12, 1700, Fulham Papers in the Lambeth Palace Library,
Box "Maryland 1696-1769," item 132, DLC transcript; Arch. Md., XXV, 95).
The office never reverted to the Church.

[2] Bray made several attempts to furnish the commissariate with a
landed estate and a plantation, but he never managed to raise enough money.
In August 1703 he tried to gain support in the Maryland legislature for a
proposal to grant the bishop of London presentation rights to a single but
lucrative parish; he even offered to stock the glebe with slaves, cattle,
and hogs. Thompson, Bray, 69-70.

[3] Arch. Md., XXIV, 288-289.

period, usually in order to greet or say farewell to a governor or to
felicitate a new bishop of London. In Annapolis on May 27, 1703, eleven
clergymen[1] met for the purpose of petitioning the legislature. Among
other requests, they asked the council to order church officers to subscribe
to the Thirty-Nine Articles (an order which would have hindered dissenters
from joining the vestries), and to prohibit unbaptized persons from
admission to government offices. The ministers also requested the enactment of an additional religion act to penalize protestants who did not
attend church services. In effect, they sought a Maryland version of the
Test and Corporation Acts which supported the Church in England. The
petition was referred to the next assembly and, not surprisingly, was
never considered.[2]

Without Bray or an acceptable substitute to uphold the interests of
the Church, the power to discipline the clergy remained in the hands of
the governor and council. In 1703 Joseph Holt became the second minister
to lose his benefice by order of the state. Holt was charged with dis-
honoring the Church by fathering a bastard child and associating with a
"Woman of ill Fame."[3] During the winter of 1702-1703 Holt appeared before
the council to answer the charges. He denied his guilt and was dismissed
with a warning to behave more circumspectly in the future.[4] He did not do
so. The following August the council ordered him "suspended ab Officio
et a Beneficio" by reason of his "ill Behaviour to the Great Scandal of his
Function" until Governor Seymour arrived in Maryland and could judge the

---

[1] There were about twenty-one ministers in Maryland at the time.

[2] Arch. Md., XXV, 160-161.

[3] Arch. Md., XXV, 135. Previously, Holt had been deprived of a
Virginia living by Commissary James Blair for adultery and drunkenness.
Bray, "Memorial," in Perry, Collections, IV, 58.

[4] Arch. Md., XXV, 135.

case for himself.[1] Sometime after his disembarkation in the spring of 1704
Seymour reinstated Holt. However, when the vestrymen of Holt's St. Mary's
County parish sent the council a letter of complaint against the incumbent
in September 1704, Seymour appointed a five man committee to hear the case.
The committee decided that Holt had so misbehaved himself that he was not
"a person fitting to be further continued in the Ministerial function in
that Parish or Else where."[2] The council then suspended Holt, stopped his
income, and took away his glebe.

The matter was not yet closed. On September 14, 1704, the council
received a petition from Thomas Cockshutt, Joseph Colbatch, and Henry Hall.
All three were ministers of parishes near Annapolis whose induction dates
preceded the final establishment. They were men of impeccable reputation.
The ministers wrote that Holt's suspension was a penalty

> we are perswaded in our Consciences cannot be
> inflicted upon him by any Civil Power whatsoever
> as such but only by his Bishop and that too
> according to the Canons of our Church and only by
> Virtue of the Authority Committed to him by Christ
> our Lord for our office as ministers of Christ is
> purely Spiritual and therefore we cannot be
> deprived of it or the Exercise thereof by any
> lay Person or Persons how great Soever without
> Sacrilegiously usurping upon the Divine Authority
> Committed by Christ to his Church which we hope
> is not designed by the late Suspension nor can we
> see how Mr Holt could in Conscience submit to it.[3]

For the first time the Church in Maryland was questioning the
ecclesiastical power of the state. According to English canon law, the
ministers had a perfectly valid case.[4] But in Maryland at this time the

---

[1] Arch. Md., XXV, 163.

[2] Arch. Md., XXVI, 33.

[3] Arch. Md., XXVI, 51-52.

[4] H. A. Wilson, ed., Constitutions and Canons Ecclesiastical 1604
(London, 1923), Canon CXXII.

state—in particular the governor—set the boundaries of Church jurisdiction, and Seymour and his council chose to interpret them narrowly. The
petition incensed Seymour. He ordered the petitioners before the council
and in scorching language berated them for exceeding their stations. The
governor threatened the men with punishment as "Contemners of Authority and
Disturbers of her Majesties peace" if they bothered him again.[1] Seymour
did not answer the specific and legitimate complaints the petitioners had
brought up. He did not say categorically that the conventions and canons
of the Church of England did not apply in Maryland. The governor did not
have to do so; his actions spoke clearly enough for themselves. The protest
of the three incumbents, however, was the only time in the history of the
Church in Maryland that clergymen challenged the authority of the executive
to deprive inducted ministers.

John Seymour died in July 1709. Between 1704 and the arrival of
Seymour's successor, John Hart, in 1714, no cases of clerical immorality
were reported to the government. There is also no evidence that the clergy
met together during this time. Two peculiar but noteworthy items remain from
this period, though. A New Jersey clergyman wrote a friend in London in 1704
that John Lillingston, a Talbot County minister, was planning to sail for
England the following year, and that many of the clergy and laity of
America wished him appointed suffragan. The minister claimed that several
clergy in New Jersey and Maryland had said they would pay their tenths to
Lillingston as the bishop of London's vice-regent, "whereby the B[isho]p
of America might have as honourable Provisions as some in Europe."[2]

---

[1] Arch. Md., XXVI, 52.

[2] John Talbot to Mr. Keith, October 20, 17-- [from context clearly
1704], Society for the Propagation of the Gospel (S.P.G.) Papers, Series A,
Volume 2, item 23, DLC transcript. Lillingston was the most senior of the
Maryland clergy.

Lillingston was not appointed commissary, much less consecrated bishop, but in 1707 Henry Hall did receive a commission from the bishop of London to act as commissary. He recorded his commission in the council journal but, like several predecessors, he did not exercise any authority.[1] His commission lapsed in 1713 when Bishop Compton died.

In his concern and zeal for the Church, John Hart resembled Francis Nicholson.[2] During his administration (1714-1720) several important structural changes took place in the Maryland Church. Finding that the ministers "were strangers to one another by their distant residence on this vast tract of Land," Hart convened the clergy in Annapolis on June 24, 1714.[3] This meeting was the first convention called by a governor of Maryland. Twenty-one of the province's twenty-three clergyman attended. Careful not to overstep the bounds of his authority as a layman, Hart translated his orders from the queen into a list of queries which he presented to the clergy. The queries indicate that Hart's ecclesiastical instructions were fundamentally the same as those given to Copley twenty-two years before. He inquired into the number of churches, the condition of the glebes, whether the minister was a member of the vestry, and whether the clergy had a due sense of the ecclesiastical jurisdiction of the bishop of London. Governor Hart inspected licenses and other documents as well, and suggested that the clergy appoint a committee to consult with

---

[1] Arch. Md., XXV, 211-212.

[2] Before he sailed to Maryland, Hart met with John Robinson, the new Bishop of London (Compton died in 1713). He later wrote the prelate that he was extremely sorry not to have had the time to show the bishop his royal ecclesiastical instructions, or to receive the bishop's own orders. John Hart to Bishop John Robinson, July 10, 1714, in Perry, Collections, IV, 77-79.

[3] Ibid., 78.

him on Church affairs.[1]   The ministers gratefully selected six men for the committee.[2]

Hart did not long escape the problem of how to deal with irregular clergymen. On September 15, 1714, the vestry of St. Paul's Parish in Baltimore County sent him a petition complaining of the life and morals of William Tibbs, their minister. The vestry sent another petition in February 1715. The petitioners accused Tibbs of drunkenness, neglecting his ministerial duties, and demanding payment for administering the sacraments. They insisted that the governor remove him.[3] Hart had deliberately ignored several other complaints against ministers but to "quiet the minds of the people" he had to take notice of the petition from St. Paul's.[4] He sent for Henry Hall, Thomas Cockshutt, Joseph Colbatch, and Jacob Henderson, the nearest members of his clerical advisory committee, to consider the case. The ministers expressed great satisfaction that the governor was "so disposed to proceed in these affairs after so just and Laudable a manner as that of Consulting the Clergy where the Cause of the Church is so much concerned." The committee examined the petitions and concluded that the charges were insufficiently substantiated.[5] They advised the governor to

---

[1] John Hart's speech to the clergy, June 24, 1714, in Perry, Collections, IV, 74-75. The queries were part of the speech.

[2] "The humble Representation of the Clergy of Maryland concerning the state of the Church in that Province....," n.d. but c. June 24, 1714, in Perry, Collections, IV, 77. The ministers chose Henry Hall, Thomas Cockshutt, and Joseph Colbatch (the three ministers who had opposed Seymour's deprivation of Joseph Holt), plus Jacob Henderson (a future commissary), Richard Sewall (the senior attending Eastern Shore minister), and Henry Nichols.

[3] "The Case against the Revd Wm Tibbs," Fulham Papers, "Maryland 1696-1769," item 133.

[4] John Hart to Bishop John Robinson, September 6, 1715, in Perry, Collections, IV, 81.

[5] Henry Hall, Thomas Cockshutt, Joseph Colbatch, and Jacob Henderson to John Hart, n.d., in "The Case Against Tibbs," Fulham Papers, "Maryland 1696-1769," item 133.

order Tibbs admonished to change his ways and to reconcile himself to his parishioners. If he failed to comply, the committee recommended that affidavits be taken and the whole case sent to the bishop of London for determination. The vestry of St. Paul's Parish was less than satisfied with the verdict, and again pressed the governor. Hart thought it might be worthwhile to summon Tibbs before the council for a hearing, and then to send the charges and the defense to Robinson, but "being advised that such acts were purely of Ecclesiastical Cognizance, tho' he has an instruction that favored it," he desisted.[1] He asked Bishop Robinson to send immediate orders on how to proceed.[2]

Hart did not like his anomalous position as a civil and an ecclesiastical officer. Unlike Seymour, he felt uncomfortable usurping the jurisdiction of a bishop even if his official orders stated he could do so. Yet something clearly had to be done to provide discipline in the colonial Church. Hart must have discussed the need for discipline and his reluctance to exercise it himself with members of the advisory committee, for in September 1715 both the governor and Jacob Henderson wrote to Bishop Robinson proposing that commissaries be sent to Maryland.[3] The two men lamented the lack of a colonial bishop, but recognized that such an appointment was "a work not easily to be effected."[4] Hart suggested that, until the investiture of an American bishop, a commissary be appointed for each side of the Chesapeake Bay with authority to inspect the affairs of

---

[1] Jacob Henderson to Bishop John Robinson, September 1, 1715, in Perry, Collections, IV, 80.

[2] John Hart to Bishop John Robinson, September 6, 1715, in Perry, Collections, IV, 81.

[3] Jacob Henderson to Bishop John Robinson, September 1, 1715, and John Hart to Bishop John Robinson, September 6, 1715, in Perry, Collections, IV, 80, 81–82.

[4] Jacob Henderson to Bishop John Robinson, September 1, 1715, in Perry, Collections, IV, 80.

the Church in Maryland and "to preserve a decorum."[1] He recommended
Christopher Wilkinson as commissary for the Eastern Shore, and Jacob
Henderson for the Western.

Four months before he wrote the bishop asking for commissaries, Hart
heard unofficially that the Calverts were again to become full proprietors
of Maryland. Benedict Leonard Calvert, the fourth Lord Baltimore, converted
to Anglicanism in 1713, and did indeed convince the Crown to restore full
charter rights two years later. His son Charles became proprietor in 1715.
Along with word that Hart would remain governor, news of the restoration
of proprietary government reached Maryland in December 1715.[2]

On February 15, 1716, Robinson signed commissions for Wilkinson and
Henderson. Wilkinson was fifty-three years old when he was appointed and
was English; Henderson was twenty years younger and Irish. Before coming to
Maryland in 1711 Wilkinson served seventeen years in English cures and had
also been a chaplain in the Navy. Henderson, on the other hand, sailed for
the colonies almost immediately after his ordination in 1710. He served
briefly as an S.P.G.[3] minister in several places from New York to Delaware
before he settled in Maryland in 1713. Temperamentally, the commissary of
the Eastern Shore was mild and considerate, and easily gained friends and
respect. Henderson had an explosive temper and was haughty, impatient,
forceful, and vindictive. The differences in personality and background
between the two officers proved very important in the following decade.

When Wilkinson received his commission he promised the bishop of London

---

[1] John Hart to Bishop John Robinson, September 6, 1715, in Perry,
Collections, IV, 81.

[2] Jordan, "Royal Period," 325, 336, 343.

[3] The Society for the Propagation of the Gospel in Foreign Parts
(S.P.G.) was founded in 1701. Its primary purpose was to underwrite colonial
missionary activity and to furnish ministers to the colonies which had not
established the Church.

that he would "execute it with that caution as may support your Lordship's Jurisdiction here and answer the ends thereof."[1] He quietly convened the clergy of his shore for a consultation.[2] After a personal inspection tour of the parishes, the commissary called a general visitation on May 8, 1717. He conducted it according to English usage: public prayers, a sermon, and an exhortation to his subordinates preceded a hearing for persons accused of moral crimes. As in England, the parish churchwardens attended the visitation and were asked to respond to queries concerning the spiritual and physical conditions of their churches. Wilkinson had previously ordered the churchwardens (who traditionally acted as the sheriffs of ecclesiastical courts) not to present for minor offenses but to concentrate on the notorious ones. In dealing with these Wilkinson "proceeded after the same manner used in the spiritual courts in England, as near as the circumstances of this country will permit."[3] Since the punishments meted out by an ecclesiastical court were neither corporal nor monetary, but only spiritual, Wilkinson's sentences did not interfere with the workings of the regular civil courts. Technically, though, the Church had managed to institute a new court in Maryland, which claimed to have jurisdiction over laymen and clergy alike.

Wilkinson was not sure how comprehensive a court system he could set up. His first session functioned without the customary proctors (attorneys) and clerks, and he probably proceeded without writs and other legal paraphernalia. The commissary did not know whether he could demand fees,

---

[1] Christopher Wilkinson to Bishop John Robinson, October 10, 1716, in Perry, Collections, IV, 86.

[2] Wilkinson to Bishop Edmund Gibson, September 9, 1724, in Perry, Collections, IV, 244. At this meeting the clergy agreed on an address Wilkinson presented to the governor. No copy has been found and its contents are unknown.

[3] Christopher Wilkinson to Bishop Edmund Gibson, September 9, 1724, in Perry, Collections, IV, 244.

or if so, whether he could call on the civil authorities to recover them.
Bishop Robinson did not help him at all. The diocesan applauded Wilkinson's
care and moderation but did not describe the limits of his commissarial
jurisdiction.[1]

The establishment of an ecclesiastical court on the Western Shore
progressed less pacifically. Henderson received his commission in April
1716, and also convened the clergy of his shore to discuss it. The ministers
thought that the country would oppose the innovation of an ecclesiastical
court and advised him not to set one up. Henderson asked Bishop Robinson's
advice and received a reply, dated March 14, 1717, which he interpreted as
a direct order to "set about Executing the Powers of my Commission." On
the strength of it the commissary summoned the clergy and churchwardens
of the Western Shore to a visitation in Annapolis on December 4-5, 1717.[2]

Henderson conducted his visitation in a regal manner, complete with
procurator (prosecutor) and a registrar. He reprimanded those of the ten
attending ministers who had failed to bring, for his inspection, complete
sets of their credentials.[3] He ordered two ministers who held pluralities
to obtain dispensations for their dual livings. Henderson's intention to

---

[1] Wilkinson to Bishop John Robinson, July 3, 1717, and May 26, 1718,
and Robinson to Wilkinson, October 7, 1717, in Perry, Collections, IV,
87-88, 89, 108.

[2] "Answers to the Queries," n.d. but 1723 or 1724, in Perry,
Collections, IV, 132. A paraphrase of the bishop's commission appears in a
later document. The bishop gave Henderson "full power & Authority (as t'was
lawfull for us to doe) to hold Visitations in Order to Inquire into to
Correct & reform all Disorders Irregularityes & Immoralityes (if any)
Committed within the sd Shore & properly belonging to an Ecclesiasticall
Cognizance." Fulham Papers, "Maryland 1696-1769," item 131.

[3] Canon CXXXVIII of the Church directed that during the first visitation of a bishop or his surrogate all ministers were to display their
orders, inductions, and licenses. Wilson, ed., Constitutions and Canons.
Whether from malice or ignorance, only two ministers at the meeting brought
complete sets of documents. The meeting, though, attracted most of the
ministers of the Western Shore; only three incumbents out of thirteen did
not come, and they sent acceptable excuses.

press charges against William Tibbs for immorality and neglect of duty
went awry when Tibbs discreetly absented himself, but the commissary made
plans to deal with the matter at a later visitation. The highlight of the
meeting, however, was the rupture between Henderson and Henry Hall, the
former commissary. When Hall brought his credentials to Henderson for
inspection the commissary rather boorishly insisted on retaining them for
perusal overnight. The implied insult enraged Hall. He left the meeting
in a fury and obtained a warrant from Governor Hart ordering the immediate
return of the documents. Henderson interpreted Hall's actions as an
assault against his authority, and ordered the procurator to draw up a
formal indictment. In the name of the bishop of London, Hall was charged
with violating his canonical oath of obedience to his superiors and dis-
puting the colonial jurisdiction of the diocesan. Henderson tried to obtain
a conviction during two subsequent visitations, in March and in May 1718,
but the hearings became snarled in disputes over procedure. Meanwhile,
the governor and many of the clergy complained to Bishop Robinson that
Henderson was treating them all inconsiderately and had bungled the Hall
affair.[1] In April 1718 the bishop informed Henderson curtly that the
commissary's "demand upon Mr Hall, of Synadodals and Procurations, is not
to be supported, being without precedent either in your or any other
Colony."[2] Reluctantly, Henderson ceased the prosecution of Henry Hall.[3]

---

[1] Bishop Robinson told Henderson that the governor and "the greatest
part of the Clergy" had protested to him that Henderson treated the government with disrespect and had offended the clergy by, among other things,
assembling them at unseasonable times of the year. Bishop John Robinson to
Jacob Henderson, April 15, 1718, in Perry, Collections, IV, 100.

[2] Bishop John Robinson to Jacob Henderson, April 15, 1718, in Perry,
Collections, IV, 100.

[3] For the Hall affair and Henderson's visitations of December 4-5,
1717, and March 13-14, 1718, see the minutes of the meetings in Perry,
Collections, IV, 92-96; the indictment is in the Fulham Papers, "Maryland
1696-1769," item 131. See also Bishop John Robinson to Jacob Henderson,
April 15, 1718, and Bishop Robinson to John Hart, April 16, 1718, both in
Perry, Collections, IV, 100-101.

Precisely what Henderson did after 1715 to antagonize Governor Hart (who remained in Maryland as governor under the proprietors until 1720) is not clear. Their differences were probably ones of personality. The commissary's relations with the clergy, however, were soured by his righteous insistence on deference and obedience. Henderson demanded all due honor as the bishop of London's accredited lieutenant. He equated acceptance of his commissarial authority with acknowledgment of the diocesan jurisdiction of the bishop in the colonies. The commissary was passionately concerned that laymen and clergymen alike should concede the authority of the bishop. Commissarial authority in Maryland hinged on the legality of the bishop's colonial jurisdiction. If the bishop was truly the colonial diocesan, then it was the duty of his commissaries to reconstruct as much as possible the usual English diocesan establishment of ecclesiastical courts, visitations, and clerical self-regulation. The efforts of Henderson and Wilkinson to do just that were thwarted by Bishop Robinson's unwillingness to assert his claims. First he told the commissaries not to insist on jurisdiction over lay moral offenses.[1] Next he made Henderson appear ridiculous by not supporting him during the Hall affair. Finally, the bishop would not even give Henderson straightforward instructions on how to prosecute William Tibbs, who prudently refused to attend visitations.[2] Two years after they had been granted their commissions, neither Wilkinson nor Henderson knew exactly what they were supposed to do with them.

---

[1] Bishop John Robinson to Christopher Wilkinson, October 7, 1717, in Perry, Collections, IV, 89; Henderson paraphrased the orders he received from Robinson (in a letter dated October 5, 1717) in the "Answers to the Queries," n.d. but 1723 or 1724, in Perry, ibid., 132.

[2] Bishop John Robinson to Jacob Henderson, April 15, 1718, in Perry, Collections, IV, 100.

With the exception of Henderson, the Anglican ministers were on excellent terms with Governor Hart. They valued his goodwill. Even though the proprietor of Maryland was now an Anglican, members of the clergy worried about Catholic plots and intrigues.[1] Worse, the ministers were beginning to realize that the Establishment Act was not the bulwark they had once thought it was. A number of delegates in the Maryland assembly did not consider the Act sacred or permanent or unalterable. In 1704 they demonstrated as much by changing the marriage fees set down in the act of 1702.[2] Rumors spread through the ministry that the assembly intended to divide their parishes and reduce their incomes.[3] Alarmed, Wilkinson consulted Governor Hart. The two men decided that the best guarantee of the establishment would be a legislative act securing the jurisdiction of the bishop of London in the colony.[4] Henderson did not agree with them. He reasoned that the bishop's jurisdiction would be completely discredited if, as he predicted, the legislature refused to pass the bill.[5] His advice

---

[1] In 1718, for instance, Henry Hall and Thomas Cockshutt reportedly tried to induce their colleagues to sign a petition asking for the replacement of Lord Baltimore as chief executive on the grounds of his alleged Catholicism. Henderson thought the governor abetted them. Jacob Henderson to Bishop John Robinson, June 17, 1718, in Perry, Collections, IV, 111.

[2] Arch. Md., XXVI, 356. Vestry oaths were amended by an act in 1715. Arch. Md., XXX, 228-229.

[3] The clergy of the Eastern Shore to Bishop Robinson, October 25, 1717, in Perry, Collections, IV, 90. The product of a convention Wilkinson called on this date, this communication asked Robinson to intercede with Baltimore to "enjoin all Gov[erno]rs for the time being not to pass any act relating to Ecclesiastical affairs without causing the Commissarys or some other Clergymen to attend, to know what they can say to the thing before them to be enacted." Ibid., 91.

[4] Christopher Wilkinson to Bishop Robinson, May 26, 1718, in Perry, ibid., 106.

[5] Jacob Henderson to Bishop John Robinson, July 17, 1718, in Perry, ibid., 110.

was disregarded. In April 1718 Hart summoned the clergy to Annapolis and
invited them to advise him how to remove obstructions to the execution of
the commissarial commissions. He promised to present their ideas and
grievances to the assembly.[1] The clergy wrote a representation listing as
the major obstruction that "the People are generally made to believe that
the Bishop of London has no Authority to Erect any Court within this
Province." Their recommended solution was "that the Bishop of London's
Jurisdiction in this Province as Contained within his Diocese be asserted
and Recognized, Except in such things as are Excepted in his Lordships
Commission to his Commissarys and his Instruction from the late Queen."[2]
Essentially the motion was an attempt to put back in the statute books the
clause concerning the liberties and rights of the Church in Maryland which
had been dropped from the establishment acts of 1700 and 1702. Apparently
the council favored the petition.[3] The joint committee assigned to discuss
the motion, however, confessed that it had no experience with an ecclesiastical court. Its members were "in a great part Strangers to it's Powers
and Authorities of punishing Crimes and Offenses," and wondered whether
ecclesiastical punishments might not overlap civil ones.[4] The assembly
thought that putting ecclesiastical laws into effect in Maryland was
"altogether impracticable."[5] Though the petition was officially referred

---

[1] Arch. Md., XXXIII, 146-147.

[2] Arch. Md., XXXIII, 154. The ministers also asked that taxes be
levied to cover some of the expenses of holding visitations and that the
county sheriffs serve citations to the ecclesiastical courts. Ibid., 154-
155. Twenty clergymen (out of twenty-two in the province) signed the representation. Henderson signed for fear he would appear disloyal to the
bishop.

[3] Christopher Wilkinson to Bishop John Robinson, May 26, 1718, in
Perry, Collections, IV, 106.

[4] Arch. Md., XXXIII, 243.

[5] Arch. Md., XXXIII, 243.

to the next session of the legislature, the assembly had plainly rejected it.[1]

During the last two years of Hart's administration the commissaries functioned very little. Wilkinson held at least one visitation on the Eastern Shore and at that time admonished an irregular minister, but he hesitated to act more decisively. His queries on how to carry out his commission elicited only nebulous replies from Bishop Robinson warning him not to irritate the public or the governor. In October 1719 he signed, probably with relish if little hope, a petition of New Jersey, Pennsylvania, and Maryland ministers for an American bishop.[2] Henderson was equally inactive. Until Hart left the country he refused to hold any more visitations. The commissary was miserably humiliated by the Hall affair, angered by the handling of the 1718 representation, and felt isolated from his ministers and abandoned by his bishop. His open contempt for the governor alienated clergymen who wished to remain on good terms with the executive. Henderson, moreover, suspected that Hart was less than completely loyal to Lord Baltimore (whom Henderson supported) and that he was secretly inciting ministers to join him in plotting the overthrow of the proprietor.[3] Henderson was in no position to attack the governor's politics, but he

---

[1] Jacob Henderson to Bishop John Robinson, June 17, 1718, in Perry, Collections, IV, 110. Wilkinson informed Robinson that some ministers, covertly against the representation, had told members of the assembly that the act was tyrannical and would drive people out of the Church. Wilkinson to Bishop Robinson, May 26, 1718, in Perry, ibid., 106-107.

[2] S.P.G. Papers, Series A, Vol. 14, fols. 144-167.

[3] Henderson to Bishop Robinson, June 17, 1718, in Perry, Collections, IV, 111.

resolutely countered open disloyalty among the clergy.[1]

"Thank God we have now got rid of him," Henderson sighed when Hart left in 1720.[2] Quickly emerging from semi-retirement, he convened the clergy of his shore to write a note of congratulations to Thomas Brooke, the new executive. From that time until the death of Bishop Robinson in 1723, when his commission automatically lapsed, he held yearly visitations. Wilkinson did the same. The visitations were quiet, orderly meetings. Occasionally the clergy formulated an address to the government, but usually they read correspondence from the bishop of London and were exhorted to do their duties well. Perhaps the commissaries made some mild attempts to discipline irregular clergy, but for the most part the visitations were professional colloquia.[3]

Edmund Gibson succeeded Robinson to the see of London in 1723. Gibson had taken an active part in England's convocation crisis.[4] He was a student of Church history, a specialist in ecclesiastical law, and an energetic,

---

[1] One instance of Henderson's action in such a situation occurred in the spring of 1720, just as Hart was preparing to leave Maryland. Henderson rushed to Annapolis when he heard that some ministers were meeting there to discuss "things of an extraordinary nature." Rumor had it that Hart had invited the clergy to the city to draft an address to the king or the bishop of London against Lord Baltimore. The eight ministers in the city told Henderson that they were simply gathering to say farewell to the governor. The meeting may well have been innocent, but Henderson rather doubted it was, and if the ministers had intended to sign a petition of that sort, Henderson's arrival convinced them to do otherwise. Jacob Henderson to Henry Hall, Thomas Cockshutt et al., May 20, 1720, and Henry Hall, Thomas Cockshutt et al. to Henderson, May 20, 1720, and Henderson to Bishop John Robinson, July 16, 1720, in Perry, Collections, IV, 118-121, 124.

[2] Henderson to Bishop Robinson, July 16, 1720, in Perry, ibid., 123.

[3] Thomas Brooke to Henderson, June 25, 1720; Henderson et al. to Brooke, June 29, 1720; Henderson to Bishop Robinson, July 16, 1720; "Articles of Enquiry Exhibited to the Churchwardens at the Visitation Held May the 30th, 1722, in St. Peter's Church in Talbot County;" "Answers to the Queries," n.d. but 1723 or 1724; all in Perry, ibid., 121-122, 124, 126-127, 133-134.

[4] For a discussion of the convocation dispute, see Appendix A.

persevering Church reformer.[1] Gibson made it immediately clear that he
intended to include the colonies in his diocese. Doubting that his
colonial jurisdiction would be valid until he held a commission under the
Great Seal, he began to pressure the Privy Council for one in 1724. Two
years passed before the order was issued on October 31, 1726. Because
Privy Council lawyers had warned that the colonists might not approve if
Gibson's jurisdiction extended to the laity, his commission limited his
regular diocesan powers. Gibson was given full authority to call visitations, to inspect church buildings, to inquire into the morals and conduct
of all priests and deacons, and to issue citations ordering them to appear
in court. He could correct and punish clerical offenses by suspension,
deprivation, excommunication, and other ecclesiastical penalties. The
bishop could appoint commissaries and delgate authority to them. Appeals
from their decisions were to a committee of the Privy Council. Gibson was
forced to seek a second commission when George I died in the middle of 1727.
It was granted on April 29, 1728, and was identical to the first one except
that it excluded oversight of church buildings.[2]

Even before Gibson was granted the first commission he alerted the
colonial clergy that a new regime had begun. Queries were sent out to
all commissaries and all ministers eliciting information on topics ranging
from the frequency of communion in the individual parishes to the size of
glebes. Gratified to learn that he was dealing with an innovative diocesan,
Henderson sent Gibson a history of the provincial Church and copies of all
laws pertaining to the establishment. He suggested that Gibson and the
Society for the Propagation of the Gospel, an organization founded by

---

[1] Norman Sykes, Edmund Gibson, Bishop of London (London, 1926), passim.
[2] Sykes, Gibson, 334-339.

Thomas Bray, talk Baltimore into conferring the commissary generalship
(now worth ₤600 sterling a year) on a colonial bishop.[1]

News circulated in the summer of 1724 that Gibson had indeed decided
to send bishops to the colonies. One was supposedly bound for the West
Indies while the second would be stationed in Virginia. Astonishingly, the
clergy in Maryland still assumed that the bishop of London--who had not
yet even received his commission--could unilaterally send a bishop if he
so desired. They did not understand Gibson's complete dependence on the
English state, nor did they comprehend how weak was his claim to colonial
jurisdiction. Both Wilkinson and Henderson believed the news.
Wilkinson advised Gibson to send the bishop to Maryland rather than to
Virginia. Henderson, for a bargain price of four thousand pounds sterling,
volunteered to sell the new prelate a suitable estate consisting of two
thousand acres of land complete with building, slaves, and livestock.[2]

During the October 1724 session of the general assembly the Church
almost lost what little disciplinary powers the commissaries had. Claiming
that clerical immorality was driving the public out of the Church in
disgust, the lower house proposed a bill to give laymen authority to
try ministers. The Maryland Church was in a very weak position. The
bishop of London had not yet secured his colonial patent, and the commissions
of Henderson and Wilkinson had lapsed the year before.[3] Nevertheless,

---

[1] "Answers to the Queries," n.d. but 1723 or 1724, in Perry, Collections,
IV, 131-187.

[2] Christopher Wilkinson to Bishop Edmund Gibson, September 9, 1724, in
Perry, Collections, IV, 245-246.

[3] As the problems of Henderson and Wilkinson demonstrated, even when
commissioned the officers' authority to discipline the clergy was weak
and disputed. The commissaries could hold a hearing to determine the guilt
of an accused minister, but they could not force him to attend the session,
nor could they remove him from his living. The right to deprive a minister
of his benefice, ultimately the most effective means of enforcing discipline,
was after 1715 the prerogative of the Maryland proprietors, and by delegation,
the governors. When Gibson's royal commission was operative (1728-1748) no
one was really sure whether it superceded Baltimore's chartered rights.

the Eastern Shore clergy hastily convened and sent Wilkinson hurrying to
Annapolis to block the measure. Henderson and three other nearby ministers
rode to the capital to protest to the council that a law which placed
jurisdiction over the clergy into lay hands would be inconsistent with
Baltimore's charter, repugnant to the laws of Great Britain, and destructive
of the constitution of the Church. They declared that they could not submit
to such an act without violating their ordination oaths.[1] When the petition
was sent down to the lower house, the delegates replied that they thought it
improbable that the provincial Church would succeed in regulating itself,
and that it was their "indisputable duty" to "put some check to parties so
destructive to our Religion."[2] The council refused to pass the bill (the
governor would have vetoed it in any case), but the lower house let the
clergy know they could expect the bill to come up again.[3] Shortly afterwards Henderson sailed to England, and it was said that he went specifically
to apply to Gibson for a patent as commissary.[4] Not yet commissioned as
diocesan himself, the bishop could not or more likely would not grant him
one.

During the late 1720s the assembly and the clergy commenced what became

---

[1] The journal of the upper house notes that the protest was lodged
October 22, 1724, (Arch. Md., XXV, 31) but does not include the text. This
is found in Perry, Collections, IV, 247-248.

[2] The response of the assembly is not in the legislative journals, but it
was copied for the bishop of London and is in Perry, ibid., 248-249.

[3] Christopher Wilkinson to Bishop Edmund Gibson, November 20, 1724, in
Perry, ibid., 246. The bill to put regulation of the clergy under lay
control was also in principle a veiled attack on Baltimore's chartered
ecclesiastical rights. The bill was formulated in the middle of a battle
between the assembly and the governor, the proprietor, and the council over
the extension of English statutes to the province. Members of the assembly
were trying to induce the government to acknowledge the extension. The
regulatory bill may have been directed more against the government than the
Church. For the constitutional dispute, see Aubrey C. Land, The Dulanys of
Maryland (Baltimore, 1955), chapter 4.

an intermittently flaring, fifty-year quarrel over the issue of clerical stipends. The annual salary of each Anglican incumbent depended upon two factors: the number of taxables in his parish, and the price of tobacco. The forty pounds of tobacco per parish taxable allowed by the establishment acts to inducted ministers was, for the early clergymen, a very small income. Though the price of tobacco fluctuated from year to year, the rapidly increasing population had considerably boosted the average clerical salary by the 1720s.[1] Many legislators thought the salaries too high, the tax too burdensome, and the parish inhabitants too many. One method of cutting clerical stipends was to subdivide the original parishes, producing a larger number of smaller units. Another was to diminish the tax outright. The assembly attempted both.

For a time it was quite successful. Between 1725 and 1729 four new parishes were created out of existing livings. Ministers accurately pointed out that they held their livings as freeholds, and claimed that efforts to deprive them of their income base, the taxables, were tantamount to robbery. Convinced that the affected incumbents could afford the loss, the assembly ignored the protests.[2]

Although the divisions troubled the clergy, they actually involved only a small number of incumbents. Far more threatening to the ministry as a group was the legislature's move to alter the forty per poll. The first attempt of this kind occurred in 1728, when the legislature passed an act to regulate the tobacco staple. The aim of the measure was to raise the quality and the price of Maryland tobacco by forcing a cut in production. To compensate for the reduced worker yield, officers' fees--which included

[1] Clerical salaries are more fully discussed in Chapter V.

[2] The parish divisions of the late 1720s are handled in Chapter V, pp. 242-243, at greater length.

court costs and other state services as well as fees for lawyers and
government officials—were decreased. Along with all county levies, they
became payable at the rate of ten shillings current money per hundredweight
of tobacco or, at the choice of the debtor, in tobacco at three-quarters
the original rate.[1] To the consternation of the clergy, their dues were
treated as officers' fees and were also reduced by the same amount.

Before the bill passed the upper house, ministers in the vicinity of
Annapolis heard of it and rushed to the city to protest. Six clergymen
informed the council that the reduction in their salaries was a "Grievous
Offense against God." They asserted that the Establishment Act was
unalterable because it had received the royal sanction.[2] The upper house,
though, agreed with the assembly that a measure to curb tobacco production
was necessary for the good of the people of Maryland. The councillors also
agreed that it was only fair that parochial fees fall in the same degree
the officers' fees did. They assured the ministers that the anticipated
rise in the price of Maryland tobacco would shortly render their salaries
even more valuable than before.[3]

The ministers did not surrender. In late November 1728 sixteen of them[4]

---

[1] The act is in Arch. Md., XXXVI, 266-275. Officers' fees had long
been a controversial issue in Maryland. They had been cut before (in 1719
by a quarter, and by another quarter in a 1725 act which was later vetoed
by the proprietor) but the clerical dues had never been associated with them.
St. George Leakin Sioussat, Economics and Politics in Maryland, 1720-1750,
Johns Hopkins University Studies, Series XXI, No. 6-7 (Baltimore, 1903), 13;
Mereness, Proprietary Province, 335-337.

[2] Arch. Md., XXXVI, 162.

[3] Arch. Md., XXVI, 162-163. At the invitation of the assembly, on
November 2 the council joined the lower house in addressing Benedict Leonard
Calvert, the governor. They stressed the importance of the act and warned
against efforts by selfish ministers to frustrate it. Arch. Md., XXXVI,
166-167, 169-170.

[4] There were about thirty-four ministers in the province at that time.

convened to prepare a countermove. They decided to send petitions and
copies of the act to the king, the S.P.G., and the bishop of London.[1]
The petitions emphasized the conviction of the ministers that the clause
which cut their dues violated the Establishment Act. Even if the clause
were legal, they argued, it placed an undue hardship on men of their order.
Salaries would not rise. Should the price of tobacco increase above ten
shillings a hundredweight, the taxables would prudently pay the dues in
money, and if the price of tobacco remained low or fell, their parishioners
would pay the thirty pounds of leaf. Either way, their incomes would be
reduced.[2]

However much members of the clergy had disliked Henderson's haughty
behavior as commissary, they realized that in this crisis his stubbornness
and determination were invaluable. Henderson was sent to London to deliver
the petitions. By October 14, 1729, he had persuaded the king to refer
the case to the Privy Council. Baltimore's agent in London became thoroughly
alarmed at the prospect of royal intervention into a proprietary matter.
He convinced the Privy Council to postpone hearings until Baltimore, who
had not been apprised of the petitions, could look into the case. The
hearings were never held. In midwinter Baltimore came to London, studied
the act, and decided the measure would not benefit the colony's economy.
Besides, he noted, "it appear'd so unjust & unreasonable the taking from
the Clergy a 4th part of their Incomes without any just grounds or

---

[1] The ministers did not address a petition to Lord Baltimore. Benedict
Leonard Calvert, the governor who signed the act, was the brother of the
proprietor; the clergy probably thought they would be more successful
petitioning for redress outside the proprietary government. Only later,
when the case was before the Privy Council, did Henderson frame a petition
to Baltimore.

[2] The clergy of Maryland to the S.P.G., November 24, 1728; the clergy
to Bishop Edmund Gibson, November 24, 1728; the clergy to King George II,
November 28, 1728, all in Perry, Collections, IV, 262-268.

Equivalent." The proprietor disallowed the act on January 30, 1730.[1]
That same day, he wrote to the Maryland clergy assuring them that he would
not tolerate any innovations in the Establishment Act.[2]

With the proprietor so conveniently available, Henderson ventured
further. He persuaded Baltimore to veto an act, passed in August 1729, which
had rearranged the boundaries of several Western Shore parishes. Henderson
informed Baltimore that the legislature had passed the act without obtaining
the consent of the affected incumbents, and told him that Parliament itself
would not dare to alter a living without the incumbent's consent. Baltimore
saw the point, vetoed the act, and ordered that in the future Maryland
parishes could be divided only with the approval of the incumbents or
during vacancies.[3] At Henderson's instigation the proprietor also disallowed another act, passed in November 1728, which had subjected ministers
to the same fines for absenteeism the other vestrymen were liable to.[4]

Henderson must have congratulated himself when he sailed back to
Maryland in early 1730. His mission had been very successful. The proprietor had promised to protect the establishment, and the legislature had
been reined in. Equally gratifying, the bishop of London had granted

---

[1] Privy Council Committee minutes, December 18, 1729; "The Humble
Representation of Cecilius Calvert Equire for & on Behalf of Charles Lord
Baltimore his Brother," n.d. but c. December 1729; "The Petition of
Jacob Henderson Clerk in behalf of Himself & the rest of the Clergy of
the Province of Maryland," n.d. but c. December 1729/January 1730; "The
Memorial of the... Traders to Maryland," January 17, 1729; all in Arch.
Md., XXXVIII, 438-441.

[2] Lord Baltimore to the Maryland clergy, January 30, 1730, in Perry,
Collections, IV, 282.

[3] The act is in Arch. Md., XXXVI, 467-469; Henderson's petition
(d. January 17, 1730) and the disallowance are in Arch. Md., XXXVIII, 442.

[4] The act is in Arch. Md., XXXVI, 276-278; Henderson's petition
(d. January 22, 1730) and the disallowance are in Arch. Md., XXXVIII,
442-443.

Henderson a patent as commissary of Maryland.[1]

The royal commission of 1728 gave Henderson's authority for the first time an unquestionably legitimate derivation. His right to discipline the clergy was firmly grounded in an act of state, which would remain in force until the death of George II or Bishop Gibson. Better yet, his diocesan was willing to spell out his responsibilities. Gibson had strong ideas on how his deputies were to exercise their commissions. The bishop thoughtfully drew up a pamphlet for colonial commissaries describing in detail the legal procedures they were to use to try immoral subordinates. Minor offenses were punishable by admonition in private. The penalty for particularly flagrant or immoral misdeeds was a public admonition or an ecclesiastical trial. Except in the most serious cases, the commissaries were to limit their sentences to suspension rather than deprivation. Gibson also ordered the commissaries to hold yearly visitations.[2]

Presumably Henderson was also cheered by the information that in early 1730, prodded by Gibson, the Board of Trade began to include in its instructions to colonial executives a notice of the bishop's royal commission, along with an order to "give all Countenance & due Encouragement to the Said Bishop of London or his Commissaries in the Legal Exercise of Such Ecclesiastical Jurisdiction." Governor Calvert of Maryland was

---

[1] By this time Wilkinson had died. Henderson may not have been the bishop's first choice. Wilkinson noted in December 1728 that a short time previously Gibson had invited the aged Joseph Colbatch to head the clergy in Maryland. According to Wilkinson, Colbatch was willing enough but a writ of ne exeat (a court order generally used to stop debtors from fleeing the country) prevented him from sailing for England. Wilkinson said Colbatch was to be suffragan--which was an impossibility--but the whole affair is rather curious. Commissaries could be appointed by mail, but any sort of consecration would indeed have required a trip to Britain. There is no other evidence of the writ or the invitation. Christopher Wilkinson to Bishop Edmund Gibson, December 10, 1728, in Perry, Collections, IV, 269.

[2] Edmund Gibson, "Methodus Procedendi Contra Clericos Irregulares in Plantationibus Americanis," in the Fulham Papers, printed in Cross, American Episcopate, 294-309. It was issued in September 1728.

sent a copy, too.[1]

The veto of the tobacco regulation act of 1728 was unpopular in Maryland. Henderson's arrival in the province almost provoked a riot, and several ministers were thrashed by furious parishioners.[2] Shortly after news of the disallowance reached the colony, however, the legislature passed another act to regulate tobacco. Again it arranged a cut in tobacco production and reduced the fees of some officers. In contradiction to the proprietor's instructions, the act included a provision that taxables could pay a quarter of the forty per poll due to ministers in grain at set conversion rates.[3] To forestall Baltimore's disapproval, the legislature drew up a petition averring the importance of tobacco regulation and the fairness of the alteration in the forty per poll. As a parting shot, the petitioners asserted that no parishes had ever been unjustly divided, and declared that even the reduced ones supplied a larger maintenance than Virginia incumbents enjoyed.[4]

Jolted out of his new complacency, Henderson quickly wrote a counter-petition to Baltimore and hired a London agent to plead the cause of the clergy. As they did before, the ministers argued that the inclusion of the clause changing their salaries required the nullification of the act. The act itself, they agreed, was perfectly laudable, and they were sure the

---

[1] The draft of the instructions, which includes a notation that Calvert received a copy, is printed in Cross, American Episcopate, 293-294.

[2] Jacob Henderson to Bishop Edmund Gibson, August 12, 1730; statement of Thomas Fletcher, n.d., and statement of James Robertson, May 22, 1730; in Perry, Collections, IV, 300, 283.

[3] The text of the act is in Arch. Md., XXXVII, 138-151. The conversion rates were given in the act and were, according to the legislature, fair ones. Wheat was worth forty-two pounds of tobacco per bushel, for instance, and oats were worth twenty pounds of tobacco for the same amount.

[4] Arch. Md., XXXVII, 60-61.

legislature could prepare a revision in short order.[1] The regulation act

was due to expire on September 29, 1731, at any rate, and perhaps mostly

for that reason Baltimore ruled on December 17, 1730, that it was to remain

in effect.[2] The proprietor did, however, write to the clergy the following

January promising them his protection in the future.[3]

The attempt to increase the price of Maryland tobacco by restricting

the size of the crop was not successful. The legislature permitted the act

of 1730 to lapse quietly. From that time through 1747 the Anglican

ministers were paid their regular forty pounds of tobacco per taxable.

During the interval, though, it became apparent that the method used in

Virginia to enhance the price of its tobacco was working very well. Rather

than cutting production, Virginia passed an act in 1730 requiring public

inspection of all exported tobacco. Quality-controlled, Virginian tobacco

was favored on the open market. In 1747 the Maryland legislature passed

"An Act for Amending the Staple of Tobacco ... and for the Limitation of

Officers' Fees" which was consciously patterned on the Virginia model.[4]

Re-enactments maintained the measure in force until 1770. The act ordered

the inspection of all tobacco intended for export and the destruction or

sequestration of below-standard tobacco. It also reduced the poll tax to

thirty pounds of inspected tobacco and gave non-tobacco producing taxables

the option of paying the tax in currency, at the rate of twelve shillings

sixpence per hundredweight of tobacco. This time the clergy did not protest.

---

[1] "The Petition of Jacob Henderson Clerk, in behalf of himself & the
rest of the Clergy of Maryland," presented by Ferdinand John Paris, agent,
d. November 18, 1730, in Arch. Md., XXXVIII, 443-448. This time the clergy
did not address their grievances to the Crown. Henderson may have anticipated on the basis of Baltimore's promises that this act also would be
quickly vetoed.

[2] Arch. Md., XXXVIII, 448.

[3] Lord Baltimore to the clergy, January 29, 1731, in Arch. Md.,
XXXVIII, 448-449.

[4] The act is in Arch. Md., XLIV, 593-638.

They realized that the legislature could not be induced to exempt the

clerical dues from the overall reduction in officers' fees. More than

that, though, the clergy were as concerned as other citizens about the

relatively low market value of Maryland tobacco. Most were probably quite

resigned to sacrificing a portion of their gross in exchange for a boosted

return on the remainder. In addition, the conversion rate of tobacco to

currency set by the legislature was a fair one for the time. Prompted by

economic motives, most ministers accepted the act and chose to ignore

the consideration that it was in effect an amendment to the supposedly

inviolable Establishment Act.[1]

Meanwhile, Henderson did not find his task as commissary an easy one.

When he returned to Maryland in 1730 he committed a serious blunder by not

bringing with him a copy of Gibson's royal patent as colonial diocesan.

Henderson did not receive a copy for several years.[2] Without proof of

---

[1] The only clerical petitions on record against the Tobacco Inspection
Act before the late 1760s were instigated by Alexander Adams. Adams wrote
Gibson's successor, Bishop Thomas Sherlock, in 1751 and again in 1752 to
complain about the alteration to the Establishment Act provisions regarding
salaries. Adams wanted Sherlock to persuade Frederick Calvert, the new Lord
Baltimore, not to approve any future acts which would change the forty per
poll. In 1752 Adams wrote a petition to the bishop making the same request,
and three other clergymen signed it also. Adams said more ministers would
have signed had he been able to travel to the individual parishes to obtain
signatures. Presumably Adams was seeking to forestall the 1753 re-enactment
of the Inspection Act. Alexander Adams to Bishop Thomas Sherlock, October
5, 1751; Adams to Sherlock, September 29, 1752; Alexander Adams, Hamilton
Bell et al. to Bishop Sherlock, n.d. but c. 1752; in Perry, Collections, IV,
326-330. Adams mentioned in his letter of 1752 that the clergy did not
convene after the enactment of the Tobacco Inspection Act because Maryland
had no commissary and they did not dare to meet without authority. Perry,
ibid., 329. A more likely explanation is that the ministers simply did not
want to meet.

[2] By March 1732 Henderson had received a copy of the patent issued by
George I. It was, of course, invalid. At that time he had heard that a
copy of the commission from George II had been sent to the colonies by
the Board of Trade, but no one seemed to have received it. Henderson
suspected that Governor Benedict Leonard Calvert had deliberately withheld
it. Jacob Henderson to Bishop Edmund Gibson, August 12, 1730, August 7,
1731, and March 13, 1732; in Perry, Collections, IV, 301, 302-303, 308.

Gibson's colonial rights, the commissary's own ecclesiastical authority
in Maryland was very weak. Though he managed to hold visitations without
difficulty in 1730 and 1731 his power to regulate the clergy was
repeatedly challenged.

Shortly after his return from England Henderson was obliged to deal
with two cases of clerical immorality. In 1730 the vestry of St. Stephen's
Parish in Cecil County complained that John Urmston was a drunkard and
neglected his duties. Henderson admonished the minister, but when Urmston
refused to mend his ways the commissary deprived him of his living in what
was apparently a full scale ecclesiastical trial. This was the only such
trial ever held in Maryland and the only time a commissary ventured to
deprive an incumbent. Charging that the commissary had exceeded his
authority, Urmston threatened to sue him for damages. Although Governor
Benedict Leonard Calvert appeared to accept the legitimacy of the sentence
by inducting another minister into Urmston's living, Henderson was
greatly relieved when Urmston died before a suit was lodged.[1]

Henderson did not even dare to order the other miscreant, William
Tibbs, to stand trial. In September 1731 the long-suffering vestry of
St. Paul's Parish in Baltimore County sent Henderson a formal petition
asking him to try Tibbs for negligence and drunkenness. The vestry vol-
unteered to testify against the minister in an ecclesiastical trial.
Henderson sent a copy of the petition to Gibson but took no action himself.
Urmston's fulminations had made him wary, and Tibbs was rich and liable
to fight any attempt the commissary made to discipline him.[2]

---

[1] Jacob Henderson to Bishop Edmund Gibson, August 17, 1731, October 11,
1731, and March 13, 1732, in Perry, Collections, IV, 302, 308, 310.

[2] The churchwardens and vestrymen of St. Paul's Parish, Baltimore
County, to Jacob Henderson, September 10, 1731; Henderson to Bishop
Gibson, October 11, 1731, and Henderson to Gibson, March 13, 1732; in
Perry, ibid., 302, 309-310.

Frustrated by his judicial impotence and the insubstantiality of his authority, Henderson wrote Gibson in 1732 that he was "quite tired out with the opposition I meet with and nothing to support me."[1] A few years later he relinquished his commission.[2]

Henderson was the last Maryland commissary. Relations between Lord Baltimore and Bishop Gibson grew very cool following a quarrel over presentation rights, and the bishop subsequently did not presume to or did not want to appoint another colonial deputy.[3] He ignored supplications from Maryland clergymen for an ecclesiastical officer authorized to control their colleagues.[4] By default, the responsibility for regulating clerical immorality returned to the state. In 1746 a minister was ordered to answer charges before the council, and in 1747 the assembly investigated and ruled on an alleged instance of simony.[5] The legislature almost institutionalized lay regulation of the clergy in a 1748 bill to "restrain the ill-behavior of clergymen," which passed the lower house and was read twice in the upper house before it was voted down.[6]

By the mid-1730s the Maryland Church had given up any real effort to discipline its own personnel. Responsibility for clerical regulation sub-

---

[1] Jacob Henderson to Bishop Edmund Gibson, March 13, 1732, in Perry, Collections, IV, 303.

[2] Although it seems quite certain that Henderson ceased to function as commissary by c. 1736, no resignation has been found.

[3] Gibson refused to license several ministers Baltimore wanted to present to Maryland parishes. The proprietor inducted them anyway. The rupture occurred prior to April 1735 but the exact period cannot be ascertained. Henderson to Bishop Gibson, April 25, 1735, Fulham Papers, "Maryland 1696-1769," item 75; Hugh Jones and Henry Addison to Bishop Thomas Sherlock, August 27, 1753, in Perry, Collections, IV, 331.

[4] See, for instance, Hugh Jones to Bishop Gibson, October 19, 1741, in Perry, ibid., 323.

[5] Arch. Md., XLIV, 291, 527-530, 534.

[6] Arch. Md., XLVI, 29, 69, 72-73.

sequently rested entirely with the state. This abdication of independence
was completely contrary to canon law and English custom. It was, however,
a concession necessitated by the position of the Anglican Church in Great
Britain as well as in Maryland. For most of the seventeenth and eighteenth
centuries the British state gave little recognition and less support to
the principle that the bishop of London was the diocesan of the colonies.
Without the backing of the state, legal quibbles hampered the colonial
churches from functioning as a part of an episcopal organization. In Maryland, furthermore, the Church was established sixty years after the executive had been granted extensive ecclesiastical powers. Though the limits
to those powers were never exactly defined, neither the bishop of London
nor the clergy in Maryland ever dared to force a confrontation between
Church and proprietor. While the Maryland executive retained the right to
induct ministers, and claimed--usually convincingly--to have the sole right
to deprive them, the Church's attempts to discipline its own personnel
were bound to be ineffectual.

The Church's frailty in Maryland was further exemplified by its
inability to protect its so-called constitution. Clergymen claimed that
the Establishment Act was permanent and inviolable; in fact, the legislature altered various of its clauses on several occasions to fit the needs
of the moment. Lacking firm support from Church or state in England,
uncertain of the durability of the establishment in Maryland, clergymen
of the Anglican Church abandoned their early efforts to construct a
colonial organization replicating the structure, jurisdiction, and the
power of the parent body. The Church remained a "Body without a head,"[1]

---

[1] Hugh Jones and Henry Addison to Bishop Thomas Sherlock, August 27,
1753, in Perry, Collections, IV, 332.

and without one, it could neither protect itself from internal nor external enemies.

Chapter II

The Church in Maryland, 1750 - 1776

Troubled Maryland clergymen hoped that the death of Edmund Gibson in 1748 would lead to the elevation of a cleric with the interest, prestige, and diplomacy necessary to lead the provincial Church. They wanted a diocesan willing to fight any further innovations to the Church's constitution. They looked for a bishop who could solve the chronic problem of clerical dicipline, and one who would speak for them to Lord Baltimore and, when requisite, to the Crown. The new bishop disappointed them. Thomas Sherlock was seventy years old when he moved to the see of London. He did not seek, as Gibson had, a royal commission recognizing him as the superior of the colonial clergy. Though he bore the title of colonial diocesan until his death in 1761, he never seriously attended to the duties of that office. Instead, Sherlock tried to relieve himself of any responsibility for the American ministry by securing the appointment of a resident colonial bishop. When the Crown denied his suit the disappointed prelate handled colonial matters with indifference.[1] He was by no means a leader of much use to the Maryland Church.

A change of personnel in the state rather than the ecclesiastical establishment was ultimately of more importance to the ministers in the colony. Charles Calvert, fifth Lord Baltimore and proprietor of Maryland since 1715, died in 1751, and was succeeded by his son Frederick. The new

---

[1] Sherlock had in mind a suffragan bishop shorn of all secular power and without authority over laymen and lay concerns. The state ministers under the Duke of Newcastle feared that the consecration of a bishop for America would arouse the dissenters and create religious and political turmoil in the colonies. See Cross, Anglican Episcopate, 58, 59, 113-125, 131-132.

proprietor was an irresponsible rake devoid of any real interest in
Maryland except insofar as the colony produced his income. He viewed the
Church less as a religious institution consigned to his care than a useful
source of patronage appointments. Quite unintentionally, though, the
sixth Lord Baltimore fostered the invention of a non-controversial method
of regulating the clergy when he sent Horatio Sharpe to Maryland as
governor in 1753.

Sharpe was a thoughtful, scrupulous, guileless administrator. He had
received no warning prior to his arrival in August 1753 that directing
the established church would absorb much of his time over the next sixteen
years. His official instructions sounded simple enough. The governor
was to "Pass no Act of Assembly by which the Provision that is made for
the Clergy in an Act Intitled An Act for the Establishment of Religious
worship may be taken away." He was not to divide parishes to the disad-
vantage of living incumbents. Sharpe was also to inform the proprietor
immediately when livings became vacant so that Baltimore could "have an
opportunity of obliging deserving Persons."[1] The instructions said
nothing about whether or in what fashion the governor was to maintain
discipline in the Church.

A couple of weeks after Sharpe disembarked in Annapolis almost half
the Anglican clergy in Maryland gathered together in the capital. The
convention was an extraordinary occurrence, for the provincial ministers
had rarely ventured to meet without the permission of the governor or the
commissary. The purpose of the meeting of August 22-23, 1753, was to

---

[1] Sharpe's ecclesiastical instructions are numbers 6 and 12, found in
Arch. Md., XXXI, 11, 12. Very curiously, the phrasing of his first
ecclesiastical instruction suggests that the proprietor or his agent did
not know that the forty per poll had been reduced in the Tobacco Inspection
Act of 1747.

discuss the state of the Church and to frame congratulatory addresses
to Baltimore and to Sharpe. The sixteen ministers[1] adopted parliamentary
procedure and came to decisions by vote of the majority. The meeting was
not peaceful. The ministers engaged in long and acrimonious debates over
whether to insert in the addresses a warning to the government that popery
and Jacobinism in Maryland were growing at an alarming rate. They finally
decided to delete all but a passing reference to the popish menace in the
messages themselves but decided to meeting again in October to address the
proprietor on that issue.[2]

The ministers also presented Sharpe with his first case of clerical
immorality. They sent the governor a remonstrance informing him that his
chaplain, Matthias Harris, labored "under a most vile & scandalous Report."
Harris was a native Marylander and was thought to have been guilty of
forgery and counterfeiting before ordination. The petitioners asked Sharpe
not to induct Harris until his innocence was proved.[3] Sharpe investigated
the charges, decided they were valid, and asked Baltimore for instructions.
The proprietor ordered Sharpe not to induct Harris into any living before
he had been cleared of any imputation of guilt.[4] The matter was handled
easily because Harris was not an inducted minister, and Baltimore was
simply exercising the right of any patron of a church living to deny a
presentation to an applicant.

---

[1] Fifteen ministers attended the first day and sixteen did so the
second. Four ministers sent proxies. There were about thirty-nine
ministers altogether in the colony.

[2] The minutes of the meeting, recorded by Thomas Bacon, are in the
Gilmor Papers, Md, 387.1, Volume 1, fols. 40 ff., MdHi. They have been
printed in Md. Hist. Mag., III (1908), 257-273.

[3] Ibid., 271-272.

[4] Horatio Sharpe to Cecilius Calvert, September 14, 1753, and Calvert
to Sharpe, January 5, 1754, in Arch. Md., VI, 6, 30; Baltimore to Sharpe,
January 5, 1754, in the Maryland State Papers, Black Books, XI, No. 25,
MdA.

In October 1753, a few days before the next convention was scheduled
to begin, Governor Sharpe was unexpectedly and publicly apprised of the
gravity of the Church's disciplinary problems. Amid much fanfare, Thomas
Cradock preached a sermon to the governor and the legislature on the
scandalous lives of his fellow ministers. Cradock held up for public view
a catalogue of corruption: a minister on trial for murder, a recent
suicide, and clerics "plunging into all manner of Debaucheries, and becoming
martyrs to their Mistress and their Bowl." He lamented the lack of an
agent or an agency with regulatory powers over the Maryland clergy. Somewhat obliquely, Cradock suggested that the proper dispenser of discipline
would be an American bishop sanctioned by Parliament. He explained that
Bishop Sherlock had requested a colonial bishop at an inopportune moment
and had been rejected, but if the colonies themselves applied for a prelate
"we are not of so little importance to the Strength, Trade and Prosperity
of Great Britain but that our Petitions wou'd be immediately granted."
Baltimore would undoubtedly agree to the proposal, he assured the audience.[1]

The assembly was so impressed by Cradock's depiction of clerical sins
that it ordered a committee of laws to draft a regulatory bill. The
measure was later referred to the next assembly and was subsequently
dropped.[2]

Sharpe had been very concerned when he heard that the clergy intended
to petition Baltimore about the growth of popery. During this period the
proprietary government was hard-put to stifle vehement anti-Catholic

[1] This sermon, delivered October 7, 1753, in St. Anne's Church in
Annapolis, Maryland, is on deposit at the MdDL. It has been edited by
David C. Skaggs and printed as "Thomas Cradock's Sermon on the Governance
of the Church," William and Mary Quarterly, 3d Ser., XXVII (1970), 630-
653. The two quotations given here may be found on pages 640 and 641,
respectively, in the printed version.

[2] Arch. Md., L, 176, 250.

legislation originating in the lower house, and Sharpe did not want the clergy to aggravate the situation. The governor asked Thomas Bacon, an Eastern Shore minister friendly to the proprietor, to discourage his colleagues from attending the meeting in October. Bacon complied with such success that only ten ministers finally came to the convention.[1] To "prevent Mischief" Bacon was among them.[2] He persuaded the ministers to defeat a motion to assert the "Rights of the Clergy," which he feared would include a protest against the Tobacco Inspection Act, then up for re-enactment. He also tempered the ferocity of the rabidly anti-Catholic ministers. A list of seventeen Catholic outrages was reduced to seven, and the memorial was addressed to Sharpe instead of Baltimore.[3] A slightly different version of the memorial was presented to the assembly's Committee on Aggrievances, but, as Bacon and Sharpe were pleased to discover, it had been signed by so few ministers that it attracted little attention.[4]

Baltimore responded to the conventions of the clergy with an order which was the equivalent of the suspension of convocation in England. "I think it Necessary of Advising You," he wrote Sharpe, "of No further Meeting of the Clergy in a particular Body. -- I observed Warmth among Them by Their Proceedings at their late meeting at Annapolis, Therefore Direct You to Stop their further Meeting until you have My Instructions thereupon."[5] Sharpe transmitted the order to the clergy and assured the proprietor that

[1] An eleventh minister arrived the second day.

[2] Thomas Bacon, "An Account of what passed at a Meeting of the Clergy in Annapolis in October 1753, with other Matters relating thereto," Md. Hist. Mag., III (1908), 364-384. The quotation is taken from p. 364.

[3] The outrages consisted of, for example, the proliferation of Catholic schoolmasters.

[4] The memorial to the committee is printed in Arch. Md., L, 199. It was signed by Thomas Chase, Hugh Deans, Thomas Cradock, James MacGill, and William Brogden.

[5] Lord Baltimore to Horatio Sharpe, January 5, 1754, in the Maryland State Papers, Black Books, XI, No. 25, MdA. For the suspension of convocation in England, see Appendix A.

"from the temper they shewed I am persuaded they will not give any room
for uneasiness or Displeasure by any more such general meetings."[1]

With the clergy silenced, the prospects for an American prelate
remote, and Baltimore's leadership less than inspiring, Sharpe made it
his own business to deal with the problem of clerical discipline. He
formulated two plans. The first went into effect in early 1754, when
the governor began demanding bonds for good behavior from applicants for
Maryland livings.[2] Requiring bonds to ensure the conduct of appointed
officials was a common practice in the colony, and Sharpe observed how
useful it could be to regulate erring ministers. Sharpe planned to deny
induction to any minister unwilling to post a large bond (£500 sterling
in the one surviving specimen) promising that he would "well truly and
faithfully exercise perform and discharge his Duties and Functions and be
& remain of Good Life Manners and Conversation and demean behavior and
carry himself with Sobriety Honesty and [...]ty and ordinarily be Resident
in the said Parish ... and not absent himself by Thirty Days altogether
in any one Year."[3] Shrewdly, the governor planned to bond as many
incumbents as possible by offering to induct them into more lucrative
livings if they would sign.[4] Sharpe hoped that his program would
"effectually prevent for the future any Complainings against Lives &
Examples of the Clergy" and would guard against the "possibility of their
future immoral or vicious Conduct."[5] Rather proud of his project, Sharpe
was dismayed when he received orders to stop bonding ministers in early

[1] Horatio Sharpe to Lord Baltimore, May 2, 1754, Arch. Md., VI, 55.
[2] Horatio Sharpe to Cecilius Calvert, February 10, 1754, in Arch.
Md., VI, 38.
[3] Bond of Edward Dingle, May 1, 1754, Gilmor Papers, Ms. 387.1,
Vol. I, fol. 25, MdHi.
[4] Sharpe to Calvert, May 3, 1754, Arch. Md., VI, 61.
[5] Sharpe to Calvert, ibid.

1755.[1] Baltimore feared that the clergy or the bishop of London would protest the bonding. Requiring a bond for good behavior from a minister was not a measure which contravened a specific canon law, but it was a somewhat questionable innovation. In addition, the proprietor could not ignore the possibility that the Church might object to the bonding on the grounds that a minister who violated the terms of the contract would be tried by a civil court for what was fundamentally failings of an ecclesiastical nature.

Sharpe's second method of dealing with clerical misbehavior proved more durable. By the time Sharpe came to Maryland applicants for the better livings exceeded the available posts. The superfluity of eager candidates enabled the governor to demand that many applicants for induction first complete a period of probation. Rather than granting an unknown newcomer a full induction into a Maryland living, Sharpe licensed him as "reader" or curate. The candidate was then installed in a parish for a probationary period, which usually lasted about a year. As a reader the clergyman enjoyed all the usual benefits of incumbency, but if his behavior was objectionable the governor could easily strip him of his readership and deny him an induction.[2]

The scheme was neither foolproof nor flawless. Baltimore, a heedless patron, frequently ordered Sharpe to induct candidates into livings immediately. The governor himself occasionally ignored evidence of profligacy or incompetence and granted inductions when he should not have. Besides, almost any candidate could conceal reprehensible characteristics

---

[1] Cecilius Calvert to Horatio Sharpe, December 10, 1754, Arch. Md., VI, 1

[2] No letter from Sharpe proposing the scheme has been found. Baltimore, however, had apparently approved it by May 1754, when Edward Dingle was granted an induction to Christ Church Parish in Queen Anne's County after serving a probationary period.

for the duration of the probationary period.

Sharpe's schemes were primarily preventive measures. He could do little to curb immorality or negligence in the inducted clergy. In spite of the governor's pointed hints Baltimore steadfastly refused to permit the trial, suspension, or removal of troublesome incumbents. Perhaps the proprietor did not care to put his family's hereditary ecclesiastical rights to the test. Although the Maryland charter could be and usually was interpreted to bestow upon the proprietor the right to suspend or deprive ministers, only one clergyman had ever been deprived of a living at the instigation of a proprietary government.[1] Baltimore's refusal to act gave credence to the idea, current in the 1760s, that he did not actually have the authority to remove incumbents.[2]

By his own account, the care the governor usually gave to the inspection of candidates resulted in a higher moral tone in the Church as he gradually filled the parishes with his personal appointees. When Sharpe wrote Baltimore's agent in 1768 to report on the current cases of irregular clerical conduct he specifically noted that all of the men involved had been inducted into their livings before the beginning of his administration.[3]

---

[1] Governor Charles Calvert deprived Charles Smith of his living in St. George's Parish, Baltimore County, on May 1, 1726, for not conforming to the government. Smith is elsewhere described as a Jacobite. It should be noted that the deprivation occurred at a time when Maryland lacked a commissary and before Bishop Gibson was granted his royal commission as diocesan. St. George's Spesutia Parish, Baltimore/Harford County, Vestry Minutes, 1718-1771, MS. 12211, d. June 14, 1726, MdA.

[2] Thomas Chandler, for instance, told the bishop of London in 1767 that ministers in Maryland could not be removed "not even by the highest exertion of proprietary power." Thomas B. Chandler to Bishop Richard Terrick, October 21, 1767, in Perry, Collections, IV, 335.

[3] Horatio Sharpe to Hugh Hammersley, June 22, 1768, Arch. Md., XIV, 507.

Even Baltimore sometimes realized that a more comprehensive method
of clerical regulation was necessary. For a short period in 1754 he
toyed with the idea of permitting a commissary to reside in the province
to supply "the place of a Bishop in the Exercise of Ecc[lesiastica]l
Jurisdiction" and to share the commissary generalship with a layman.[1]
He apparently talked with Bishop Sherlock about a plan to discipline the
clergy using authority granted to him in the charter.[2] Neither plan (or
perhaps it was one plan) was ever implemented. Baltimore offered no
explanations, but he probably concluded that the measures would eventually impinge on his own ecclesiastical prerogatives. One alternative
Baltimore had no intention of supporting was the establishment of a
colonial bishop. "His Lordship," Secretary Hugh Hammersley wrote Sharpe
in 1767, "by no means wishes to see an Episcopal Palace rise in America,
or to have St Peter's Chair Transferred to Maryland."[3] For his part,
Sharpe believed that an American prelate would interfere with Baltimore's
ecclesiastical rights and that his investiture would upset the provincials.[4]

The inadequacy of the proprietary regime's regulatory measures
became embarrassingly evident during the late 1760s. Until that time the
Sharpe administration had been spared any exceptionally notorious cases
of immorality or negligence. For a while, indeed, it seemed possible that
clerical regulation would become less vital as erring ministers inducted
previous to the introduction of the probationary system died off and were
replaced by tested (and presumably more virtuous) former readers. Sharpe

---

[1] [Cecilius Calvert?] to Horatio Sharpe, January 5, 1754, Sharpe
Papers, MS. 1414, MdHi.

[2] Calvert to Sharpe, December 10, 1754, Arch. Md., VI, 129.

[3] Hugh Hammersley to Sharpe, November 10, 1767, Arch. Md., XIV, 431.

[4] Sharpe to Baltimore, June 11, 1767, Arch. Md., XIV, 401.

soothed complaining congregations with promises of future pulpit paragons.
In 1767, however, a parish refused to be mollified. The ensuing uproar,
exacerbated by an inopportune scandal, turned clerical discipline into an
issue of political importance. For what they reveal of the complexity of
the relationship between proprietary government and established church,
both incidents are worth recounting in detail.

The attack on the government's ecclesiastical dispositions originated
in Coventry Parish, in Somerset and Worcester counties on the lower Eastern
Shore. The parish incumbent of over twenty years, Nathanial Whittaker,
died in November 1766. He was, as Sharpe described him earlier, "a Person
of a most abandoned & prostituted Life & Character," who had "forfeited
not only the Character of a Clergyman but even of a Christian."[1] Despite
urgent and repeated applications by the vestry, Sharpe had not succeeded
in convincing Baltimore to deprive the minister. When Whittaker died,
the vestry immediately wrote Sharpe to remind him of their many tribula-
tions and their most remarkable display of patience. The vestrymen told
the governor that they expected that no minister would be inducted into
Coventry before he had served a trial period and had earned the approbation of the congregation. The vestry wanted the benefit of Sharpe's
probationary scheme. "We hope Sir that you will not conceive that we claim
this as an absolute right," the group explained, "but that we expect it
and hope your Excellency will be perswaded to think we merit this
Indullgence when you recolect that we have been more than twenty years
without having the Gospel preached to us or any other religious exercise
performed."[2] The letter also informed Sharpe that the parishioners had

---

[1] Horatio Sharpe to Lord Baltimore, June 6, 1754, Arch. Md., VI, 69. The
governor told Baltimore that if the proprietor moved to deprive Whittaker
"the whole Parish" would send affidavits certifying his disgusting behavior.

[2] The vestry of Coventry Parish to Horatio Sharpe, November 25, 1766,
Arch. Md., XIV, 349.

in mind several candidates for the living.[1] In January 1767 Sharpe
licensed Robert Reade to Coventry Parish as reader.[2] The parishioners
interpreted his appointment as a temporary engagement, and the vestry
initiated a search for an acceptable minister. On May 16, 1767, the
vestry and over 170 parishioners wrote the governor that they wished to
present Dr. Thomas Bradbury Chandler for induction.[3] Chandler's reputation
was excellent. He was also one of the key colonial agitators for a
resident bishop, and given Baltimore's sentiment on that subject, Sharpe
naturally refused to induct him. When news of the refusal reached
Coventry, "the whole parish appeared struck with Surprize and filled with
discontent."[4] Sharpe calmed the dissidents by promising that he would not
induct Reade, but would appoint a worthy gentleman the parishioners were
certain to endorse. When the governor heard, however, that some of the
vestry began to promulgate the notion that parishioners should rightfully
present ministers, he hastily inducted John Ross, minister of a neighboring
parish, into Coventry.[5] This action "struck the whole parish with horror
& dispair" and infuriated the vestry, for Ross's character was not
especially admirable. The parishioners decided not to accept the induction
without a protest. The thought of the hardships they had endured under
Whittaker, the vestry wrote Sharpe, and

[1] Arch. Md., XIV, 349-350.

[2] Horatio Sharpe to Lord Baltimore, March 31, 1768, Arch. Md., XIV, 480.

[3] The vestry of Coventry Parish to Sharpe, May 16, 1767, Arch. Md., LIX, 513-517.

[4] The vestry of Coventry Parish to Sharpe, n.d., c. late 1768, Arch. Md., XIV, 365.

[5] Horatio Sharpe to Baltimore, March 31, 1768, and Sharpe to Hugh Hammersley, April 1, 1768, Arch. Md., XIV, 480, 488.

the prospect of continuing in the like Situation
occasioned the utmost discontent both with
Vestry & People from which they were restrained
to the disagreeable necessity of forming some
resolutions among themselves to endeavor to find
out some relief, reason and humanity without the
consideration of the least idea of religion
declared that none should be stript of their
Substance without some consideration and that in
every Secular Imployment all were at Liberty to
share in every contract which should bind them.

The vestrymen concluded that they should

take the matter under our most serious consideration as an affair of the greatest importance both
to ourselves and posterity and to loose no time
or pains in being fully instructed with the right
of presentation Admission and Induction under the
laws of this Government as also the operation and
construction of his Lordships Charter relative to
the right of Advowsons.[1]

Apparently the vestry hired lawyers to investigate the issue of who had
the right to present ministers in Maryland. The attorneys concurred with
the vestry's conclusion that ecclesiastical law and tradition predating
the Maryland charter and the Establishment Act gave the people, the true
founders and maintainers of the churches, the sole right of presentation.
The vestry freely admitted that the people had not claimed the right to
present for a long time and that other agents had commonly exercised it.
This did not, the vestry argued, vitiate the people's original privilege.
The parishioners supported the vestry's ideas and ordered it to take the
case to court and to deny Ross admission into the church until the matter
was settled.[2]

---

[1] The vestry of Coventry Parish to Horatio Sharpe, n.d., c. late 1768,
Arch. Md., XIV, 366. An advowson was the right to present to an
ecclesiastical living.

[2] The vestry of Coventry Parish to Sharpe, n.d., Arch. Md., XIV, 367.

Hearing of the commotion in Coventry, Ross resigned his induction.[1] Because he could not permit the vestry's challenge to Baltimore's prerogative to remain unanswered, Sharpe promptly inducted Philip Hughes into the living on December 5, 1767. Hughes was a former army chaplain with battle experience, and Sharpe hoped that a man who had been at the affair of the Monongahela would not be frightened by a few threats from overly excited parishioners.[2] Hughes met with the Coventry Parish vestry on December 21 in the yard of the locked and bolted church. Determined to "use him [as] a Gentleman and do him any good natured Act in our power, except that of giving up what we thought our right," the vestrymen explained their views on proprietary presentations. They proposed that Hughes resign his induction and come to the parish as a licensed probationer. If his work pleased them, they promised that the parish would in due course recommend him to Governor Sharpe for an induction. Hughes rejected the proposal. The vestrymen told him that they would not permit him to officiate as incumbent before the parishioners had voted to receive him. A voting day was scheduled. Before it came, however, Hughes broke into the parish church and read the forms which legitimized his induction. During the next two Sundays he forced his way into the parish's two chapels, "with Weapons," as the vestry commented, "unbecoming the Character of a Minister."[3]

On January 11, 1768, at a meeting Hughes did not attend, the vestry and a considerable part of the congregation gathered and unanimously

---

[1] Ross was inducted into Coventry on November 9, 1767, and resigned before December 5. Horatio Sharpe to Hugh Hammersley, April 1, 1768, Arch. Md., XIV, 488.

[2] Sharpe to Lord Baltimore, March 31, 1768, and Sharpe to Hugh Hammersley, April 1, 1768, Arch. Md., XIV, 480-481, 488.

[3] The vestry of Coventry Parish to Sharpe, n.d., Arch. Md., XIV, 367-368.

decided not to approve Hughes's induction.[1] Hughes was then forcibly

prevented from entering the church buildings and was, in addition,

harassed when he moved about the parish. He finally went to Annapolis

for advice. Daniel Dulany, the eminent lawyer and provincial secretary,

considered the case. In his written opinion he sympathized with Coventry's

misfortunes under Whittaker, but declared that the "Reins of Government

are not to be surrendered into the Hands of any Vestry." He stated that

Baltimore's right to present ministers derived from the Crown and was

unassailable. Though Dulany admitted that canon law and Lord Coke said

that the founders, benefactors, and maintainers of churches had the right

of patronage to those livings, he disputed the idea that English custom

was valid in Maryland.[2]

Hughes sent a copy of the opinion to the vestry at Coventry and

asked the governor and council for redress. The vestry sent back a

defense expressing their disbelief that the proprietor's charter abrogated

the fundamental constitution of the Church and their doubt that a dispen-

sation had nullified canon law.[3] In late April 1768 the council read the

pertinent papers. It recommended that Hughes immediately lay the case

before the attorney general and prepare to testify in the Provincial

Court against his principal antagonists.[4] The dispute never reached the

---

[1] Arch. Md., XIV, 368. Hughes told Sharpe that 200 men had agreed to oppose his attempts to preach, which gives some indication of how many parishioners attended the meeting. Hughes was told that not all the parishioners were against him but that those who dare to speak on his behalf ran the risk of retaliation against their bodies and property. "Remonstrance of the Reverend Philip Hughes," April 29, 1768, Arch. Md., XXXII, 223.

[2] Dulany's opinion, which is not dated, is printed in Arch. Md., XXXII, 224-228.

[3] The vestry of Coventry Parish to Philip Hughes, n.d., Arch. Md., XXXII, 228-231.

[4] Arch. Md., XXXII, 231.

court. Sharpe ordered peace in the parish, deprived the leading vestryman of his civil office, jailed some of the troublemakers, and pressured
county delegates to stifle unrest.[1] Hughes, however, never felt safe or
at ease in Coventry, and he resigned his induction in July 1769.[2]

During this same period a second incident, which became known as the
Allen affair, disrupted the establishment. In 1766 the governor received
several letters from Baltimore ordering him to reserve a lucrative living
for the proprietor's "particular freind [sic]" Reverend Bennet Allen,
Fellow of Wadham College, Oxford.[3] Allen arrived in Maryland in late
December of that year with permission from Baltimore to hold two livings
if a single large one was unavailable. Sharpe hastily wrote to Baltimore
to remind him that the Establishment Act forbade pluralities except for
adjacent parishes and by permission of the two vestries. Offered his
choice of the available livings, Allen spurned the more lucrative in
favor of St. Anne's, the parish in which Annapolis was located, for the
advantages it offered of convenient access to the governor and a
relatively sophisticated social life. After his induction on January 1,
1767, Allen became discontented with his mediocre stipend and demanded
that Sharpe give him a second living. Consternated, Sharpe went so far
as to offer Allen ₤50 out of his own pocket if the minister would just remain
quietly at St. Anne's. Allen refused to drop his demands. St. James's
Parish, just north of Annapolis, became vacant in October 1767, and a very
reluctant Sharpe licensed Allen there as reader although the minister

---

[1] Horatio Sharpe to Hugh Hammersley, October 30, 1768, and June 22,
1768, Arch. Md., XIV, 509, 548.

[2] Outerbridge Horsey to Sharpe, October 15, 1768; Philip Hughes to
Sharpe, December 16, 1768, and June 13, 1769; all in Arch. Md., XIV, 533-
534, 560-561, 562-563.

[3] Lord Baltimore to Horatio Sharpe, August 2, 1766, Arch. Md.,
XIV, 323.

retained his Annapolis living. Allen was not satisfied with his readership and pressed Sharpe for a full induction. Worried that Baltimore
would be angry if he failed to carry out the proprietor's original
instructions, Sharpe inducted Allen into St. James in February 1768.
Shortly afterwards, he learned that Baltimore had changed his mind and had
decided not to provoke a dispute about pluralities.[1] The news arrived too
late.

While Allen had been pressuring Sharpe for an induction into the
second living, he composed a long position paper arguing that Baltimore
inherited through his charter the king's prerogative, as supreme ordinary,
to dispense with the canonical and Establishment Act rules concerning
pluralities.[2] In spite of his theories, though, Allen decided to comply
with the strictures in the Act and to obtain the consent of the two
vestries. Apparently St. James's Parish initially agreed to the arrangement
on Allen's promise to furnish a curate during his absences. The vestry
of St. Anne's indignantly refused to concur. Constrained by parishioners,
the vestrymen at St. James's changed their minds. Allen, in public, blamed
this development on collusion between vestrymen Samuel Chew of St. James's
and his stepbrother Walter Dulany of St. Anne's. Allen declined the
resulting challenge of a duel with Chew. In retaliation, though, he
questioned in an article in the Maryland Gazette whether Dulany, as a
member of the council, had the right to be a vestryman--a nonsensical
query which invited a retort, and got it.[3] From late January 1768 to early
June Walter Dulany, Allen, and their various supporters dominated

---

[1] Sharpe recapitulated the whole affair in a letter to Hugh
Hammersley, October 30, 1768, Arch. Md., XIV, 538-547. See also Sharpe
to Baltimore, October 29, 1767, Arch. Md., XIV, 425.

[2] Bennet Allen to Horatio Sharpe, n.d., Arch. Md., XIV, 437-456.

[3] "A Bystander," Maryland Gazette (Annapolis), January 28, 1768.

practically every issue of the Gazette.

In the beginning the debates were confined to the questions raised by Allen's plural livings: what constituted a legal induction, what were the rights and duties of a vestry, how Baltimore's presentation and induction powers compared with English practice. Very shortly this legal and philosophical tone was abandoned for the charms of muckraking. Allen's sexual life (it was rumored that he lived with a "sister" who was as much a sister to him as "Sarah was to Abraham")[1] was by no means exemplary for a clergyman. He drank heavily, had a wicked temper, and brawled in public. The Gazette articles revealed to the public that Baltimore's most favored protégé was a man totally unfit for his ecclesiastical office.

Having learned of Baltimore's change of heart, Allen resigned St. Anne's in March 1768 to retain the more lucrative post at St. James's. On March 26 he was consoled for his loss with the civil office of receiver general of revenue. Though he was deprived of it several months later, his new-found contentment led Sharpe to hope that the affair would soon be forgotten.[2]

On the contrary, matters became worse. Thomas Bacon, rector of All Saints' Parish in Frederick County, died May 24, 1768, leaving the richest living in Maryland vacant. Baltimore had at one time promised the parish to Allen. Several weeks before his death, Allen heard that Bacon was dangerously ill and informed Sharpe that he expected to succeed the incumbent.[3] This

---

[1] Jonathan Boucher to Reverend M. James, March 9, 1767, Md. Hist. Mag., VII (1912), 341.

[2] Commission Record, 1733-1773, fols. 207, 208, 209, MdA.

[3] Bennet Allen to Horatio Sharpe, May 8, 1768, Arch. Md., XIV, 494.

placed the governor in an uncomfortable position because he knew that
the parishioners of All Saints' planned to ask the assembly to divide
their oversized parish when Bacon died.[1] He sympathized with their wishes
but believed he had to induct Allen into the undivided parish. Three
days after Bacon's death Allen rode off to Frederick County with his
induction. He arrived at the church the day of Bacon's funeral, just
hours after the parishioners had signed the petition for division. He
refused to support it. Unluckily, a few days later the newest editions
of the Gazette arrived, filled with calumnies against Allen. The minister
"saw the Storm & anticipated it."[2] Not daring to wait for his scheduled
investiture the following Sunday, he obtained the church keys from the
sexton's serving maid and entered the empty building to read his induction
forms.[3] The vestry was outraged by his effrontery and later bolted the
church shut from the inside. Nothing daunted, Allen climbed through a
window before dawn on Sunday morning and opened the door. Before church,
the vestry remonstrated with Allen, telling him that the parishioners did
not want to acknowledge him until they knew the response of the legislature
to their petition. During the service the vestry called the congregation
out of the church, and a group of brawny men attempted to pull Allen from
the pulpit. They stopped only when the minister pulled a pistol and swore he
would shoot their leader. When the congregation outside began to pelt him
with stones through the windows and door, Allen fled the building. Following another riotous demonstration Allen went to Philadelphia, leaving

[1] Sharpe to Hugh Hammersley, May 27, 1768, Arch. Md., XIV, 494.

[2] Bennet Allen to Sharpe, June 6, 1768, Arch. Md., XIV, 501. In this
letter (the whole of it covers pp. 501-503) Allen reported most of the
particulars which follow here.

[3] "A Parishioner of All Saints," Maryland Gazette, September 1, 1768.

Bacon's popular curate in charge in his stead. Once again the Gazette
printed long and damaging reports on the conduct of an inducted minister.

The Coventry and Allen affairs were not the first times that vestries
and ministers in Maryland had clashed, or that parishioners had locked
ministers out of their pulpits. What was significant about these events
was their timing, notoriety, and ramifications. During the Stamp Act
crisis the proposition that taxation without the consent of the governed
constituted a violation of basic political rights gained much currency.
It was not a large step for disgusted churchgoers to conclude that supporting an undeserving minister was a form of illegal taxation.[1] The publicity
generated by the two incidents demonstrated to a large audience that
Baltimore was an insensitive and overbearing ecclesiastical patron, and
that Sharpe, however personally well-meaning, was a mere puppet. The
newspaper articles, the rallies, and the public discussions had also
provided Marylanders with an education in the particulars of the charter,
the Establishment Act, and canon law. In this atmosphere of public outrage
the legislature once again intervened in Church matters.

"The Publications with which the Maryland Gazette was for some time
filled & the bad Conduct of some among the Clergy seem to have made them
& their Thirty p[e]r poll more thought of lately than ever they were before
since the Law was made for the Support of an Established Clergy in the
Province," Sharpe warned Baltimore in June 1768.[2] The Tobacco Staple Act
was not due to expire for another year, however, and the assembly focused
on the old problem of disciplining the clergy. On June 8, 1768, a
committee introduced into the lower house a bill intended to supplement

---

[1] Oddly, the attacks on the Anglican Church seem to have come almost
exclusively from within the fold, despite the fact that people of all
denominations had to pay the clerical dues.

[2] Horatio Sharpe to Lord Baltimore, June 23, 1768, Arch. Md., XIV, 510.

the Establishment Act. Designed to go into effect in March 1769, the
bill called for the constitution of a special court to try ministers. The
governor, three clergymen, and three laymen were to form a board with
authority to judge ministers and punish them by suspension or deprivation.
The bill passed the lower house by a margin of 35 to 2 and swept through
the upper house on June 20.[1] The governor completely agreed that "something is necessary to be done" to discipline recalcitrant ministers, but
since the bill was an innovation he did not dare to sign it without hearing
from Baltimore.[2] He put it aside to await instructions. The delegates
promised that the bill would be re-submitted every session until it passed.
They underlined their determination to curb the clergy on the last day of
the session when they heard and applauded a report from the Committee of
Aggrievances on the misdoings of Richard Brown. Three of St. Mary's
County delegates charged that Brown, minister of King and Queen Parish,
had not been in residence in his parish for more than three years. Worse,
he had long been guilty of execrable conduct and was also being prosecuted
for murdering a slave. The lower house concurred with the committee's
conclusion that "the growth of popery and superstition are, as may be
expected, attendant consequences of such remiss and immoral conduct."[3]
The Church had to be protected from its own ministers.

The near-enactment of the regulatory bill roused the Maryland clergy out
of their now customary quiescence. Many of them began to think that only
the presence of a bishop in America could restrain the legislature from
imposing lay controls on ecclesiastical personnel. Of themselves only a

---

[1] Arch. Md., LXI, lxxi-lxxxii, 304, 315, 319, 361, 383, 400, 405,
406, 412, 420. The provisions of the bill are discussed in Horatio
Sharpe to Hugh Hammersley, June 15, 1768, and June 22, 1768, in Arch. Md.,
XIV, 503-504, 507.

[2] Sharpe to Hammersley, June 22, 1768, Arch. Md., XIV, 507.

[3] Arch Md., LXI, 410-411.

small number of Maryland ministers had ever been strong proponents of a colonial episcopate. They rather liked their freedom from diocesan supervision. The usual passivity of the majority was in marked contrast to their northern brethren. During the 1760s some of the clergy in the middle colonies and New England worked for the investiture of an American prelate with a unity and vigor never before achieved.[1] Their cause won the support of Archbishop Thomas Secker (who was elevated to Canterbury in 1758) and the acquiescence of Richard Terrick, Bishop of London from 1764 to 1777.[2] The cause was irreparably hamstrung by the late colonial crises, the rapidly changing British ministries, and the professed unwillingness of the colonials to accept a bishop. Uncertain of his overseas authority, Terrick, like Sherlock, refused to seek royal permission to send commissaries.[3] However, heartened by constant reports that a bishop was imminent, the northern S.P.G. clergy politicked, convened, and petitioned for his investiture. In October 1766 delegates from five middle and northern colonies met in Shrewsbury, New Jersey, to plan their strategy. In May the following year, the clergy of New York and New Jersey united their annual meetings and began to seek support from the unenthusiastic southern clergy. The conference members voted to send

---

[1] See Carl Bridenbaugh, Mitre and Sceptre: Transatlantic Faiths, Ideas, Personalities, and Politics 1689-1775 (Oxford, 1962), 178-182, 214-221, 229, 246-250, 266-270, 289-296, 315-316; Cross, Anglican Episcopate, 133-134, 164-172, 186-189, 215-225, 243-246; Frederick V. Mills, Sr., "The Internal Anglican Controversy over an American Episcopate 1763-1775," Historical Magazine of the Protestant Episcopal Church, XLIV (1975), 257-276; Don R. Gerlach, "Champions of an American Episcopate: Thomas Secker of Canterbury and Samuel Johnson of Connecticut," HMPEC, XLI (1972), 381-414; Edgar Legare Pennington, "Colonial Clergy Conventions," HMPEC, VIII (1939), 178-218.

[2] Prodded by Secker, Terrick asked the Board of Trade for permission to form an American see in March 1766. Gerlach, "Champions of an American Episcopate," HMPEC, XLI (1972), 405-406. Secker left ₤1000 to the S.P.G. for a colonial bishop when he died in 1768. Bridenbaugh, Mitre and Sceptre, 270.

[3] Gerlach, "Champions," HMPEC, XLI (1972), 406; Cross, Anglican Episcopate, 245-246.

Myles Cooper, president of King's College, and Robert MacKean, a New Jersey missionary, to Governor Sharpe with a plan to establish episcopacy without hurting anyone else's religion, pocketbook, or civil rights. They hoped for permission to hold a convention with the Maryland ministers to discuss the state of the Church in America.[1]

In Virginia, Jonathan Boucher heard that Cooper and MacKean had visited Maryland in June 1767, and guessed correctly that the missionaries' proposal would not "go down well."[2] The two representatives met with the governor, gave him a copy of the plan, and asked for his approval. Sharpe told them that he could not approve or disapprove of the plan without hearing Baltimore's opinion, but that he would not permit the clergy to convene for this or any other purpose. Disappointed, the two men asked Sharpe to transmit the proposal to Baltimore and left for New York. Personally the governor suspected that the successors of the first, very limited bishop would find their restricted authority unsatisfactory and would soon invade Baltimore's ecclesiastical prerogatives. Sharpe told the proprietor that he would be happy to put the matter before the legislature if Baltimore so desired, but he really thought that the colonists would prefer that disciplinary power over the clergy be lodged in the hands of a temporal authority.[3] Baltimore's secretary responded that the proprietor did not want the clergy to gather, most emphatically spurned the idea of colonial bishops, and would resist all Church attacks on his charter rights. He also did not want the legislature queried. Not only the proprietor's rights would be affected if the religious structure in Maryland changed,

---

[1] Bridenbaugh, *Mitre and Sceptre*, 268.

[2] Jonathan Boucher to Rev. James, July 4, 1767, *Md. Hist. Mag.*, VII (1912), 350.

[3] Horatio Sharpe to Baltimore, June 11, 1767, *Arch. Md.*, XIV, 401.

the secretary reminded Sharpe: "Should you be Blessed w[i]th a Bishop will he not want your Excellencys Perquisites arising from Marriage Licenses?"[1]

The regulatory bill of 1768 drew protests from the clergy. Ironically, the first to object was none other than Bennet Allen, who told the governor that an ecclesiastical commission of that type was a direct attack on the liberties and property of the clergy infringed on Baltimore's prerogative, and was contrary to canon law, which forbade a separate jurisdiction over church personnel.[2] Hugh Neill wrote to Bishop Terrick in September 1768 that no one disputed the necessity of disciplining the clergy, but the bill

> was a presbyterian form of ministers and ruling lay Elders, and laying a foundation for the presbyterian Government in the Church of England in Maryland, as well as subversive of the canons of the Church, which give the Bishop alone power to pronounce sentense [sic] in such cases.

Such a law, he continued,

> would be establishing Presbyterianism in this Colony upon the neck of the Church, and an effectual Bar to the introduction of Episcopacy, which is generally wished for by the Clergy of this Provence [sic].[3]

Neill neglected to mention that for many (if not most) of the clergy the preference for episcopacy was a recent acquisition, which developed in proportion to their fear of lay control.

The clergy felt sufficiently endangered to ignore Baltimore's prohibition and once again began to hold conventions. The first meeting since 1753 probably occurred in May 1769, when outgoing Governor Sharpe

---

[1] Hugh Hammersley to Sharpe, November 10, 1767, Arch. Md., XIV, 431.

[2] Bennet Allen to Sharpe, June 21, 1768, Arch. Md., XIV, 504-505.

[3] Hugh Neill to Bishop Richard Terrick, September 20, 1768, in Perry, Collections, IV, 338.

was presented with a farewell address signed by thirty-five clergymen.[1]
On June 15 an advertisement in the <u>Maryland Gazette</u> asked all the clergy
to meet July 2 in Annapolis. The object of the convention was probably
to discuss the state of the Church and possibly to plan an address to
Robert Eden, the new governor. There is no evidence, however, that the
meeting took place, and it may have been cancelled following an announce-
ment in the paper on June 29 that the appointment of American bishops
was certain.

At least three and possibly four meetings took place before the end
of September 1770. The excuse for the gatherings was that many of the
clergy wished to form and incorporate a society for the support and
relief of the widows and children of deceased clergymen. During this
same period, when Anglican ministers in other colonies were also forming
relief societies, there was nothing unusual in the Maryland meetings--but
they did enable the ministers to gather and there was no reason for them
to restrict their discussion to the business at hand. Seventeen clergymen
met in November 1769 to address a petition to Governor Eden concerning the
society, and an unknown number met again during the summer of 1770 on the
same business.[2] In September 1770 the clergy earnestly discussed the
situation of the Maryland Church. "After the fullest and maturest
Deliberation," they reported to the governor,

---

[1] The petition is in Arch. Md., XXXI, 566-567. There were about fifty-
four clergymen in Maryland at the time.

[2] The petition, dated November 17, was printed in the <u>Maryland
Gazette</u>, November 23, 1769; Henry Addison, Bennet Allen, and Jonathan
Boucher to Robert Eden, September 17, 1770, and Addison, Allen, and
Boucher to Rev. --, September 16, 1770, in <u>Arch</u>. <u>Md</u>., XXXII, 386-387;
Hugh Neill to Dr. Daniel Burton, July 18, 1771, in Perry, <u>Collections</u>, IV,
342.

> We have unanimously resolved that it is highly
> becoming us to make an Effort as far as in Us lies
> to introduce if possible Episcopacy into America:
> a Measure so highly reasonable, so absolutely
> necessary at this Crisis to the Colonies in general,
> and we add to Maryland in particular and so
> peculiarly befitting the Clergy of this Province to
> be amongst the foremost in soliciting that we cannot
> doubt of its meeting with your Excellency's perfect
> Approbation.

Listing the growth of sectaries and their impertinent, increasing tendency
to call Baltimore's presentation rights into question as signs of trouble,
the clergy noted that "It must then be obvious to your Excellency that the
Establishment here cannot subsist much longer without some form of
Government." They added that

> Whether this shall be that constitutional one by
> Bishops to which alone a Clergyman of the Church
> of England can in Conscience think it his Duty to
> Submit, or the unconstitutional and palpably
> Presbyterian System not long ago warmly contended
> for by both Houses of Assembly, is a Question
> hardly less interesting to the Civil Government
> of this Province than it is to its Clergy. The
> Jurisdiction of a Presbytery and every other
> Jurisdiction in its Principles akin to it is so
> adverse to the Frame and Scope of our excellent
> Establishment both in Church and State that in
> attempting to keep it forever at a distance from
> Maryland we trust your Excellency will consider us
> doing what most undoubtedly is our Duty.[1]

The clergy included in their report copies of petitions asking for a
bishop, which they intended to submit to the king, the proprietor, the
archbishop of Canterbury, and the bishop of London.[3] All the petitions
stressed the same themes: the danger of a presbyterian or puritanical
scheme to control the clergy, the need for discipline, the attacks on or

---

[1] The clergy to Robert Eden, n.d., but read in the council September
15, 1771, Arch. Md., XXXII, 380. The complete letter is on pp. 379-381.

[2] The petitions are printed in Arch. Md., XXXII, 381-384.

threats to the Church's establishment and Baltimore's presentation rights, and the clergy's conviction that a resident bishop was the sole viable means to bolster the constitution and regulate the ministers. The petitioners even promised the king that they would donate a proportion of their livings for the financial support of the bishop.

When nine of the clergy brought the address and the petitions to the council on September 15 the governor received them "very coldly," Hugh Neill reported, "and let us know, by the advice no doubt of his Council, that the Livings in Maryland were Donatives, and stood in no need of the aid of Episcopacy, &c. This casts a damp upon many."[1] Eden disputed the right of the eleven petition signers to speak for the whole clergy. The governor did not think that the religious establishment was in the least danger, but because the investiture of an American bishop was a matter of such momentous concern he declared that he would put the petitions before the assembly.[2] The council in turn advised the governor to delay the execution of the charter for the relief society because the clergy were using it as a pretext for frequent meetings.[3]

The September conference members appointed three ministers to act for the clergy as an executive committee. Jonathan Boucher, recently arrived from Virginia and incumbent in St. Anne's, Annapolis, thought of himself as the leader of the pro-bishop group.[4] Henry Addison, scion of an old and wealthy Prince George's County family, had been concerned with clerical regulation for almost two decades. He was Boucher's

---

[1] Hugh Neill to Dr. Daniel Burton, July 18, 1771, in Perry, Collections, IV, 342-343.

[2] Robert Eden to the clergy, September 15, 1770, Arch. Md., XXXII, 385.

[3] Arch. Md., XXXII, 385.

[4] Jonathan Boucher, Reminiscences of an American Loyalist, 1738-1789 (Cambridge, Mass., 1925), 65.

friend, patron, and later relative. Bennet Allen's past was rather
disreputable, but he had a facile pen and some claim to Baltimore's
attention. These men answered Eden's letter with a firmly worded protest
that the clergy's petitions were not intended for the eyes of the assembly,
whose members might be riled by the frank but unguarded language used.
Furthermore, they informed Eden, during the three meetings held a majority
of the whole clergy had attended and they had approved the application for
a bishop.[1] The committee and Governor Eden may have reached a compromise.
Eden did not, it seems, submit the petitions to the assembly, and the clergy
did not send them to England, either. Both parties went back to waiting
to hear what Baltimore would say about the 1768 regulatory bill.[2]

The committee of clergymen was not quite as certain of its mandate as
the members implied to the governor. During the September meeting the
three men sent letters to all Anglican ministers to tell them that, on the
authority of the eleven attending ministers, petitions for a bishop had
been drawn up. The committee intended to submit the petition to the
assembly, and asked the clergy to sign individual statements approving
the proceedings. The three men promised that dissenting voices would be
heard.[3] Since the replies have been lost, it is impossible to say just
how many clergy were prepared to live under a prelate's supervision in
order to escape lay jurisdiction. There were about fifty-six clergymen
in the province in 1770. Of these, eleven are known to have been pro-
bishop, and two ministers certainly opposed the installation of an

---

[1] Henry Addison, Bennet Allen, and Jonathan Boucher to Robert Eden,
September 17, 1770, Arch. Md., XXXII, 386-387.

[2] There is no evidence in the assembly journals that the petitions
were submitted to the house. Hugh Neill said that after Eden replied to
the clergy, "the Addresses were continued over till our next meeting."
Hugh Neill to Dr. Daniel Burton, July 18, 1771, in Perry, Collections, IV,
343. This prospective meeting does not appear to have taken place.

[3] Henry Addison, Bennet Allen, and Jonathan Boucher to the clergy,
September 16, 1770, Arch. Md., XXXII, 387-388.

episcopate. The petitions "greatly disgusted" John Gordon and David Love.
They drew up a counter-petition to the governor, and planned to submit it
to the chief executive with as many signatures as they could obtain. Gordon
thought that in this matter the interests of the Church and the interests
of mankind in general clashed, and he refused to propose anything as a
clergyman which he would think unreasonable as a layman.[1]

Later in the autumn the Church's constitution came under attack from
a different quarter. The Tobacco Inspection Act expired for good on
October 22, 1770, when a re-enactment failed because the two houses could
not agree on whether or not to cut officers' fees.[2] For the sake of the
inspection system, assemblymen until this time had overlooked their rising
dissatisfaction with proprietary rates and had periodically re-enacted
the Inspection Act without strife. Officers' fees and clerical dues
remained stable. In October and November 1770, however, the assembly
scrutinized the poll tax rates and decided to make some changes. On
November 10 the lower house voted 25 to 9 to permit anyone who wished to
pay the tax in money to do so, provided they paid at the rate of
twelve shillings sixpence per hundredweight of tobacco on thirty-two
pounds of tobacco instead of the standard thirty. Those who paid in
tobacco would continue to pay thirty pounds per poll. The upper house
agreed with the measure.[3] The reason for the change was that the amount of

---

[1] John Gordon to Walter Dulany, October 11, 1770, Dulany Papers, MS.
1265, Box 5, MdHi. No evidence as to whether or not the petition was
circulated among the clergy or presented to the governor has been found.

[2] The act expired in the fall of 1769, was renewed until October 1, 1770,
and extended until October 22. The lower house signified its discontent with
fees in 1769, but did not force a stalemate until the following year.

[3] Arch. Md., LXII, 232-233, 353, 356-357, 390-391, 429. The new
money tax came to four shillings per poll.

tax paid in tobacco by planters and the amount paid in money by non-
producers, as specified in the 1747 Act, were no longer congruent.
Originally, the exchange rate of twelve shillings sixpence per hundredweight (which came to three shillings ninepence per taxpayer) was a fair
assessment of the price of tobacco. But Maryland tobacco prices began
to rise extraordinarily in 1766, and when the boom peaked in 1770 tobacco
planters were paying about 300 percent more to the clergy than non-growers.[1]
The assembly measure was an attempt to equalize the two types of tax payments
and to ease the rigidity of the old system by leaving the medium of payment
up to the individual taxpayer. Although the two houses agreed on the
issue of clerical dues they could not come to a consensus on officers' fees.
No new Inspection Act was passed in 1770 and the rate change in clerical
stipends did not become official.

The legislature did not pass new measures fixing clerical dues
until November 1773. In the meantime, the ministers were obliged to protect
their income by asserting that the poll tax clause of the 1702 Establishment Act was once again in force. Because the amending Inspection Act had
expired, the clergy claimed forty pounds of tobacco per poll as the
original act stipulated. Characteristically, Bennet Allen voiced this
opinion first, in a notice in the Maryland Gazette which was published on
November 22, 1770, the day after the abortive assembly session ended. A
month later Thomas Chase argued the same thing. Both men, though,
asserted their legal right to the forty per poll at the same time that
they proclaimed their willingness to accept their dues at the rates the

---

[1] Jean H. Vivian, "The Poll Tax Controversy in Maryland, 1770-76: A
Case of Taxation with Representation," Md. Hist. Mag., LXXI (1976), 158,
159. Vivian's excellent article (pp. 151-176) provides the best examination of the controversy yet written and should be read for a more
comprehensive treatment of the clergy's money woes in this period.

assembly had just decided on.[1]

The two men were not really being magnanimous and public-spirited. The validity of the Establishment Act itself was being questioned in the colony. In their petition to the archbishop of Canterbury in September 1770, the clergy mentioned that prejudiced people were raising doubts about the legality of the act.[2] That same fall a handbill was distributed which declared that the Act had been void from the beginning. The death of William III on March 8, 1702, automatically dissolved the provincial assembly then sitting, the anonymous pamphleteer argued, and the council had not approved the religion bill until March 23. The act had always been invalid.[3] Though the argument was rather specious, it was seductive and rapidly gained popularity. Clerical stipends dipped as taxpayers, citing the illegality of the Act as justification, refused to pay the poll tax. Sheriffs were uncertain whether or not to force the taxables to pay, and if so, how much.

The debates about the validity of the Establishment Act remained fairly subdued until late 1771. Most people probably expected that the fall 1771 session of the assembly would obviate the need to come to terms with the Act by setting new tax rates. The clergy, nonetheless, heard worrisome rumors that the lawyers in the assembly were preparing to force them to give up all claim to the forty per poll.[4]

During the summer of 1771, when they should have been trying to present

---

[1] _Maryland Gazette_, November 22, 1770, and December 20, 1770.

[2] Arch. _Md._, XXXII, 383.

[3] The original handbill, by a "Church of England Planter" has been lost. Its contents, however, were summarized in "A Constitutionalist," _A Reply to the Church of England Planter's First Letter Respecting the Clergy_ (Annapolis, 1770). A copy of the _Reply_ is in the MdHi.

[4] For an example of the rumor, see the anonymous letter in the _Maryland Gazette_, March 7, 1771.

a united front, members of the clergy indulged in a silly and vindictive
internecine quarrel. To the amusement of its readers the Maryland Gazette
published all the relevant materials. Matthias Harris, the minister
accused of forgery in 1753, had finally been granted a small living by
Governor Eden after many years as a probationer in various parishes. His
benefice was very small, but he valued it, and was loath to risk offending
the administration. When Harris was informed that the clergy of Kent,
Queen Anne, and Talbot counties were planning a convention in January 1771
to discuss their financial strategy he sent his regrets. He did not want
to join in any petitions to the governor and assembly because he considered
"the supreme Legislature to be the sole Judges of what is a proper Allowance
to the Clergy, & to have an absolute Right to repeal any former Act."[1] His
pious declaration that the clergy should be satisfied with what the legislature deigned to grant them was read amid great hilarity at a second
meeting of the Eastern Shore ministers on May 22 and 23, 1771, attended by
fifteen ministers.[2] Remembering Harris' past, his colleagues thought him a
hypocrite and wondered if he had been drunk when he wrote the letter. The
secretary of the convention officiously told Harris that the calumnies
voiced against him were on the offical minutes of the meeting--which was not
true--and this prompted Harris to publich the correspondence and a defense
in the Maryland Gazette. The Eastern Shore clergy appeared extremely
foolish and childish as recriminations, accusations, and vindications
were interspersed between sober articles debating the Church's financial
establishment.[3]

---

[1] Harris sent a copy of his letter (d. January 21, 1771) to the
Maryland Gazette. It was published June 13, 1771.

[2] Two more attended by proxy.

[3] See the letters and affidavits by Matthias Harris, John Gordon and
John Montgomery, and Hugh Neill in the June 23, 1771, August 1, 1771,
August 15, 1771, and October 3, 1771, issues of the Maryland Gazette.

When the assembly reconvened in October 1771 members of the clergy
had two petitions prepared for submission. Governor Eden received one,
signed by twenty-one ministers, which expressed their concern that the
proposed tobacco inspection bill would reduce their incomes considerably.[1]
Another petition was submitted to the legislature, asking that attention
be given to the legal rights of the clergy in framing a new stipend bill.[2]
The protest must have reminded Eden that his instructions from Baltimore
prohibited him from allowing the clergy's income to be reduced, for he
told the upper house that he would veto any bill that did so. His statement
caught the upper house by surprise. The lower house had already reapproved
the 1770 tax measure and was disgruntled and uncooperative when the upper
house proposed several alternate schemes. These included leaving the clergy
out of the proposed new act altogether, retaining the provisions of the
original inspection act, and allowing the old act's financial arrangements
to remain in force in each parish until the incumbent died or left, when
the taxables would be free to pay in money or tobacco at the rates agreed
upon in 1770.[3] The lower house declared that the "Clergy are too much
connected with Tobacco to leave them out of the Bill," and refused to
consider any of the other proposals.[4] On the last day of November the
assembly, immovably stalemated, was prorogued.

Late in the session the houses passed an "additional supplementary
act" to the 1702 Establishment Act. This replaced the regulatory bill of
1768 which Sharpe had refused to sign and to which Baltimore had never
replied. To be in effect for seven years, the act ordered all ministers

---

[1] Henry Addison, James MacGill et al. to Robert Eden, October 5, 1771,
in the Vertical File, MdDL.

[2] Eighteen clergymen signed the petition. Arch. Md., LXIII, 10, 101.

[3] Arch. Md., LXIII, 19-20, 46-50, 54, 62-63, 107, 146, 155.

[4] Arch. Md., LXIII, 205.

to take an oath denying simoniacal contracts. It forbade them from will-
fully absenting themselves from their parishes for more than two months
per year. Clerical discipline was put into the hands of the local courts
and the governor's ecclesiastical commission. When a majority of the
vestry and churchwardens thought a minister guilty of immorality or neglect
of his duties, they were entitled to send a written complaint to the
governor and the assize or provincial court. A grand jury would be called
to examine the case. If they indicted the defendant, the case went to
the governor who, on the advice of the council, would promptly appoint a
commission of three beneficed ministers and three Anglican laymen. The
commission was granted authority to admonish, suspend, or totally deprive
ministers found guilty of the charges.[1]

The clergy remained curiously unaroused when Governor Eden signed
the bill. Perhaps news had filtered into Maryland that Frederick, Lord
Baltimore, had died on September 14, and that his death automatically
invalidated the fall assembly session. The lower house recognized the act
as void in June 1773 for this reason.[2] There is no evidence that Eden
ever appointed an ecclesiastical commission between the enactment of the
bill and the annulment. This last attempt to establish a means of
disciplining irregular clergy was as much a failure as all of its predecessors.

From December 1771 to June 1773, when no general assembly convened,
clerical incomes were at best insecure, at worst non-existent. Taxpapers
were confused and uncertain as to what law was in force and how much the
clergy were owed. Lawyers pronounced contradictory opinions, Baltimore
residents joined an association which refused to pay ministers more than

---

[1] Arch. Md., LXIII, 290-293.
[2] Arch. Md., LXIII, 347.

four shillings each, and a minister, in the name of the proprietor,

sued his county sheriff for not collecting the forty per poll.[1] Court

cases which hinged on the validity of the Establishment Act proved incon-

clusive because the lower courts were hesitant to grapple with the issue

before the Provincial Court made a decision. The higher court was expected

to rule on the Establishment Act but somehow never got around to hearing

the case. The general assembly, not the court, made the final decision.[2]

The _Maryland Gazette_ was the main forum for debate on the Establishment

Act. In October 1771 a minister warned that a reduction in the clergy's

income would be the equivalent of theft against their absolute freeholds.[3]

The following summer several articles examined the case against the Act.

Some of the positions were facetious--if the 1702 Act was not in effect,

did that not mean that the 1700 Act was?--but the defenders of the Act had

fairly secure ground to stand on when they pointed out that the Act had

been accepted without question for seventy years, and that the assembly had

implicitly acknowledged its validity in subsequent legislation. The 1747

Inspection Act, for example, specifically amended the Establishment Act,

thereby confirming its legality.[4] In September William Paca argued that

---

[1] Vivian, "The Poll Tax Controversy," _Md_. _Hist_. _Mag_., LXXI (1976) 163-170, deals at length with the court cases involving taxables, sheriffs, and ministers.

[2] Three important court cases handled the topic. Rev. David Love instigated two suits (Lord Proprietary v. John Clapham) against the Sheriff of Anne Arundel County for non-collection of his forty per poll. These cases were appealed to the Provincial Court but never heard. The case of Harrison v. Lee, in Charles County, in which the sheriff was sued by a tax-payer (charging assault and battery) when he arrested him for not paying the forty per poll, was expected to be the test case. The court, however, would not permit the sheriff to plead the Establishment Act as justification. Sheriff Lee was found guilty of the charge but the court agreed not to act further on the case until the Provincial Court had decided on the Establish-ment Act. Vivian, _ibid_., 163-170; Maryland Gazette, March 4 and 11, 1773.

[3] "An Eastern Shore Clergyman," October 17, 1771.

[4] "Expositor," August 13, 1772. See also issues of July 30, August 6, August 20, August 27, and September 3, 1772.

no subsequent legislation could confirm an act inherently invalid. A
week later, an anonymous writer agreed with him, adding that the "Clergy
have no Right to One Penny more than we think they merit, and I believe
most People think 3/9 per Tax a great Plenty."[1] Jonathan Boucher entered
the lists on behalf of the clergy in December 1772, beginning an acrimonious debate with William Pace and Samuel Chase, the anti-Establishment Act
champions, which lasted through the following April. Touched off when
Boucher asked Pace and Chase how they could justify acting as vestrymen
of St. Anne's if the Establishment Act was void, the debate did not merely
cover the Act. Chase and Pace made Boucher's agitation for a resident
bishop a central issue. He was lambasted for his role in the 1770
petitions, asked to explain who was going to pay for the bishop's expenses,
and essentially depicted as a man who wanted to import a new type of
slavery into the colonies.[2]

A resolution of the stipend issue did not emerge from the legislature
when it met in June 1773, again because of a deadlock between the houses.
The lower hourse dealt swiftly with the issue. Five days after the
session opened the assembly resolved that the Establishment Act was not
enacted by legal and constitutional authority, but was void. The delegates
decided unanimously that a new establishment bill should be passed, in which
the provision for the clergy would be modeled on the Virginia system of
flat, equal payments.[3] June 25 the lower house voted thirty-nine to six

[1] William Paca letter, September 10, 1772; "Reconciliator," September 17, 1772.

[2] Jonathan Boucher letter, December 31, 1772. The Boucher-Chase-Paca debates were printed in almost every issue of the Maryland Gazette from January 14, 1773, to April 29, 1773.

[3] Arch. Md., LXIII, 347.

to pass the new bill, which assured each minister 32,000 pounds of
tobacco annually, payable in currency at twelve shillings sixpence per
hundredweight. The next day the upper house declared that as far as it
was concerned the basis for the new bill was defective because the original
Establishment Act was still perfectly valid. The council refused to pass
the legislation.[1]

During the two fall sessions of the assembly the two houses argued
cajoled, changed their minds. The tobacco boom was over. In the face of
falling prices and a teetering economy, the houses agreed to separate the
clerical dues from a new tobacco inspection act, which was promptly
enacted. The lower house again voted that the 1701 Act was void (34:1)
and the upper house disputed their decision, but they both knew that a
revenue bill could be passed without reference to this touchy point. When
the lower house gave up all the more recent proposals and voted (28:11) to
pass a bill which supported the clergy at the rate of thirty pounds of
tobacco or four shillings currency, at the option of the taxpayer, the
other chamber accepted and Eden signed it.[2]

Probably many of the clergy greeted the act with resigned relief. A
petition from fifteen clergymen was submitted to Governor Eden on December 8,
at the height of the legislative debates, lamenting the lack of
public peace and tranquillity and offered to "relinquish some of our
undoubted Rights." Three proposals were offered on how to restructure

---

[1] Arch. Md., LXIII, 323-324, 359, 365. Though the lower house passed
the whole bill 39:6, the vote on accepting the stipulated rate was affirma-
tive 26:23. The records do not mention whether the rate was thought too
low or too high by the negative voters.

[2] Arch. Md., LXIV, 12-13, 37-38, 45-46, 77, 81, 96-97, 132, 134, 139.
The act is on pp. 254-256. I am indebted to Ms. Vivian for the information
on the tobacco depression. See also Ronald Hoffman, A Spirit of Dissension:
Economics, Politics, and the Revolution in Maryland (Baltimore, 1973),
101-102.

the clerical revenue system. The ministers proposed that when the taxables
of a parish exceeded 2,200 the taxes from the excess be put into a fund
for disseminating religious instruction. Secondly, they suggested that
the disparity between tobacco growers and non-growers could be removed by
computing the sum due each minister according to the old inspection act
and dividing the total equally among all the parish taxables. The third
proposition was that every taxable have the option of paying forty per
poll or five shillings currency. If none of these proposals was accepted,
the ministers assured the governor that they would abide "without Devia-
tion" by the 1702 Act.[1] Their position was a last ditch-effort to preserve
the Establishment Act. In spite of the humble preface the petition offered
to give up scarcely anything. Considering the mood of the country, it was
an ill-advised move which practically begged the legislature to chop down
the Establishment Act--and the lower house promptly obliged. The new
clerical revenue act, however, was only valid for twelve years, and a clause
specifically noted that it was not to be construed as validating or
invalidating the original religion act, a sop to the clergy. Moreover,
the new bill ended the period of indecision and gave the clergy an
unquestionable legal right to press for their salaries; after years of
uncertain stipends, this alone was no small relief. At least two of the
clergy who signed the seemingly uncompromising petition to Eden ended
up by urging members of the upper house to approve the bill because public
harmony demanded this private sacrifice.[2]

---

[1] Thomas Thornton, Henry Addison et al. to Robert Eden, n.d., but sent
to the assembly December 8, 1773, Arch. Md., LXIV, 119-120.

[2] The two ministers were John Montgomery and David Love. David Love to
Horatio Sharpe, May 23, 1774, in James High, ed., "Letters from the Reverend
David Love to Horatio Sharpe, 1774-1779," HMPEC, XIX (1950), 361. Love's
letter indicates that Governor Eden thought of the bill as a stopgap measure,
and expected that the proprietor would disallow it. Love to Sharpe, May 25,
1774, ibid., 363.

The enactment of the revenue bill was the last time the legislature concerned itself with the clergy or the Church before the disestablishment of November 1776. The unresolved problem of clerical discipline and the debatable question of stipends were submerged as more pertinent issues seized the attention of the public. Had the Revolution not occurred, the relationship between Church and state would probably have continued to change along the lines indicated during the troubled times of the late 1760s and the 1770s. Baltimore would undoubtedly have had to forfeit his presentation rights.[1] Maryland would most likely have instituted a presentation system very much like the one in force in Virginia, which allowed the vestries to select the parish incumbents. By the mid-1770s it was also clear that, unless an American bishop were consecrated, the state would have shortly taken over the task of regulating clergy. However, had the Revolution not taken place the establishment itself would probably have ended during the 1780s. The legislature had decisively asserted its right to alter the Establishment Act, and very little hindered it from abolishing the institution altogether. The salaries act was due to expire in 1785 in any case, and, given the increasing reluctance of the public to pay the clerical dues, the governor and the upper house, still defenders of the Act in 1773, may well have joined the assembly in declaring the Establishment Act void.

---

[1] Protest against his ecclesiastical authority mounted. For example, in May 1772 St. George's Parish, in Baltimore County, informed its new minister that "the vestrymen object to his Excellencys haveing rights of Presentation" and promised they would not accept the chosen incumbent unless he agreed to certain conditions they laid down. Vestry proceedings, St. George's Parish, Baltimore County, May 17, 1772, fragment, Vertical File, MdDL.

Part Two

THE ANGLICAN CLERGY IN MARYLAND

Chapter III

Recruitment

No more than five Anglican ministers officiated in Maryland when the
first Establishment Act was signed in June 1692.[1] Isolated, cut off from
their fellow priests and the parent Church, these men had chosen to serve
in a colony where their religious affiliation provided neither state
patronage nor public support. Most of their colleagues had judiciously
elected to live in Virginia or in various colonies in the British West
Indies, under governments which had already established the Church.
Virginia in 1692 boasted from six to eight times more Anglican clergymen
than Maryland.[2] The lure of a guaranteed annual salary--Virginia, for
instance, offered 13,333 pounds of tobacco--was irresistible to most
prospective missionaries.[3] The Anglican churches in the colonies were not
staffed by fiery-tongued, passionate proselytizers determined to wrench
souls from the very clutch of the devil. Anglicanism was the religion of
the famed "middle way." By the late seventeenth century the church
founded by Henry VIII had developed a theology which its adherents
believed was the epitome of moderation and rationality. Carefully avoiding
doctrinal extremes, its tone was dignified and low-key. The colonial

---

[1] They were John Hewitt, James Clayland, John Leach, John Lillingston,
and John Turling. John Coode, leader of the anti-proprietary rebellion in
1689, was an ordained minister but apparently renounced his vows before
1692. Arch. Md., XIX, 435-436.

[2] This estimate is based on two surviving lists of Virginia clergymen.
A 1680 list notes 48 parishes and 34 clergy, and a 1702 list notes 49
parishes and 37 clergy. These lists suggest that during the 1690s the
number of Anglican clergy in Virginia ranged between 30 and 40. Brydon,
Virginia's Mother Church, I, 241.

[3] In 1698 the stipends were raised to 16,000 pounds a year plus
1,280 pounds for marketing costs.

ministers shared this disposition. They were not zealous missionaries willing to endure great hardships to convert unbelievers to the best of religions. They much preferred to settle in the colonies where they could quietly serve members of the Anglican community while enjoying the comforts of a regular income and perquisites such as a house or glebe. Before 1692 Maryland could offer no inducements to such men. The Calverts were Catholic and merely tolerated the Anglicans as they did all other Christian denominations. The ministers of the English Church could not rely on the state for their salaries. At best they could hope to make a meager living from voluntary subscriptions, gifts, and the occasional fees they received from the Anglicans in their community. If the ministers had families to support, or if they desired a better fate than semi-starvation, they were obliged to acquire plantations and, like their neighbors, to work the soil. For any reasonably conscientious clergyman the combination of pastoral duties and farming was an exhausting, debilitating life. Few essayed it.

With the establishment of Anglicanism the Church in Maryland began to compete more successfully for its share of the incoming colonial clergy. The key was the "forty per" proviso. Based on the number of parish taxables as well as the price of tobacco, Maryland's system of generating clerical salaries produced a hierarchy of incomes rather than the fixed, uniform stipends given to ministers in Virginia and other colonies. If the unequal size of the parishes in Maryland meant that some parishes were usually worth less than the Virginia norm, the larger, more populous parishes were--even during the 1690s--worth a good deal more.[1] By the late 1720s

---

[1] The value of the Maryland livings during the establishment period is discussed in Chapter V.

the average clerical salary in Maryland was considerably above that offered in any other colony and, boosted by a ceaselessly increasing population, it continued to rise. As the mean salary increased, so did the number of men willing to serve in the province. During the last fifteen or twenty years of the establishment the supply of applicants consistently exceeded the number of available parishes. Initially unable to attract more than a handful of men to its service, the Church in Maryland eventually held the most sought-after livings in the colonies.

The number of parishes organized at any given time essentially determined the size of the clerical job market in Maryland. Each parish provided a living for one incumbent.[1] The county commissioners, justices, and principal freeholders obligated by the Establishment Act of 1692 to divide the province into parishes laid out thirty.[2] By 1776, fourteen more were available, carved out of the original parishes or organized along the expanding frontiers. This rather inelastic market could be somewhat loosened if incumbents were willing to hire private curates as their assistants. Inducted clergy, however, tended to employ curates only when their own salaries exceeded their needs, and curacies were really a phenomenon of the later, wealthier decades. During the 1760s and 1770s such subordinate positions expanded the formal market by no more than five to ten posts, or at most just over a fifth.

---

[1] Or, after 1754, a living for a licensed probationary curate.

[2] The Establishment Act did not stipulate how many parishes were to be formed. The boundaries of the original thirty were determined by the collaboration of those ordered by the act to undertake the division.

| Maryland Parishes, 1694–1776 | | | |
Date	No. Parishes in Maryland	No. Western Shore Parishes	No. Eastern Shore Parishes
1694–1703	30	17	13
1704–1706	31	18	13
1707–1725	32	18	14
1726–1727	34	19	15
1728–1742	36	20	16
1743–1744	38	22	16
1745–1748	42	24	18
1749–1765	43	24	19
1766–1776	44	24	20

About two hundred men served as Anglican ministers in Maryland between the passage of the Establishment Act in 1692 and the enactment of the Maryland Bill of Rights in 1776.[1] Though they differed in social background, ethnic origin, intellect, and piety, they were bound closely to each other by their choice of professions. In their own eyes and in the eyes of the general public they were men set apart from their fellow human beings. Ministers were men of God, authorized by Jesus Christ (acting through the bishops of the Church) to perform the sacred rites forbidden to ordinary

---

[1] 193 men definitely served in the Maryland Church as incumbents, probationers, and salaried curates. This figure is based on evidence of service derived from parish and vestry records, the legislative journals, the colonial executive papers, the S.P.G. and Fulham Library papers, provincial court and land records, and various miscellaneous documents in the MdDL, the MdHi, and the MdA. Other men undoubtedly officiated. They were probably not inducted clergy but itinerant curates or men who died shortly after their arrival in Maryland. I estimate that there were about ten of these.

people. Whatever their personal inadequacies or idiosyncracies, priests
were the dispensaries of the means of grace and therefore very special men.
They were members of a caste as well as a profession. With the exception
of a bishop, no agent or agency on earth could deprive an ordained man of
his priesthood. Spiritual authority was conferred on priests for life.
As the Maryland assembly noted in 1696, while discussing whether John
Coode's renunciation of his ordination vows was valid, priesthood was "an
indeleble Character stamped upon them which cannot be taken of but by the
Ordinary or Power by which the same was Conferred."[1]

The rite of ordination transformed a man into a priest. This ceremony
was the solemn conclusion to a (theoretically) lengthy process of examination and scrutiny designed to weed out the immoral, the unlearned, and the
questionably orthodox. A candidate for the priesthood was required to meet
criteria testing his character and his fitness to enter the profession.
Some of the rules for attaining ordination dated back to the early days
of the Christian church or to pre-Norman British rulers. Most of them,
though, were delineated in the 1604 Constitutions and Canons Ecclesiastical,
the fundamental rule book of the Anglican Church.

The English Church has two sacerdotal orders. Ordination to the
diaconate is the preliminary step to full priesthood. Deacons are
consecrated in a public ceremony by the imposition of episcopal hands. The
rite gives them the authority to help a priest during services, to read the
Scriptures and homilies, to preach (with a bishop's permission), and to
baptize, catechize, marry, and bury. A deacon may not consecrate the bread
and wine during Communion. He could not hold a benefice or a donative.[2]

---

[1] Arch. Md., XIX, 437.

[2] Robert Phillimore, The Ecclesiastical Law of the Church of England
(London, 1895), I, 108-110. The regulation concerning benefices effectively
prevented deacons from holding Maryland livings.

Since the Canons specifically recommended a year in the diaconate (so that "there may euer be some time of trial of their behauiour")[1], deacons could usually expect to remain in their office for at least that long before a bishop would permit admission to full priesthood. Bishops were, however, granted permission to ordain candidates to both orders in a shorter period of time if they found good cause to do so. This dispensation was very important to the colonial churches. The prospect of a lengthy period in the diaconate would have reduced the number of British candidates willing to seek ordination in order to serve overseas, and it would have deterred most interested Americans, short of funds and friends in Britain, from applying for orders at all. Most men in a rush to sail for the colonies were ordained deacon and then priest on successive Sundays.

The personal prerequisites for both ordinations were generally the same except for the regulations concerning age. A deacon had to be twenty-three years old, a priest twenty-four. The age requirement for deacons could be waived if the archbishop of Canterbury approved, but the minimum for priesthood was canonically absolute and supposedly inviolable.[2] Unless granted a dispensation by a bishop, candidates for both sets of orders were to be legitimate by birth, baptized, and without crippling or disgusting corporal infirmities. Bigamists, criminals, and the ordained ministers of other denominations were also excluded.[3]

The canons of 1604 established specific educational requirements and demanded character references and titles for those men seeking employment in the Church. A university degree was not necessary for ordination, though the canons advised that "some degree of Schoole in either of the saide

---

[1] Wilson, ed., Constitutions and Canons, Canon XXXII.

[2] In practice, bishops in the eighteenth century were often less than scrupulous about observing these and most other canons.

[3] Phillimore, Ecclesiastical Law, I, 93-95.

Vniuersities" of the realm was desirable.[1] At the very least a candidate
had to display a minimum of learning by giving the bishop a Latin account
of his faith, supported with appropriate scriptural references. Candidates
also had to produce letters affirming their good lives and conversations,
either under the seal of a university college or from three or four "grave"
ministers and other respectable persons.[2] Along with these documents,
candidates were required to bring titles to an ecclesiastical or scholastic
post.[3] This was a sensible, if discriminatory, rule designed to avoid
unemployment in the Church.

When a candidate presented himself to the bishop, armed with proper
testimonials and certificates, he faced an examination by the bishop or an
episcopal surrogate. The inquiry checked the authenticity of his credentials and probed the applicant's knowledge of Scriptures, divinity, and
classical learning.[4] If the candidate passed the tests, he was permitted
to take the oaths which qualified him for service in the Anglican Church.
He swore that he believed the king was the only supreme governor of the
realm and the Church. He repudiated all foreign princes and powers of any
sort. The candidate assented to the Thirty-Nine Articles, the Book of
Common Prayer, and the episcopalian structure of the Church.[5] He was then
ready for ordination. Except when a bishop had reason to hold a special

---

[1] Wilson, ed., Constitutions and Canons, Canon XXXIV. By the late
seventeenth century, however, candidates knew that a degree was a virtual
prerequisite to advancement in the Church.

[2] Ibid., Canon XXXIV. The attestors to the certificates were required
to have known the applicant for a minimum of three years.

[3] A title was a promise from the patron of an ecclesiastical living or
a university post that the applicant would receive employment if he
entered orders.

[4] Wilson, ed., Constitutions and Canons, Canon XXXV; Phillimore,
Ecclesiastical Law, I, 100.

[5] Wilson, ed., Constitutions and Canons, Canon, XXXVI.

ordination, the ceremony was supposed to take place only during four
Sundays of the year at roughly three month intervals.[1]

The canons gave the primary responsibility for approving and performing
ordinations to the bishops. Indeed, episcopal ordination was the hallmark
of Anglicanism. Since the bishops were few, and the candidates many,
this practice created many problems. As members of the House of Lords,
bishops were expected to spend a good part of the year in London, attending
to their parliamentary duties. They were often aged or infirm. Because
they frequently could not attend examinations and ordinations in their own
particular dioceses, various expedients, such as requiring all candidates
to journey to London to meet with their bishop, were adopted. Ordinations
celebrated on other than the four canonical Sundays were common.[2] Busy
prelates and indifferent surrogates did not devote sufficiently scrupulous
attention to the examination of candidates. Careless administration of
the tests permitted badly educated men to enter the ministry. Compromises
were made; an unsatisfactory education could be discounted by a bishop if,
for instance, he was convinced the candidate wanted to serve in a colony
which desperately needed ministers. One of the greatest difficulties in
examining candidates from the colonies and from distant parts of Britain
was that testimonials of character and titles to livings could be forged.
By the end of the colonial period elaborate precautions had been devised
to avoid flagrant counterfeiting. Such criminal activity, though, was one
of the more egregious forms of violating the canons. The ordination procedure
was really so full of loopholes and dispensations, so pegged to the whimsy or
credulity of a handful of bishops, that it is debatable whether it really
weeded out many unfit candidates.

---

[1] Wilson, ed., Constitutions and Canons, Canon XXXVI.

[2] Sykes, Church and State, 97-98.

The minister who wished to officiate in the colonies had to complete another requirement before sailing. A license from his diocesan, the bishop of London, was formally necessary to serve in America. A few ministers ventured to the colonies without the license, but they risked being denied a living by royal or proprietary governors whose orders forbade the induction of uncertified clergymen. Most licenses granted permission to officiate in one specific colony.[1] However, the Church had no sure means of ascertaining that ministers really went to their designated colonies or that they remained at their posts. Moving from colony to colony without a proper license was quite easy, and few men bothered to ask the bishop for permission to travel. Ministers with licenses to other colonies were normally accepted without fuss in Maryland.

Obtaining a license authorized a minister to collect the so-called "King's Bounty." This was a £20 gift from the Crown to clergymen bound for the colonies and was normally used to pay travel expenses.

Before the restoration of proprietary government in 1715 an episcopal license was the only certification needed for induction into a Maryland living. After 1715 ministers were required to procure a permit from Lord Baltimore empowering them to officiate in Maryland before they asked the bishop of London for a license to the colony. Though the document was supposedly the equivalent of a title to a living, it was not normally a promise to supply the applicant with a specific living. Rather, it was a general authorization to go to Maryland and to ask the governor for ecclesiastical employment.[2]

---

[1] Occasionally, licenses were issued authorizing the holder to officiate anywhere in the colonies.

[2] Ordained ministers who removed to Maryland from other colonial livings were usually inducted into Maryland benefices without waiting for special permission from Baltimore. Sometimes, though, the governors gave them temporary appointments while awaiting Baltimore's consent to a full induction. Horatio Sharpe and Robert Eden seem to have been less inclined to induct without the proprietor's permission than their predecessors were.

A permit to officiate in Maryland was rarely difficult to obtain, and the Calverts seem to have denied few applications for one. Apparently the barons relied on their secretaries to carry out a perfunctory screening of the candidates and then signed the authorizations quite mechanically. Most British applicants probably just showed the secretaries the recommendations and other documents they had mustered for ordination or for licensing by the bishop of London. Candidates from the colonies usually produced a letter of introduction from the Maryland governor, sometimes supplemented by a title of curacy from a provincial incumbent. Although most of the applicants were strangers to Baltimore and his secretaries, some candidates were university chums of the proprietor, friends of his family, or protégés of people he was happy to oblige.

Once a candidate had procured Baltimore's permit to officiate in Maryland little could be done to prevent him from entering the colonial Church. If the bishop of London thought him unfit for orders, the permit could be used to persuade a less obstinate or less informed prelate to perform the rites of ordination. When the bishop refused to license a Baltimore protégés already in orders, the proprietor simply ignored the colonial diocesan and installed the minister in a Maryland living without benefit of the episcopal license.

The process of becoming a Maryland clergyman took time, money, and effort, but it was not particularly troublesome or complicated. The greatest hazard was not that one would fail to meet the requirements but that one would die at sea or, in the case of colonials, of unfamiliar diseases encountered in England. The people in Maryland, however, inherently prone to respect the cloth, knew as well as any in England that the ordination and licensing procedure was more a formality than a true test of character and learning.

The Inflow of Ministers

Recruiting ministers for the colonies was not always an easy task.
Three thousand miles of ocean sufficed to give any man pause, and candidates
who were in the colonies before ordination had to make the voyage twice.
Pirates, hostile navies, disease, and the inherent dangers of sailing
in leaky vessels deterred many. Cost was a problem as well. The King's
Bounty was frequently an inadequate sum to pay for the voyage and all its
concomitant expenses, particularly if the ship's sailing was delayed by
unfavorable winds or war. Room and board in London while awaiting
ordination or licensing were a heavy expense. The danger and the cost
which were the unavoidable preliminaries to acquiring a Maryland parish
discouraged many ministers who might otherwise have been attracted to what
the Church could offer. Indeed, the recognition that the voyage was "a
difficulty that has and always will prevent the growth of the Church in
America," as Hugh Neill put it in 1766, was one of the chief arguments
for the consecration of a resident colonial bishop.[1]

Attracting ministers to Maryland was not only a matter of convincing
them to risk the journey and the expense but persuading them to select
Maryland over one of the other colonies where the Church was established.
During the 1690s a missionary could choose to serve in the settled
churches of Virginia, Maryland, part of New York, and several colonies in
the British West Indies. By 1706 North and South Carolina had been added
to the selection. After the S.P.G. was formed in 1701 more adventurous
ministers could apply for the society's £50 annual stipend and ensconce
themselves in missions scattered from Newfoundland to Barbados. The
colonies offered parsons with the itch to travel a vast choice of climates,

---

[1] Hugh Neill to the Secretary of the S.P.G., May 19, 1766, in Perry,
Collections, II, 404.

locations, societies, and opportunities. The initial difficulty and the later facility the Maryland Church experienced in staffing its livings must be viewed in the context of intercolonial rivalry for a limited number of clergy.

Certainly the Establishment Act of 1692 did not transform Maryland into a Mecca for overseas clergymen. In all probability, hardly anyone outside of Maryland, the Privy Council, and Lambeth Palace in London was even aware of the existence of a religious establishment in the colony. In addition, any prospective candidates would have known that the permanence of the establishment was in doubt so long as the Crown failed to ratify the act. The act could promise ministers nothing more solid and secure than the hope of an eventual stable settlement. Understandably, few clerics chose to accept the risk. The bishop of London himself was apparently hesitant about recruiting missionaries for Maryland while the fate of the act was uncertain. During the first two years after the enactment of the bill only one minister joined the Maryland Church: a Dutchman, Lawrence Vanderbush, who was wandering south from New York.

When Francis Nicholson--energetic, dedicated, fiercely Anglican--took over the governorship of Maryland in July 1694 his arrival was a promising omen. He brought with him a private chaplain who was promptly installed in the church in the capital city. The governor pressed Bishop Compton and Archbishop Thomas Tenison to send ministers, fretted when fleets arrived without them aboard, and gave a hearty welcome to the men when they came. To protect their salaries, he engineered the enactment of the 1696 establishment bill.[1]

---

[1] For an example of Nicholson's requests, see Francis Nicholson to Thomas Tenison, Archbishop of Canterbury, June 30, 1697, in the Fulham Papers, "Maryland 1696-1769," item 167. His solicitous welcomes are noted in several sources, including "An Account of George Trotters Mission into Maryland," n.d. but c. 1707, S.P.G. Papers in the Lambeth Palace Library, Volume XII, fols. 73-74, DLC microfilm.

110

Annual Inflow of Ministers into Maryland, 1692-1776			
Year	Arrivals	Year	Arrivals
1692	1	1735	2
1693	0	1736	1
1694	2	1737	1
1695	1	1738	2
1696	4	1739	4
1697	4	1740	2
1698	8	1741	0
1699	0	1742	7
1700	5	1743	0
1701	6	1744	3
1702	1	1745	4
1703	2	1746	0
1704	1	1747	0
1705	2	1748	3
1706	0	1749	3
1707	0	1750	4
1708	4	1751	4
1709	0	1752	0
1710	1	1753	3
1711	3	1754	1
1712	4	1755	2
1713	2	1756	0
1714	3	1757	3
1715	0	1758	0
1716	0	1759	0
1717	1	1760	2
1718	4	1761	5
1719	0	1762	2
1720	1	1763	0
1721	3	1764	1
1722	1	1765	3
1723	1	1766	7
1724	2	1767	5
1725	1	1768	3
1726	5	1769	5
1727	0	1770	6
1728	4	1771	1
1729	0	1772	1
1730	2	1773	3
1731	1	1774	2
1732	3	1775	4
1733	2	1776	1
1734	3		188*

*Five clergymen were serving in Maryland in 1692 when the Establishment Act was signed.

```
┌─────────────────────────────────────────────┐
│         Total Arrivals per Decade             │
│      Period                       Ministers   │
│      1690-1699  .................    20*      │
│      1700-1709  .................    21       │
│      1710-1719  .................    18       │
│      1720-1729  .................    18       │
│      1730-1739  .................    21       │
│      1740-1749  .................    22       │
│      1750-1759  .................    17       │
│      1760-1769  .................    33       │
│      1770-1776  .................    18       │
│                                     ───       │
│                                     188       │
└─────────────────────────────────────────────┘
```

*The five ministers serving in Maryland in June 1692 had all arrived in the colony previous to 1690.

During the first two years of his administration a total of two ministers came from England. Compton was probably to blame for the disappointing turnout. A prelate with so many temporal as well as ecclesiastical duties could not spend much time drumming up missionaries for the colonies. The bishop was simply not in the position to do the time-consuming drudgery of recruitment--first searching out candidates, then checking their credentials, nursing them out of their fears, arranging their voyage, and looking after them until they boarded their ships. This problem was solved when Compton appointed Thomas Bray commissary in 1696. Bray immediately threw himself into the task of recruiting clergymen for Maryland. He scoured the universities for promising candidates. A forceful, talented pamphleteer, the commissary must have also been a mesmerizing talker. From 1696 through 1701 he sent no less than twenty-one

missionaries to parishes in Maryland. The obstacles he faced were
daunting. England was at war for part of the period, the second and third
establishment acts were never ratified, and the tobacco market was not
particularly encouraging. Moreover, one disgruntled former Maryland
minister was in London by 1698, "prating ag[ain]st yo[u]r Plantation," an
irritated Compton wrote Nicholson.[1] Still, Bray managed to send over four
ministers in 1696 and another four the following year. Eight men arrived
in the colony in 1698, six of whom sailed in a single fleet. Nicholson
was delighted to see them. They were entertained in Annapolis at his own
expense and when they went off to their assigned destinations he put money
in their pockets.[2] No ministers came in 1699, the year Nicholson left
Maryland, but five did so in 1700 and six arrived the next year. This
last group came as a unit, carrying with them Bray's draft of what became
the final Establishment Act of 1702.[3] The commissary had an eye for the
value of propaganda.

The difficulty Bray faced in persuading men to commit themselves to
service in a distant, almost primitive colony is illustrated by the high
pre-induction attrition rate. The ministers who signed for the King's
Bounty in essence contracted with the Crown to sail for the colonies as
swiftly as possible. It was almost a bond for their future services. Most
of the Maryland-bound signers fulfilled the contract and officiated in
Maryland. A significant minority did not. Fourteen men signed for the
Bounty between 1692 and the end of 1699 but have left no indication that

[1] Bishop Henry Compton to Francis Nicholson, n.d. but read to the
Maryland upper house April 1, 1698, in Arch. Md., XXII, 59.

[2] "An Account of Trotters Mission," n.d., S.P.G. Papers in the Lambeth
Palace Library, Volume XII, fols. 73-74.

[3] Thomas Bray to the Secretary of the S.P.G., March 24, 1705, in
Perry, Collections, IV, 55-56.

they appeared in Maryland. Ten did so during the next decade, and five

in the following one. Thereafter the rate drops steadily to zero by the

1740s.[1] Undoubtedly some of these men died during the voyage or met some

other mishap. In a large number of the cases, though, the men probably

never sailed in the first place. Last-minute discouragements and second

thoughts were not uncommon. Even Humberstone Baron, the man Bray selected

as his deputy commissary, changed his mind about sailing after waiting two

months in port for a ship.[2] Particularly during the war years, when ships

did not always depart on schedule, long delays dissipated lean purses and

drained enthusiasm. In May 1707 Robert Walker, marooned in Portsmouth

because the ship he had intended to sail on had "gone a Cruizing," wrote

to the bishop of London to ask his advice as to what he should do in this

"dejecting Extremity," adding that "my necessity urges to me this

Presumption; I being drove in a manner to the want of Food."[3] Five months

later Walker was still in Portsmouth, writing petitions for a subsidy.[4]

His case was probably one of the more extreme ones, but travel problems

were frequent and enervating. There were also disheartening family

troubles. Wives could weaken or puncture a minister's resolution to sail

by refusing to accompany him to Maryland. John Urmston's wife was, he

reported, "a tender & timorous poor Creature" who "hath never been upon

the salt water & has a strange notion of my undertaking."[5] Daniel

---

[1] The lists of the men who signed for the receipt of the Bounty may be found in Gerald Fothergill, A List of Emigrant Ministers to America, 1690-1811 (London, 1904).

[2] Thompson, Bray, 63.

[3] Robert Walker to Bishop Henry Compton, May 12, 1707, S.P.G. Papers, Series A, Volume 3, item XLVII.

[4] Walker to the Secretary of the S.P.G., October 1, 1707, S.P.G. Papers, Series A, Volume 3, item CXVII.

[5] John Urmston to the Secretary of the S.P.G., September 28, 1709, S.P.G. Papers, Series A, Volume 5, item XII.

Maynadier was preparing to load his belongings onto a ship in 1712 when he heard that his wife had been persuaded by friends not to leave Great Britain. Her refusal cost Maynadier his S.P.G. post.[1] The minister, a very determined man, sailed to Maryland somewhat later as a non-S.P.G. affiliated clergyman. Similar circumstances would have impelled other men to give up the project entirely. Though the reasons for the high pre-embarkation attrition rate during the first decades of the establishment are readily understandable, it is less clear why the numbers dropped so rapidly from the 1720s on. Perhaps Bishop Gibson was less tolerant of backsliding, and pressured the ministers to live up to their contracts. Declining opportunities for clerical employment in England probably boosted incentive to seek the jobs and the salaries Maryland could offer. Moreover, by the 1720s Maryland was not the barbaric, mysterious territory early ministers had steeled themselves to encounter.

Ascertaining that ministers sailed to the province was one problem, keeping them there was another. Indeed, the impact of what one could term the first great clerical migration (1696-1701) was considerably blunted by the proclivity of Maryland clergy to abandon their livings. Six of the twenty men who arrived during the 1690s left the colony, and five of the twenty-one men who came between 1700 and 1710 did the same. Thus about a quarter of the ministers who came to Maryland prior to 1710 did not stay.[2] About half of these returned to Britain, and the rest removed to other colonies, usually to Virginia. One of the eleven men who went elsewhere was in Maryland for almost eight years before deciding to leave, but

---

[1] Memorial of Daniel Maynadier to the Secretary of the S.P.G., n.d. but 1712, S.P.G. Papers, Series A, Volume 7, item XXVIII. The S.P.G. preferred that married ministers bring their wives and families with them to the colonies.

[2] Joseph Holt, deprived in 1704 for incompetence and immorality, was probably the only minister who did not leave voluntarily.

another left the province in less than half a year.[1] The average sojourn

of the men who eventually left Maryland was just over three years, long

enough to become thoroughly disenchanted with the real situation of the

Church in the province. Some of the men who left before 1702 may have

despaired that the Church would ever be securely established. Usually,

though, when reasons for the removals are given, they are almost exclusively

financial in nature. Greedy inhabitants, tax evasion, and fraud made it

difficult for many early ministers to count on an adequate yearly income

regardless of how high their hypothetical salaries would have been. If they

were paid the correct amount of tobacco, what they often received was the

trash of the crop, worth only a fraction of the regular market price.[2]

George Trotter, the minister who served in Maryland for almost eight years

before returning to England, was cheated out of most of his lawful income

by his parishioners, the vestries, and the county sheriff of his Somerset

County pluralities. When he became too poor to pay for his lodgings, and

had grown tired of "being harassed with envious and rapacious officers and

people," Trotter bid Maryland a weary farewell. He was as destitute when

he left as when he arrived.[3] Other ministers were equally hard put to

survive. In 1711 Alexander Adams received only ten shillings remuneration

for nine months' service.[4] Several Maryland ministers asked the S.P.G. for

---

[1] Thomas Clayton, the minister who left in under six months, may not
actually have been intended for a Maryland parish although he is listed
as a Maryland incumbent on a contemporary list of ministers in the Fulham
Papers. Clayton went to Philadelphia. List of Maryland parishes and
ministers, n.d. but 1698, Fulham Papers, "Maryland 1696-1769," item 127.

[2] For a detailed discussion of the financial troubles of the early
ministers, see Chapter V.

[3] "An Account of Trotters Mission," n.d., S.P.G. Papers in the Lambeth
Palace Library, Volume XII, fols. 73-74.

[4] Alexander Adams to Bishop Henry Compton, July 2, 1711, S.P.G.
Papers, Series A, Volume 6, item CVII.

special subsidies.[1] One of the depressing aspects of the financial
squeeze of the first twenty-five years or so of the establishment was that
ministers feared to send for their families in Britain, but could scarcely
afford to maintain two separate households.[2] Unable to live comfortably
on their stipends, plagued by running battles with sheriffs and taxables,
separated from their families or too poor to marry, overworked, and
lonely, the men so carefully recruited left the Church in large numbers.

The exodus of incumbents slowed after about 1708. Only two
of the eighteen men who arrived during the 1710s left the colony. Three
of the eighteen arrivals of the 1720s moved away, but one was forced out
of the province for his Jacobite principles and another was only serving
part-time in Maryland. From 1730 to 1775 about nine men (out of 111
arrivals) departed. All but one of them were curates, ministers without
settled parishes, who had little hope of a permanent induction and went
to find livings elsewhere. In contrast to the men leaving during the
early decades of the era, they traveled out of Maryland not because they
wanted to abandon their livings but because they couldn't acquire them.

After 1701 the influx of ministers to Maryland dropped considerably.
Bray effectively resigned the Maryland commissariate in 1702 and turned
his attention to recruiting for the S.P.G. rather than the provincial Church.
The absence of the former commissary was immediately apparent in the annual
recruitment figures. The peak of eight new incumbents, set in 1698, was

---

[1] The S.P.G. was reluctant to aid Maryland ministers because the society
preferred to subsidize clergymen in the colonies where the Church was not
established. However, the officers of the society recognized the destitu-
tion of many Maryland incumbents and apparently did provide some Maryland
men with special grants.

[2] Though most of the ministers in the province came to America as
bachelors, some left wives and families in Britain permanently or until
the ministers themselves were settled. Complaints about the high cost of
maintaining households may be found in Peregrine Coney, John Lillingston
et al. to Bishop Compton, May 18, 1698, in Perry, Collections, IV, 10.

never equalled. Ministers sailed or rode into the colony at the rate of about twenty per decade until the 1760s. Since fewer left, the available parishes were gradually staffed and long-term vacancies became uncommon after the mid-1730s. The fact that the ministers came to Maryland by the ones and twos, rather than by the half dozens, and that they increasingly came from the distant reaches of the British Isles instead of the vicinity around London, Oxford, and Cambridge, indicates that a change in the style of engaging ministers took place by the late 1710s. The recruiter no longer sought out suitable candidates; they came to him. Bishop Compton, who died in 1713, was kept intermittently informed of vacancies in Maryland and sent out ministers specifically for those parishes.[1] During the early part of his term Governor Hart "employed his friends every where, to look out for and recommend Clergy men of good characters."[2] After the restoration of the proprietary government, however, such activity apparently ceased. Filling vacancies in Maryland was no longer the responsibility of the bishops of London and there is no indication that the governors or the proprietors exerted any energy to enlisting clergymen. Word of mouth seems to have sufficed.

What was being said was very encouraging: the value of Maryland parishes was rising with every passing decade.[3] The news traveled up and down the coast to ministers in the other colonial churches. As the average Maryland salary slowly, then decisively, outstripped what could be earned in most of the other American parishes the province became a magnet for Anglican ministers already on the continent. Of all the priests who arrived

---

[1] See, for example, Bishop Henry Compton's recommendation for Thomas Phillips to Shrewsbury Parish, in Bishop Compton to the Secretary of the S.P.G., November 19, 1711, S.P.G. Papers, Series A, Volume 6, item CXLV.

[2] William Keith to (?) Bishop John Robinson, November 3, 1714, Fulham Papers, "Maryland 1696-1769," item 171.

[3] See Chapter V for more on this subject.

Period	No. Arrivals From Colonial Livings	% of Total Arrivals	No. Arrivals Formerly With S.P.G.*
Influx of Ministers into Maryland from Other Colonial Livings			
1690-1699	2	10%	0
1700-1709	3	14%	1
1710-1719	6	33%	5
1720-1729	8	44%	3
1730-1739	9	43%	4
1740-1749	2	9%	0
1750-1759	0	0%	0
1760-1769	7	21%	2
1770-1776	4	22%	2
Total	41		
Percent of total Maryland clergy		21%	

*These are included in the figures for arrivals from colonial livings.

in Maryland in the 1690s, only two, Lawrence Vanderbush from New York and Peregrine Coney, Nicholson's chaplain, were not sent via the bishop of London from Britain.[1] During the following decade three men left S.P.G. missions or posts in other colonial churches to come to Maryland. From 1710 through 1719 a third of the men who entered the Maryland Church (six men out of eighteen arrivals) left other colonial livings to remove to the province. The trend reached its peak during the 1720s and 1730s, when forty-four percent (eight out of eighteen) and forty-three percent (nine men out of twenty-one), respectively, came to Maryland from other American

[1] The number may actually be three. William Davis may not have been sent by Bishop Compton.

posts. The influx from colonial livings into Maryland fell sharply during
the 1740s and 1750s--perhaps a product of the saturated Maryland job
market--but rose again during the 1760s (seven out of thirty-three men,
or twenty-one percent) and 1770s (four out of eighteen, or twenty-two
percent), probably due to expanding employment opportunities offered by
the proliferation of private curacies.

For several of these men Maryland was the termination point to a long
trek across the Eastern seaboard. Three ministers came overland from the
Carolinas, stopping briefly to officiate in Virginia but then moving north.
One of the two men who arrived from the West Indies had previously served
in Newfoundland. Massachusetts lost one Anglican incumbent to Maryland.
Generally, however, the men originally served in parishes more adjacent
to Maryland. Twenty of the estimated forty-one ministers who came from other
colonial posts left Virginia, and Pennsylvania lost seven.

Most of them were lured to the Maryland Church by the salaries and
the security. Climate, reasons of health, political stability, and the
lack of social tensions were also reasons the ministers noted. Virginia
clergymen were irritated by the induction system in that colony, by which
strong vestries could postpone inductions (and thus job security)
indefinitely. Quarrels with James Blair, the Virginia commissary, caused
at least one minister to remove himself to Maryland. The clerics from the
Carolinas disliked their enormous parishes, the climate, the stipends
which were never paid, and the unceasing "civil divisions and animosities."[1]

Yet the underlying motivation was financial. Clergymen from Massachusetts to the West Indies echoed the idea that by the late 1720s salaries

---

[1] Peter Tustian to the Secretary of the S.P.G., July 19, 1721, S.P.G.
Papers, Series A, Volume 15, fol. 168.

elsewhere simply could not compare with what Maryland promised. The

secretary of the S.P.G. and the bishop of London received both mildly

embarrassed and hotly forthright letters from colonial clergy pointing

out that since heathens and sin abounded in Maryland, the ministers might

as well go where they could raise their families respectably without being

forced to beg for every shilling.[1] Most did not inform the Society or

the bishop of their plans to leave their parishes before they were safely

inducted into Maryland livings. John Humphreys, an S.P.G. missionary in

southern Pennsylvania, was one of those who simply left his post.

Offered St. Anne's Parish in Annapolis, which was worth ₤65 annually even

in the worst economic times, he accepted with mixed emotions. "I embraced

this providential opportunity of delivering my Self from a State of Life

distress'd enough," he wrote the Society afterwards. "I cañot sufficiently

lam[en]t the dismal necessity w[hi]ch constrain'd me to leave an Employ

so very hon[ora]ble so very suitable to my inclination & I am full of

grief whilst I reflect on the difficultys w[hi]ch impeded my longer stay."

After fourteen years as an S.P.G. missionary, Humphreys said that he was

never able to support himself decently "not-withst[an]d[ing] I almost

starved my Self for 7 Years to accomplish it."[2] To ministers struggling

to survive on the Society's ₤50 stipends Maryland must have taken on the

appearance of the promised land. No doubt the figures circulated as the

average for Maryland livings expanded the further removed from the source.

The total decadal arrivals fluctuated from seventeen to twenty-two

between 1692 and 1759. For the first five years of the 1760s the rate

---

[1] For example, a letter written from St. Margaret Westminster Parish in Anne Arundel County by a former South Carolina minister, states: "there is no where, I am sure not in Carolina more want of Orthodox clergy than there is here (for to saying nothing of the Ignorance & Sensuality of our people here)." Peter Tustian to the Secretary of the S.P.G., July 19, 1721, S.P.G. Papers, Series A, Volume 15, fol. 168.

[2] John Humphreys to the S.P.G., July 6, 1725, S.P.G. Papers, Series A, Volume 19, fol. 196.

remained much the same. Beginning in 1766, however, ministers flooded
into the province at rates reminiscent of the late 1690s. Twenty-six
came from the beginning of 1766 through the end of 1770. What drew them
to the province in spite of the relative shortage of jobs and the
institution of the probationary period was the fabulous and unprecedented
boom in the price of tobacco, which began in the summer of 1766 and
bottomed out in 1772. Ministers in other colonial Churches, anxiously
awaiting a summons from the Maryland governor, were no doubt further
encouraged by news of the high mortality rate for ministers during the
1760s. The richest parish in the province plus a good many other
lucrative livings, formerly under the control of a group of long-lived
incumbents, came back on the market.[1] The escalation in salaries and the
somewhat more flexible job market combined to make the period from 1766
through 1770 a half decade of high migration.

The inflow slowed to more normal rates after 1770. Fears concerning
the security of the Church's financial establishment, then being debated
in the legislature, probably had much to do with this. The new financial
settlement of 1773 reduced what one could call the gold fever hysteria of
the previous years. The slackening was not particularly important. The
Church was overflowing with young ministers , and employment opportunities
for new arrivals would have been extremely slim. In this sense, the Maryland
Church was a triumph beyond anything that Bray and Bishop Compton could
have dared to dream. Yet if the Church is considered as a body of men
charged with responsibility for ministering to the spiritual needs of the
laity, rather than a closed organization with personnel slots to be filled,
it was much less successful. Fifty-odd clergymen serving a population

---

[1] Twenty-three men died or left during the 1760s; nine parish
incumbents died between the beginning of 1766 and the end of 1770.

which, by the 1770s was well over two hundred thousand, was by no means a number sufficient to fulfill the pastoral function of the Anglican ministry.

Ethnic Origins

The geographic backgrounds of the Maryland ministers was of significance to the men themselves, both in professional and social terms, and to their parishioners. In those days of local culture a minister betrayed his origins with the first words of the service. His accent told the audience where he came from and could cause immediate feelings of antagonism or sympathy. Ethnic prejudices were common, frequently bitter and indelible, and could thoroughly estrange parishioners from the local minister. The ethnic origins of the clergymen never became an overt issue in Maryland, but everyone from the governors to the bishops of London knew it was a smoldering one.

The influx of ministers of different nationalities divides the establishment era into three periods. During the initial decade the English predominated, both in terms of their proportion of the arriving ministers and in their control of the livings. From about 1701 to the mid-1760s the Scots, and to a lesser extent the Irish, came to Maryland in such numbers that they rivaled the English hegemony and then broke it. Beginning in the years following the Stamp Act crisis, Americans--chiefly Marylanders, Pennsylvanians, and Virginians--swiftly took over a large share of the market. Almost half the ministers in the province were native Americans when the Revolution began. Had the war not occurred, the Maryland Church would have rapidly reached the point where non-American ministers were not needed and, perhaps, not wanted.

Period	Total Arrivals	England and Wales	Scotland	Ireland	Other European Countries	The Colonies	Unknown
Incumbents, 1692*	5	2					3
1692-1699	20	16	1		2		1
1700-1709	21	11	9		1		
1710-1719	18	5	7	3	1		2
1720-1729	18	9	3	4		1	1
1730-1739	21	6	3	6	1	2	3
1740-1749	22	4	8	4		3	3
1750-1759	17	4	5	1		6	1
1760-1769	33	6	8	2		15	2
1770-1776	18	2	4	1		10	1
Total	193	65	48	21	5	37	17
% Total Ministers		33.7	24.9	10.9	2.6	19.1	8.8

Ethnic Origins of Maryland Ministers

*These were the men serving in Maryland in June 1692.

Fifteen out of the twenty clergymen who arrived in Maryland through the end of 1699 were English. They were joined by a Welshman, a Frenchman, a Dutchman, and one Scot. The homogeneity of these original missionaries was a unique phenomenon. Never again would so many English clergymen disembark in Maryland in such a short time period, nor would the English again constitute anywhere near eighty-seven percent of all Maryland ministers, as they did in 1699. No other nationality ever dominated much more than half of the market.

That Bray and Bishop Compton sent almost exclusively ministers of
English and Welsh birth was probably not an accident. The appointment of
James Blair, a Scot, as commissary of Virginia in 1691 had aroused a good
deal of resentment among the English there. Some considered his nationality
"a high affront made to their nation," as Bishop Compton was told, and they
wondered why in all of England no suitable commissary could be found.[1]
In a meeting with Bishop Compton and the archbishop of Canterbury in 1697,
Blair was queried about charges that he had filled the Virginia Church
with his fellow Scots. According to Blair's accusers, the Scottish
ministers were "discontented troublesome Men" who bothered the governor
and the Burgesses with salary disputes. They were also supposedly prone
to immorality. Compton defended Blair by stating that the Scottish
Episcopalians could expect little advancement in their own country and he
considered it "both a Charity to the Men and that it was a piece of good
service to the plantations" to send them there.[2] However, the clamor
from Virginia, an awareness that Nicholson had no liking for the Scots,
and perhaps latent fears of Jacobite contamination were in all likelihood
reasons which induced Bray and Compton to restrict the entry of Scots
into Maryland. Future colonial parishioners were least offended by English
clergymen, and the recruiters knew they needed a fund of goodwill during
this critical period.

The lone Scot of the 1690s, however, was a harbinger for the future.
Another Scot came over in 1700. When Bray desperately searched for an
impressively large contingent of ministers to send to the colony with the

[1] Nicholas Moreau to the Bishop of Lichfield and Coventry, April 12,
1697, in Perry, Collections, I, 31.

[2] "A true Account of a Conference at Lambeth, Dec. 12, 1697," in
Perry, Collections, I, 37-39.

1702 Establishment Act he was obliged to send two Scots and a Frenchman
to obtain a total of six men. Thereafter, with Nicholson out of the
province, the establishment secured, and Bray removed for the commissary-
ship, Maryland was open to those who spoke with a northern burr.

Many Scots came. Out of the total number of ministers who served
the Church, at least a quarter were Scots. They trickled slowly into the
colony, never more than two per year or nine per decade. No Scot arrived
during the Jacobite uprising of 1715, nor did any come in 1716. A
similar hiatus occurred after the 'Forty-Five rebellion.[1] Through the
1730s the English decadal influx generally topped or matched that of the
Scots, but the reverse was true for all the following decades. The percentage of Englishmen among the total Maryland clergy dropped from the
high of eighty-seven percent in 1699 to seventy percent in 1704 and fifty
percent in 1715; the rate dropped steadily until they comprised only
thirteen percent of the total ministry in 1775. The Scots, on the other
hand, were only five percent of the clergy in 1700. By 1714 they constituted
thirty-three percent of the total and remained roughly at that figure up to
the Revolution. Until the Americans began to enter the Church, the English
and the Scots together generally comprised from two-thirds to three-
quarters of the total officiating ministry. After 1705 there were usually
between nine and twelve English clerics in the colony. Ten to twelve
Scottish ministers were the norm until the late 1750s, when fourteen to
seventeen became the more common total.

The large number of Scots in the Church did not go unnoticed or
uncriticized. In 1718, when over one-third of the ministers were Scottish,

---

[1] Though these hiatuses may not have been related to the rebellions,
it seems likely that they were.

Christopher Wilkinson wrote to the bishop of London saying that he thought
it was better that the vacant parishes remain without ministers rather
than to fill them with Scotsmen. Voicing complaints which became the
standard litany against them, Wilkinson said the Scottish university men
usually "come young, raw, and undisciplined, tainted with Presbyterian
principles, and no real friends to our Episcopal Government." He declared
his conviction that "necessity, not choice, has induced them to seek for
preferment among us."[1] The necessity Wilkinson spoke of was of two kinds,
religious and economic. During the eighteenth century the less prosperous
Scots, already buffeted by a series of crop failures, were hurt by an
escalation in rents, a movement among landowners to consolidate their
holdings, and the conversion of arable to sheep pasture.[2] The prospects
for young men of humble social background were not encouraging. The
Church, in England the classic refuge for poor, ambitious men, was
Presbyterian in Scotland and could not offer the security and salaries
of the Anglican. The Scottish Episcopal Church was disestablished in June
1689. At least one of the early Scottish missionaries in Maryland had
been harried out of the north because of the "Rage of the Presbiterian
Party, with whose measures and Principles, he could not comply."[3] As a
religious exile, however, he was in the minority. Most of the Scottish
clerics were young men who never served in Scotland at all. Whether most
of them were members of the Anglican community in Scotland is unknown but
improbable. Wilkinson was not given to exaggeration, and the charge that
the Scots were generally "converted" Presbyterians was repeated by other

---

[1] Christopher Wilkinson to Bishop John Robinson, May 26, 1718, in
Perry, Collections, IV, 108.

[2] Henry Hamilton, An Economic History of Scotland in the 18th Century
(Oxford, 1963), 7, 13, 14.

[3] John Makqueen to the Secretary of the S.P.G., January 16, 1703,
S.P.G. Papers, Series A, Volume 1, item XLVII.

observers. Almost fifty years after Wilkinson's letter Jonathan Boucher
remarked that one of the causes of the public's low opinion of clergymen
was the large number of Scotsmen "who, f[ro]m rigid, true-blue Presbyterians, converted by the convinc[in]g Argum[en]t of a Stipend (enormous to
Them) become ignorant and debauched Episcopal Pastors."[1] Though many
Scottish Episcopalian ministers were presumably former Presbyterians
(given the religious complexion of their homeland), the clear evidence
for this cannot be found. Only two people of positive Scottish birth,
Patrick Glasgow, who arrived in 1742, and John MacPherson, who came in
1753, are known to have been Presbyterians who later conformed. Glasgow
was a minister in the New Side Presbyterian Church and MacPherson joined
the Anglican Church specifically to become a priest. Nonetheless, the
idea that the Scots converted out of greed colored their relations with
their parishioners.

The Scottish clergymen aroused other prejudices. Some people feared
them for suspected Jacobite leanings.[2] Their education was sneered at and
their general moral character held in contempt. A Scottish accent
alienated many. Governor Sharpe complained in 1764 that the Scottish
clergymen spoke English so badly that "near half of the Inhabitants have
some Room for saying they are obliged to pay their Minister for preaching
to them in an unknown Tongue."[3]

---

[1] Jonathan Boucher to Rev. John James, March 9, 1767, in "The Letters
of Jonathan Boucher," Md. Hist. Mag., VII (1912), 337.

[2] In a curious, anonymous list compiled about 1722 and sent to the
bishop of London, the political leanings of many of the clergy are noted.
Of the eight Scots mentioned, four were called Whigs, four Tories. The
Tories were generally vilified as idiots or rakes as well. Of all the
other clergymen of various ethnic backgrounds on the list, only an Irishman--
Jacob Henderson--was also termed a Tory; the other men were all "sticklers
for the establishment" or "Whigs of the first rank." Perry, Collections,
IV, 129.

[3] Horatio Sharpe to Cecilius Calvert, July 10, 1764, Arch. Md., XIV,
166.

Apparently the Irish clergy enjoyed more prestige than the Scots. Less numerous in the Church, they may have been given some protection by the fact that Baltimore's estates were in Ireland. Though complaints against them were few and muted, the Irish did occasionally suffer from ethnic discriminations. Henderson was the chief and natural target of complaints. His fierce and intolerant personality virtually invited people to attack him on any grounds they could think of, and his nationality was a convenient handle. The most invidious charge against him was a variation of the accusation most injurious to the Scots, that of religious insincerity. In his case, however, it was rumored that he was exceptionally partial to Catholicism.[1] The legislature fostered this prejudice by persistently equating "Catholic" with "Irish" in its numerous anti-Catholic bills.

The Irish began to serve in the Maryland Church somewhat later than the English or the Scots. Henderson, who came to the province in 1713, was the first full Irishman to officiate.[2] Twenty-one came in all, composing about eleven percent of all ministers. Irish migration reached its peak during the 1730s, when six men arrived in one decade to briefly swell the proportion of Irishmen among the incumbents to something over a fifth. From 1740 to the Revolution, however, men of this ethnic background gradually disappeared from the Maryland Church. By 1775 there were only two of them.

A few representatives of non-British European countries joined the Church as well. Somehow two Frenchmen, a Swiss, and a Dutchman were

---

[1] See Thomas Bordley to the Secretary of the S.P.G., August 9, 1725, in Perry, Collections, IV, 254.

[2] Two Scots-Irish arrived in 1708.

motivated to conform to Anglicanism and were granted Maryland parishes. All of them, however, came to Maryland before 1740 and all were dead by 1745. During the last three and a half decades of the establishment, the Maryland Church belonged entirely to those born in British territories.

The juggling between the English and the Scots for predominance in the Maryland Church was upset by the appearance of large numbers of native Americans during the latter years of the establishment. George Murdoch, a tailor in Virginia who went for ordination in 1724, may have been the first native clergyman. A second Virginian arrived in 1733, and the first Marylander took a living in 1736. Three native colonials came during the 1740s, six during the 1750s. These 1750s arrivals marked the beginning of the American takeover of the market, for the six Americans were one and a half times the number of Englishmen who came during that decade and they matched the combined Scottish and Irish contribution. Fifteen Americans came back in orders during the 1760s, and ten did so from 1770 to the Revolution. The American influx was only slightly less than the combined British one of the 1760s, and during the 1770s, native arrivals topped the British by ten to seven.

Twenty of the thirty-seven American ministers were born in Maryland. Pennsylvania produced about a fifth (eight men), Virginia slightly less (six men), and Massachusetts, Connecticut, and New Jersey each contributed one man.

In 1775 forty-six percent of the colony's fifty-two ministers were natives of America. Their proportional representation in the Church had more than doubled since 1760 and the trend showed no signs of slackening. In the fight for parishes Americans had a natural advantage over everyone except Baltimore's favorite protégés: the proprietor liked to induct

Americans into the livings, they had the opportunity to cultivate the governor's interest before they sailed for ordination, and they could garner titles to curacies on the spot.

Social Origins

When a man acquired the dignity of a Maryland parish and wished to be treated with suitable respect by his parishioners he was not apt to mention that his mother had kept a tavern or his father had tilled a small farm as a tenant. Because Maryland society grew steadily more stratified and class-conscious as the decades passed, the advantages of a respectable ancestry increased. The ministers were as conscious of this as any rising planter-cum-gentleman. The social origins of more than half of the clergy are hidden behind a discreet silence.[1]

Though so much evidence is missing it is not unreasonable to conclude that most ministers in Maryland came from the middling or lower middling ranks of society. One reason is that the information on the clergyman of known social origins is culled from sources which are biased towards the upper ranks of society. If a man's family was prominent or in the professions the chances are quite good that this would have been mentioned in university registers, if he matriculated, or would appear in the testimonials and recommendations he gave to the bishop of London. The man himself was more likely to talk of his ancestry in correspondence, in parish records, or in an autobiography.[2] The list of ministers of gentle family

---

[1] The social origins of about 45% of the British, and about 60% of the Americans, are known. Since the matriculation and graduation records of the Scottish universities only rarely mention a student's social background, little can be said in the following discussion about this ethnic group. University records and grammar school records provide much of the material for this section.

[2] Of all the Maryland ministers who mentioned their parents, only one, Jonathan Boucher, admitted to humble birth.

and those with a father in one of the professions is, therefore, probably quite complete. Secondly, conditions in the Church in England were such that precisely the poorer, less respectable clergy were the ones naturally attracted to Maryland.

The lowborn Britisher who dreamed of ordination and a comfortable life as a parish incumbent faced two obstacles. If he wanted to be more than a humble, pennypinching curate he had to have a university degree, or even better, degrees. To acquire a parish, he had to find a patron. The first requisite was no small hindrance. Canon law did not require a degree for ordination, but in practice just about everyone earned one.[1] Indeed, an M.A. was almost a standard accomplishment. This degree included theological training, tended to impress the bishops and other patrons, endowed the recipient with the right to hold pluralities, and gave him some cause to term himself a gentleman. However, beginning in the later seventeenth and continuing through the entire eighteenth century young men of plebeian origins found it increasingly difficult to earn scholastic degrees. Institutions such as the grammar schools, which previously furnished poor students with the classical education necessary for the university, declined in numbers after the Restoration.[2] Rising costs and fewer available scholarships deterred poor boys from entering the universities themselves. The number of plebeians who attended the English universities during the eighteenth century declined in both absolute and

---

[1] In Leicestershire, for instance, a fairly average English diocese, 65% of the incumbents held the M.A. in 1714 and another 26% held a B.A. In 1750, the ratios were 52% and 26%, respectively. John H. Pruett, "The Clergy of Leicestershire and the Clergy of Lincoln Cathedral, 1660-1714" (Ph.D. diss., Princeton University, 1973), 55.

[2] W.A.L. Vincent, The Grammar Schools: Their Continuing Tradition 1660-1714 (London, 1969) discusses the financial problems and the academic ones which led to the decline.

relative terms.[1]

If a poor student did manage to get a degree his chances of induction into something more lucrative than a small curacy were slim. Even though the changes in English education were shutting out the lower ranks of society there were still many more clergymen than there were parishes. Not only did the production of ordinands exceed the demand, but the market was shrinking constantly due to the growing tendency to hold parishes in plurality.[2] It was hard to find a vacant parish and even harder for a plebeian to receive an induction. During this period the ministry was becoming a popular career for the gentry and the upper middle class. The profession, after all, had some status. It did not smack of trade, the incomes could be most adequate, and, if handled correctly, it left plenty of leisure time for gentlemanly pursuits. Since the younger sons of the gentry and the sons of clergymen were far more likely to know or have some influence on the patrons of livings, they tended to squeeze the poor, unknown, and unconnected clergymen out of the better market opportunities.[3] What was left for these ministers were by and large the smaller parishes or the curacies.[4]

---

[1] Lawrence Stone, "The Size and Composition of the Oxford Student Body 1580-1910," in Stone, ed., The University in Society (Princeton, 1974), I, 38-45.

[2] Sykes, Church and State, 215-218. In Leicestershire the proportion of parishes held in plurality rose from 13% in 1603 to 32% in 1670, and to 49% in 1750. Pruett, "Leicestershire Clergy," 67.

[3] Stone, "Oxford Student Body," in Stone, ed., The University in Society, I, 38-39; Sykes, Church and State, 190, 197-200, 206, 213. Pruett, "Leicestershire Clergy," 76, found 75% of the county's advowsons in the hands of laymen who were usually members of the social and economic elite. These patrons tended to favor their own kind.

[4] In Ireland, the situation was aggrevated by English dominance of the better livings and the upper ranks of the clergy. Constantia Maxwell, Country and Town in Ireland under the Georges (Dundalk, 1949), 326.

These trends in educational and employment opportunities in large measure determined the type of man who would be prone to ask for service in the Maryland Church. One would not expect to find many sons of gentlemen or well-connected professionals in the colonies because these men had the best chances of finding parishes in Britain. Unless they had an adventurous spirit, thought it wise to leave the Isles, or were completely overcome by the thought of the fat Maryland stipends, ministers with influence would tend to stay at home. The poor, plebeian, or indifferently-educated man, on the other hand, who could not obtain a title or was trapped in a small curacy, had everything to gain and little to lose by venturing across the Atlantic.

Sons of European esquires and gentlemen, then, were not common in the Maryland Church. Only two of the British-born ministers had fathers who were listed in the university records as esquires.[1] About twelve ministers, or roughly eight percent of the immigrants, were of gentle birth. One or two of them, never more, entered the Maryland Church every decade. Generally there were no more than three or four non-native gentlemen in the ministry at one time. The evidence indicates that almost all of these men originated from the ranks of the lower or middle gentry. John Hamilton and John Vaughan, Irishmen, and George Cooke, of Devon, are the only ministers known to have had immediate family relations entitled to display a coat of arms.[2]

---

[1] A Scot, John Barclay, called his father "Esq." in a parish register but this appears to be a self-bestowed courtesy title. St. Peter's Parish, Talbot County, Register, 1716-1819, M295, MdA. The entry is dated May 4, 1768.

[2] According to his family, Rev. James MacGill was the heir to the Scottish Viscountcy of Oxford. When he was informed of his inheritance he went to Scotland to investigate, only to find that the title had no concomitant estate. He refused to accept it. MacGill was indeed distantly connected with the title but his claim to it is obscure. His father was not a peer. John MacGill, The MacGill-McGill Family of Maryland (privately printed, 1948), 8, 12.

The social ranking of the American ministers is strikingly different. At least eleven ministers, well over a quarter of the total, came from families in the gentry or esquire class. These nine were scions of the colonial social and economic elite. Their families were noted for their wealth, their public service, and their style of living. The names of clergymen who came from this class reads like a roll call of the planter aristocracy: Addison, Claggett, Hindman, Fendall, and Harris are some of the names represented. Ministers from these families were on equal speaking terms with almost everyone in the colony and enjoyed a measure of personal prestige which only a true British gentleman-cleric could duplicate.

The percentage of the American ministers belonging to the gentry class is practically identical to the number of British gentry serving in a typical English diocese at approximately the same period.[1] By the early 1770s the social composition of the Maryland Church was rapidly duplicating that of the parent Church. Most of the gentry who entered the colonial Church were younger sons, sometimes rather far down the line of inheritance.[2] For them, as for their contemporaries in England, the Church was an ideal solution to the problem of what to do with a very respectable family position but a small or middling personal fortune.

The number of Maryland ministers who came from professional families was only slightly above those of gentle status. Fourteen British ministers had fathers who were clergymen, professors, or doctors. Nine Americans had the same. The vast majority of both groups (ten of the British, and eight of the Americans) were clergymen's sons. The fathers of at least

---

[1] Pruett finds that the gentry contributed about a quarter of the total county ministers by 1705 and that the proportion remained quite constant well into the century. "Leicestershire Clergy," 48.

[2] Henry Addison was a third son, as were Samuel Claggett, John Bowie, Henry Fendall, and Walter Hanson Harrison. Thomas Hopkinson, Matthias Harris, and Jacob Henderson Hindman were younger sons.

half of the British ministers were not among the more prosperous members of their profession. Only one clergyman sent his son to the university as a pensioner, or one who paid his own expenses. Four ministers' sons attended the university as sizars, students who did menial tasks in return for their education. One scion of a minister was listed in the matriculation records as a pauper. If their fathers were too poor to pay their way through school they probably could not afford to give their sons a curacy, either, and a Maryland post would have been as tempting to these young men as it was to other poor candidates. The economic background of the sons of clergymen officiating in the colonies was quite different. Five of the eight clerical fathers were well-to-do or even downright wealthy.[1] All of these fathers had acquired their fortunes primarily from the proceeds of their livings; their sons, no doubt, hoped to emulate such success. No group other than Baltimore's special appointees had more advantages than the sons of Maryland ministers in the fight for parishes. They had access to the governor, easy titles to curacies from a happy parent, and they could draw on their fathers' knowledge of classical studies and divinity.

Only a few of the Maryland clergy had fathers in the professions other than the ministry. Four sons of physicians (three British, one American) and a son of a Glasgow University professor joined the Church. All of them attended a university. With one exception, they arrived in the colony in the 1750s and 1760s.

Though the recruits from the professional classes compose only about twelve percent of the total provincial ministry they are of interest

---

[1] Of the eight fathers who were incumbents in American livings, five served in Maryland. They were Alexander Adams I, James Williamson, Joseph Holt, Samuel Claggett, and Hamilton Bell I. Adams, Williamson, Bell, Claggett, and James Scott of Virginia were the very prosperous clerical fathers of Maryland ministers.

because, like so many of the gentry, they joined the Church after mid-century. This large influx of ministers from the more esteemed social classes raised the prestige and the social tone of the clergy during the last two decades of the establishment period.

In all probability most of the remaining ministers came from the middle or lower middle classes. Though their social backgrounds are in many cases unknown, circumstantial evidence supports this hypothesis. The cost and the difficulty of acquiring a classical education would have kept most of the really poor from even aspiring to the profession. Studies required large chunks of time out of a young man's life, a loss of labor that was hard for a working family to manage. It was not impossible for a poor man's son to enter the Maryland ministry, for several are known to have done so. In most of their cases, however, they either were ordained at a more advanced age than was usual or attracted the attention of a patron who helped them with educational costs. Far more common were ministers from middling families whose economic circumstances ranged from very comfortable to just getting by. The parental occupations of about twenty of these ministers are known. They include merchants, some aldermen --occupations with some prestige--alehousekeepers, soldiers, small land-owners, a bookseller, tailor, bricklayer, saddler, and a commissioner of highways/farmer. Seemingly unprestigious careers were no reliable indication of the fathers' wealth, for one Dublin alehousekeeper could afford to send his son to Cambridge as a fellow commoner, and the saddler put one son through Eton and Cambridge and sent a second to Oxford.

Once a B.A. had been earned the plebeian or middle class young man faced the problem of finding a decent Church living. Many of them must have strained their family resources to the limit just attending school

and could neither afford to spend another year at the university earning
an M.A. nor engage in a costly and often time-consuming search for a
patron and a benefice. With the employment market in England very much
prejudiced against them, poor clerics would be the class most drawn to
the opportunities for wealth and upward social mobility offered by the
Maryland Church. Unless dozens more ministers had fathers in the gentry
or the professions than the research indicates, men of humble birth
always dominated the Church in Maryland.

Education

If learning is gauged primarily on the basis of a university education,
then the Maryland clergy were always less erudite than their English
counterparts. Compared to members of the English ministry, proportionately
fewer Maryland clergymen were university graduates and a smaller percentage
earned advanced degrees above a B.A. From the late seventeenth through at
least the first half of the eighteenth century, for example, ninety-five
percent or more of the parish incumbents in Leicestershire were university
graduates. Two-thirds of all incumbents had received an M.A.[1] In
Maryland, only fifty-three percent of the clergy (103 out of 193 men) had
graduated from a university, and about a quarter of the ministry (forty-
nine men) had earned a master's degree. An additional fifteen percent (twenty-
nine men) had matriculated at a university but had failed to graduate.
These drop-outs and the sixty-one men (thirty-two percent of all ministers)
who did not attend a university were the castoffs of the English Church.
Without a degree, their chances for induction into a British parish were
almost nonexistent, and a living in one of the colonial churches was really

[1] Pruett, "Leicestershire Clergy," 54-55.

their only option. Ministers with a B.A. or an M.A. degree, on the other hand, were less common in Maryland than in Britain and hence enjoyed a natural advantage in the colonial job market. The governor was far more likely to be impressed with university credentials than a contemporary English ecclesiastical patron would be.

As a group, the Maryland clergy were better educated during the first few decades of the establishment period than at any later time. The selective recruiting of Thomas Bray and Bishop Compton was undoubtedly one reason for the relatively higher scholastic achievements of the early Maryland ministers. Another reason may have been that news about the provincial Church was disseminated through the universities. Then too, during the early period poor students acquired a university education with greater ease than their successors did. By the 1720s, when only half of the incoming Maryland clergy had earned a bachelor's degree, poor students were harder pressed to enter a university or to remain in the institution long enough to graduate. Given the degree requirements for a position in the Church in Britain, those who wished for orders and a subsequent appointment to a decent living were well-advised to volunteer for a colonial post--and Maryland, of course, offered the best prospects of advancement. Market conditions in England were not, however, the main reason for the low percentage of degree-holders among the clergy who came to Maryland during the 1750s. Many of these men were Americans, not British, and, rather than attending one of the few Anglican colleges in the colonies, had received theological training from relatives who were themselves members of the Maryland clergy.

During the 1760s and the 1770s the proportion of incoming clergy with university degrees rose markedly. This suggests that the increasingly

The Education of Maryland Clergy by Arrival Date

(Inclusive Degrees)

Arrival Date	Number Incoming Clergy	% Arrivals With University Experience	% With B.A.*	% With M.A.**	% With D.D., L.L.D, M.D.	% With University Training But No Degree	% Without University Training
1690–1699	20	85	65	20	5	20	15
1700–1709	21	86	81	33	5	5	14
1710–1719	18	89	66	44	5	23	11
1720–1729	18	72	50	17	0	22	28
1730–1739	21	62	43	24	5	19	38
1740–1749	22	54	36	9	0	18	46
1750–1759	17	47	35	18	6	12	53
1760–1769	33	70	54	27	3	16	30
1770–1776	18	67	67	44	0	0	33

* Included in this group are all M.A., D.D., LL.D., and M.D. degree holders.

** Included in this group are all D.D., LL.D., and M.D. degree holders.

Education of Maryland Clergy by Arrival Date

(Terminal Degrees)

Arrival Date	Number Incoming Clergy	% With B.A.	% With M.A.	% With D.D., LL.D., M.D.	% Total Graduates
1690–1699	20	45	15	5	65
1700–1709	21	48	28	5	81
1710–1719	18	22	39	5	66
1720–1729	18	33	17	0	50
1730–1739	21	19	19	5	43
1740–1749	22	27	9	0	36
1750–1759	17	17	12	6	35
1760–1769	33	27	24	3	54
1770–1776	18	22	45	0	67

congested employment market in Maryland--duplicating conditions in the
English Church--was forcing applicants for ecclesiastical posts to arm
themselves with degrees. By the late colonial era the provincial governor,
like the English patrons overwhelmed with eager candidates, could afford
to choose his appointments with more discrimination.

By a slight margin the English and Welsh members of the colonial
Church had the best record for university attendance. Prior to 1730 only
one man of this ethnic background came to Maryland without some university
training. However, compared to the Scots and the Irish clergy with
university experience, more Anglo-Welsh ministers left college without a
degree, and fewer of them remained there to earn an M.A. Just under half
of all the Scottish ministers in Maryland and almost a third of the Irish
had obtained an M.A., a degree taken by less than a fifth of the English
and the Welsh. English and Welsh M.A.'s, moreover, came to Maryland more
frequently during the first two decades of the establishment period than
they did during succeeding ones.

During the eighteenth century a Scottish university such as Edinburgh
provided a more modern education and demanded more of its graduates than
did Oxford or Cambridge.[1] Nevertheless, many of the colonies had a poor
opinion of the scholastic achievements of ministers educated in Scottish
institutions. In 1697 the Scottish clergy in Virginia were considered
"basely educated," and Commissary Wilkinson thought them "raw" in 1718--
although sixteen of the seventeen Scottish ministers in Maryland at that

---

[1] For a description of Edinburgh University at this time, see
N. T. Phillipson, "Culture and Society in the 18th Century Province:
The Case of Edinburgh and the Scottish Enlightenment," in Lawrence Stone,
ed., The University in Society (Princeton, 1974), II, 407-448.

Education of Maryland Ministers by Ethnic Background

Degree (Inclusive)	English and Welsh N=65 %	Scots N=48 %	Irish N=21 %	Other European * N=5 %	Colonials N=37 %	Unknown N=17 %
Attended University	85	77	80	20	62	--
B.A.	63	64	76	20	54	--
M.A.	18	45	29	20	35	--
D.D., LL.D., M.D.	3	4	5	--	3	--

* Since these men probably attended continental European schools, their education level must be higher than indicated here.

time had studied at a university and ten of them held M.A.'s.[1] The complaints concerning the learning of the Scots, prompted as they often were
by prejudice, indicate a problem in describing the educational level of
the clergy in Maryland. The proportion of degree-holders among the ministers can be charted without much difficulty, but evaluating what the
degrees meant in terms of learning is much harder. Degree requirements
varied from university to university, and recipients of the same degree
from the same university varied in quality as much as they do today. Not
enough evidence remains to hazard an opinion on the scholastic standards
of the Maryland clergy. Some ministers wrote elegant, witty sermons,
owned large libraries, and corresponded with savants. Others mumbled
printed homilies, made do without a single book, and scrawled atrocious
English. What the median level was can only be guessed at. If the surviving complaints against the learning of the clergy are any indication,
then ironically the earlier period of the establishment, when the
proportion of university students and M.A. recipients was the highest,
was also the time of greatest parishioner dissatisfaction. Governor John
Hart, for one, wondered in 1714 how "such illiterate men came to be in
holy orders," and was appalled by the number of clergymen whose learning
was "a scandal to their profession."[2] After the first quarter of the century,
however, extant criticism of the education of the ministers is very rare.[3]

---

[1] Nicholas Moreau to the Bishop of Lichfield and Coventry, April 12,
1697, in Perry, Collections, I, 30; Christopher Wilkinson to Bishop John
Robinson, May 26, 1718, in Perry, Collections, IV, 108.

[2] John Hart to Bishop John Robinson, July 10, 1714, in Perry,
Collections, IV, 78.

[3] One of the few surviving complaints was voiced by Hugh Jones and
Henry Addison, prominent Maryland ministers and both M.A.'s from Oxford.
They told the bishop of London in 1753 that the education of some ministers
did not support their professional requirements. Addison and Jones to
Bishop Thomas Sherlock, August 27, 1753, in Perry, Collections, IV, 331.

Never, though, did the learning of the provincial clergy match English standards.[1]

Of all the ethnic groups the American-born clergy had the smallest proportion of university graduates. A few of the wealthier natives went to Britain for their education, but most studied at the colonial colleges. The College of Philadelphia, which offered tutorial classes in divinity from several distinguished Anglican ministers, was the favorite choice. Nine men, a quarter of all American clergy in Maryland, studied there. Princeton educated four future ministers, and the College of William and Mary produced two.[2] One minister went to Harvard and another studied at King's College.[3] Perhaps because an M.A. from an American institution was granted for the asking after the lapse of a stipulated period following the B.A., about a third of the American ministers in Maryland had one.

---

[1]
Degree Holding Incumbents
in Maryland and Leicestershire
By Terminal Degrees

	1714		1750		1771
	Maryland	Leicester-shire	Maryland	Leicester-shire	Maryland
Degree	N=24 %	N=175 %	N=42 %	N=159 %	N=54 %
M.D., D.D., LL.B., LL.D.	0	6	2	17	5
M.A.	42	65	26	52	24
B.A.	46	26	21	26	22
No Degree	12	3	51	5	49

Note: The figures for Leicestershire are derived from Pruett, "Leicestershire Clergy," 55.

[2] The figure for William and Mary graduates is surprising. Between 1723 and 1776, 45 clergymen who joined the Church in Virginia were graduates of the College. Joan Rezner Gundersen, "The Anglican Ministry in Virginia 1723-1776: A Study of Social Class" (Ph.D. diss., Notre Dame University, 1972), 86, 89.

[3] The graduate of King's College, William Hanna, received an M.A. from Yale.

A number of the fourteen Americans who did not attend a college were in a position to acquire a classical education on their own. Most of them qualify as scions of the great Maryland planter families, or were the sons of colonial clergymen. The gentry could afford to hire private tutors for their sons, and the ministers could educate their own. Several provincial clerics ran schools or gave divinity lessons to interested students. University degrees, however, were a sign of status if not educational excellence, and ministers without them eagerly snapped up honorary ones when they could.

***

During the course of the eighteenth century the Church in Maryland developed several characteristics which resembled those of the parent institution. Initially plagued by chronic underemployment, the Church became oversupplied with ministers for the available livings. A two-tiered system of inducted incumbents and hired curates resulted, duplicating the situation in the English Church. Fierce competition for vacant positions became normal. Certain groups, particularly the native candidates and those especially favored by the proprietor, were naturally advantaged and could squeeze into the market while others failed. After mid-century the Church attracted growing numbers of clergymen from the native gentry and professional classes, the same groups who were crowding into the Church in England. They tended to join for the same reasons: in Maryland, as in Britain, the Church became a respectable, well-paying gentlemanly profession.

In other respects the Church in the colony remained quite different from the English Church. Its ministers were from a far more diverse ethnic

background, and they were more likely to be from the middle or lower-
middle social classes than their British contemporaries were. Until
nearly the end of the colonial period Maryland took in the dregs of the
British market, those who by reason of their class or their education had
little chance of acquiring an English or Irish parish, and the educational
attainments of the colonial ministers consequently lagged far below the
standards in Britain.

Chapter IV

Professional Careers

The Anglican Church, so prudently undogmatic on many matters, was
assertive on the subject of the duties and the obligations of priesthood.
The office of the minister--its biblical justification, its authority,
and its function--was a crucial topic of debate during the Reformation and
the Church could not avoid taking a stand. The Anglican position regarding
the sacerdotal and the pastoral duties of the ministry took shape under
Edward VI and Elizabeth and was hammered out by the early seventeenth
century. The Book of Common Prayer of 1559 and the Canons of 1604
delineated clearly and simply what every minister had to do to fulfill his
"sacred function" to the satisfaction of God, the state, and the
episcopate.[1]

The most important duty of an Anglican priest was to administer the
sacraments of baptism and communion. These two rites were the only ones
the Church considered necessary for salvation, and ministers performed a
pivotal role in the celebrations.[2] If he did nothing else for his
parishioners the Church demanded that a cleric make certain that his charges
were baptized before their deaths and that they had the opportunity to

---

[1] A good discussion of the Reformation debates regarding the role
of the ministry may be found in David Hall, The Faithful Shepherd: A
History of the New England Ministry in the Seventeenth Century (Chapel
Hill, N.C., 1972), 4-67.

[2] Article 25 of the Church of England's Thirty-Nine Articles;
Phillimore, Ecclesiastical Law, I, 112. The Thirty-Nine Articles are
discussed and printed in E.J. Bicknell, A Theological Introduction to the
Thirty-Nine Articles of the Church of England (London, 1955).

receive the Eucharist at least three times a year.[1] Ministers were expected to serve the sacrament to bedridden communicants in their own homes and to perform emergency baptisms whenever and wherever needed.[2]

Catechism, confession, matrimony, and burial were the secondary rites or ceremonies of the Church of England.[3] Ministers presided at all of them. The last three were ceremonies performed on demand, and the number of times any given minister was asked to officiate at them depended largely on the size of his parish population. Catechism, however, was an office which was supposed to be observed at uniform times throughout the realm. Recognizing the importance of instructing young people in the tenets of the faith, the Church fathers ordered all parsons, vicars, and curates to teach the catechism for at least half an hour every Sunday or holy day before evening prayers.[4]

The canons gave very specific instructions on how and when ministers were to serve their parishioners in the role of pastors and teachers. Clergymen were ordered to offer at least one service every Sunday and to observe the holy days and their eves by reading the proper prayers and lessons from the Book of Common Prayer. On Wednesdays and Fridays the

---

[1] Wilson, ed., Constitutions and Canons, Canon XXI; The Book of Common Prayer of 1559, section "The Ministration of Baptism to be used in the Church." The Prayer Book of 1559 has been reprinted in William K. Clay, ed., Liturgies and Occasional Forms of Prayer Set Forth in the Reign of Queen Elizabeth (Cambridge, 1847); the section referred to here may be found in that source, 199–210.

[2] Wilson, ed., Constitutions and Canons, Canons LXXI, LXIX. Lay persons could perform baptismal services in emergencies but the practice was discouraged. Phillimore, Ecclesiastical Law, 491–492.

[3] In Britain confirmation would be included in this group. Normally performed by bishops, it apparently was perforce discarded in the colonies.

[4] Wilson, ed., Constitutions and Canons, Canon LIX.

ministers were to say the litany at the parish church or chapel.[1] State-

ordered fast days or thanksgiving days were also occasions when the

ministers gave special prayers or sermons. Though the canons decreed that

the local clergy exhort from the pulpit a minimum of three times a week

(Sundays, Wednesdays, and Fridays) the pastoral duties of a minister did

not end when he left the church. He was further commanded to "labour

diligently" for the conversion of any non-Anglicans in his parish "by

instruction, perswasion, and all good meanes he can deuise." Visiting

the sick "to instruct and comfort them in their distresse" was another

obligation.[2]

As the mien of a minister was considered an expression of his piety

and his behavior was expected to jibe with his professed religious

beliefs, the Church did not neglect to set standards for clerical dress and

deportment. Exclusively "decent and comely Apparell" fit to command "the

honor and estimation due to the special Messengers and Ministers of

Almighty God" was to be worn. Not only were the excesses of fashion con-

demned, but the canons ordered ministers to display their calling by wearing

bands and distinctive gowns. Clergymen were further forbidden to resort

to taverns or alehouses except for their "honest necessities." The Church

demanded that they avoid servile or undignified labor and refrain from

drinking, rioting, wasting time, and gaming.[3]

All ministers vowed in their ordination oaths to fulfill their clerical

---

[1] Wilson, ed., _Constitutions and Canons_, Canons XIII, XIV, XV. The
Elizabethan and Jacobean clergy were divided--usually on the basis of
education--into preachers and non-preachers. Preaching required special
licenses. The rules concerning the content of the services were different
for both types of clergy. By the eighteenth century, however, most
beneficed clergy were university graduates and they were expected to preach.
All the ministers in Maryland did.

[2] _Ibid._, Canons LXVI, LXVII.

[3] _Ibid._, Canons LXXIV, LXXV. Ministers were supposed to wear special
"Priests' Cloaks" when they traveled and were forbidden embroidered night-
caps and light colored stockings.

obligations as well as they possibly could. In practice, the standards set
forth in the canons and the Common Prayer Book were frequently difficult
to achieve. More than conscientiousness and dedication were necessary for
a minister to complete his canonical duties with any degree of success.
The intellectual and religious climate of the period and the physical
environment of the individual parish greatly influenced a minister's
ability and his inclination to maintain the letter of the canons. This was
as true for clergymen on the Maryland frontier as it was for the dean of
St. Paul's Cathedral in London. Often it was simply not enough for a
minister to be literate, diligent, hardy, and personable. Frequent church
services were of no consequence if the people were disinclined to attend
at all, and sending for the minister when an emergency baptism was necessary
was of little use if the minister lived too far away to come quickly. In
England as in the colonies the propensity of the parishioners to accept
the services of their Anglican minister determined to a considerable extent
the perimeter of the professional ministrations offered on a regular basis.
Parishioners may have been enthusiastic about gathering at the local church
three or more times a week during the sixteenth and early seventeenth
centuries, when religious passion ran high, but by the eighteenth century
the spiritual zeal of the British was much subdued and parishioners
generally declined to attend services as often as the Church recommended.
Maryland ministers discovered that their assigned charges were, if anything,
even less interested in religious matters than their English counterparts.
Besides, most English parishes were manageable in terms of their geographic
size and their population. Parishes in Maryland were impossibly large
and no minister, even with a stable of horses and the constitution of a
champion athlete, could fully satisfy the dictates of the canons.

Though recognizably an offshoot of the parent institution, the Church in Maryland, tailored to fit the political, economic, and physical environment peculiar to the colony, was a unique structure. The professional careers of its clergy, therefore, were in many ways quite different from those of their British-based colleagues. Geographical limitations altered the traditional scope of the job. The induction procedures, the lack of ecclesiastical supervision, and the arrangements regarding clerical salaries resulted in novel relationships with the state and the public. Maryland ministers played a new role in local government as members of the vestry, a parish body with authority and duties indigenous to the colony. In short, the colonial Church and its environment were simply inimical to attempts to duplicate the leisured life styles of British country parsons. Maryland ministers lived in a separate world and their professional careers reflected that fact.

***

The basic unit of individual clerical operations was the parish. Headed by an incumbent or any one of several types of curates, most English parishes boasted a church and provided a house for the resident clergyman.[1] All of England and Wales were divided into these units, and seen on a map, the effect is that of a crazy quilt of irregularly shaped pieces.[2] There were over ten thousand parishes in the eighteenth century. In terms of

---

[1] The houses, however, were not always habitable. See Diana McClatchey, Oxfordshire Clergy 1777-1869 (Oxford, 1960), 19-21, for a report on the parsonages of that county.

[2] McClatchey, ibid., 13, presents such a map of the parishes of Oxfordshire.

size, the average parish covered slightly under five square miles.[1]

Individual parishes, of course, varied in size, but compactness was the

general rule. Oxfordshire, for instance, contained 192 parishes in a land

mass of 750 square miles, or about 3.9 square miles per parish.[2] Leicester-

shire's 205 parishes averaged 4.05 square miles in size.[3] If the population

of England and Wales has been correctly estimated at about 5.5 million in

1700 and roughly a million more in 1750, then the average parish of 1700

contained some 550 inhabitants and that of 1750, about 650.[4] Though non-

residence, pluralism and other evils reduced frequent contacts between some

ministers and their parishioners, clergymen were generally nearby and easy

to reach. The ministers, in turn, were responsible for parishes small

enough so that they were not unduly strained in coping with their clerical

obligations.[5]

In Maryland, however, the ministers did not reside in tiny parishes

they could walk across in a few hours, nor did they serve a population

---

[1] During the 18th century there were somewhat over 10,000 parishes in
the 50,873 square miles of England and Wales. The exact number of parishes
is somewhat uncertain, but in c. 1835 there were 10,298 benefices in the
territory. Given the rigid advowson system in England, the number is not
likely to be more than a fraction higher than it was a hundred years
before. The census is in G.F.A. Best, Temporal Pillars: Queen Anne's
Bounty, the Ecclesiastical Commissioners, and the Church of England
(Cambridge, 1964), 545. The figures for territorial sizes used here are
from the Columbia Desk Encyclopedia, 3d ed.

[2] McClatchey, Oxfordshire Clergy, 3.

[3] Pruett, "Leicestershire Clergy," 77.

[4] Population figures are from T.S. Ashton, The Industrial Revolution
1760-1830 (London, 1968), 2. In reality, the parish populations varied
enormously. For instance, 49 parishes in Devon in 1779 contained twenty
or fewer families, yet others had two hundred and more. Arthur Warne,
Church and Society in Eighteenth Century Devon (Newton Abbot, Devon, 1969),
40, 45, 46.

[5] It should be noted that the number of clergymen who served in
England was actually about one and a half times the number of benefices,
or about fifteen thousand men. The ratio of Anglican ministers to population, then, was actually even better than the population per parish
figures given here.

so often clustered conveniently in villages. The culture of tobacco
fostered a settlement pattern which was decentralized and dispersed. Such
diffusion fit the exigencies of the plant and the trade admirably but
complicated the lives of the clergy. "The inhabitants of this Country
having (many of them) vast tracts of land, live at least a mile asunder
from their next neighbours," ministers complained in 1698, noting that one
or two horses per minister were an absolute necessity.[1] The terrain made
travel difficult and hazardous. Rivers and marshes fissured the landscape.
Roads were non-existent or frequently impassable. Worse, the parishes in
Maryland bore no resemblance to the tidy units of England. In compliance
with the Establishment Act of 1692, county commissioners, justices, and
freeholders laid out the boundaries of the first parishes between 1692 and
1694. The officials and inhabitants created thirty. The criteria they
employed in deciding where to place parish boundaries appear to have been
considerations of population (some of the parishes were obviously designed
to include sufficient taxables to produce incomes very attractive to
incoming ministers), administration (most parishes fit neatly within the
borders of one county), and some concern for geographic unity. Depending
on the parish, one or another of these seem to have been the dominant
factor. What emerged in 1694 was a network of parishes shaped like strips
or wedges radiating inland from the Bay and, on the Western Shore, from
the Potomac River. Long and narrow, their boundaries were often set along
the wide rivers which spilled into the Chesapeake. Compared to the usual
British parish they were monstrously large, ranging up to hundreds of
square miles in size. In a 1723 query Bishop Edmund Gibson asked for the
dimensions of the Maryland parishes and received responses from twenty-two

---

[1] Peregrine Coney, John Lillingston et al. to Bishop Henry Compton,
May 18, 1698, in Perry, Collections, IV, 10.

out of the thirty-two parishes in the colony.[1] The lengths reported varied

from a minimum of sixteen miles all the way up to seventy miles for one

of the frontier parishes. Widths ranged from two or three miles to forty.

Most of the parishes were between twenty and forty miles long and ten to

twenty miles wide.[2] The smallest parish in the province, Christ Church in

Queen Anne's County, was sixteen to twenty miles in length and three to

seven in width and covered about 33 square miles of territory.[3] All Hallows

Parish in Anne Arundel County, also one of the little parishes, extended

over eighty square miles.[4] The frontier parishes, stretching away from

the Bay towards the borders of Delaware, Pennsylvania, or Virginia, could

be over ten times the size of the small ones. King George's Parish in

Prince George's County on the Western Shore was about a thousand square

miles in area, and the rector of St. Paul's in Baltimore County implied

that his parish extended sixteen hundred square miles.[5] Most of the

parishes, though, seem to have ranged between two and three hundred, and

the average size of the first thirty parishes was roughly 250 square miles.

As new parishes were formed the geographic areas included in the original

[1] The responses, sent to Bishop Gibson in the summer of 1724, are reprinted in Perry, Collections, IV, 190-231.

[2] The incumbents tended to report the dimensions of their parishes at their longest and widest extents, and so these figures represent the extreme measurements of the parishes.

[3] The response of Thomas Phillips, Rector of Christ Church Parish, June 3, 1724, in Perry, Collections, IV, 214.

[4] Carville V. Earle, The Evolution of a Tidewater Settlement System: All Hallow's Parish, Maryland, 1650-1783 (Chicago, 1975), 7.

[5] Response of John Frazer, rector of King George's Parish, Prince George's County, and of William Tibbs, rector of St. Paul's Parish, Baltimore County, in Perry, Collections, IV, 206-190. The commissaries collected the responses to Bishop Gibson's queries and probably checked them against their own information. The individual reports, then, in all likelihood were reasonably accurate. In 1729 or 1730 the governor of Maryland asked for reports on the dimensions of the parishes measured at their greatest extents; the figures he received agree well with the measurements sent to London. Arch. Md., XXXVIII, 449-452.

ones were reduced until, with the inclusion of the forty-fourth parish in 1765, average size had dropped to two hundred square miles.[1]

The size of the parish alone did not determine how well a minister could carry out his responsibilities. The number of parishioners and where they were located within the parish boundaries were also decisive considerations. Within the borders of many of the early parishes were large tracts of uninhabited territory which the incumbents could justifiably ignore. These areas, however, shrank as the population expanded and the frontiers to the north, east, and west were settled and civilized. Though the government organized additional parishes in some of the rapidly developing regions, the demands made on the ministers did not diminish. In terms of land area, the clergymen of the later period often supervised technically smaller parishes than their predecessors, but they also dealt with a much larger population within the parish limits. The addition of fourteen new parishes after 1694 did little to stabilize the ratio of ministers to people at a reasonable level. Individual parishes have left documentary evidence of ever-increasing congregations but the trend is easiest to discern when the total population of Maryland is compared to the number of Anglican ministers in the province. When the first complete

---

[1] These figures are extremely rough and I give them only to provide a basis for comparison with the dimension of the English parishes. The boundaries of many parishes simply extended vaguely into the interior of either shore and were cut off only by the borders of a neighboring colony. For much of the eighteenth century the boundaries between Maryland and Pennsylvania were disputed and therefore the boundaries of the parishes touching the boundaries are somewhat unclear. The present land mass of Maryland is 9,874 square miles. The figure given as the average parish size for 1694 is obtained by excluding from the total area the land now in Garrett, Alleghany, Washington, and Frederick counties (the far western territories of the province, then hardly considered part of Maryland) and dividing the result (7,654 square miles) by 30. The area of Maryland in 1765, though, included what are now Washington and Frederick counties, and I have retained this territory in my calculations. As I compute, the settled regions in Maryland in 1765 covered approximately 8,780 square miles.

census was taken in 1700–1701 the population in Maryland was approximately

34,200 persons, black and white.[1] The mean population for the thirty

parishes stood at about 1,140 people, and each of the twenty-one ministers

was responsible for an average of 1,628 persons. Maryland parishes were

already twice as populated as those in Britain. In 1704 the ratio of

ministers to people was even worse--one to 1,811. On these parishioners,

about 1,531 were white.[2] By 1755, when British parishes contained a mean

population somewhere in the neighborhood of 650; Maryland parishes held

3,570. The forty-one provincial ministers served an average of 3,744

parishioners, of whom 2,640 were white. By the Revolution, the proportion

of ministers to parishioners had reached a ludicrous ratio of one to 4,400

or one to 3,080 whites.[3]

Had the population of Maryland been distributed in parishes the size

of those in England the province in 1755 would have had 351 units instead

of forty-three. To match the English ratio of clergymen to population at

mid-century the Maryland Church would have been obliged to employ 528

------

[1] The census material given here and in the charts is taken or inter-
polated from several sources. The original censuses of 1700–01, 1704, 1710,
and 1712, and 1755 may be found in the Arch. Md., but have been conveniently
gathered in Evarts B. Greene and Virginia D. Harrington, American Population
Before the Federal Census of 1790 (New York, 1932), 124-125. They are also
available in Robert V. Wells, The Population of the British Colonies in
America before 1776: A Survey of Census Data (Princeton, 1975), 144-158.
Several flaws in the censuses of 1700–01, 1704, 1710, and 1712 have been
corrected by Russell R. Menard, "Economy and Society in Early Colonial
Maryland" (Ph.D. diss., University of Iowa, 1974), 396-413, and I have used
Menard's figures for these enumerations. The population data for 1775 is
taken from A.E. Karinen, "Numerical and Distributional Aspects of Maryland
Population, 1631-1840" (Ph.D. diss., University of Maryland, 1958), 74.

[2] The figures for white population probably reflect with greater
accuracy the real dimensions of ministerial responsibility. Interaction
between most ministers and the blacks in their parishes appears minimal.

[3] Naturally not all parishioners were white Anglicans. However, the
ministers, in a strict canonical sense, were responsible for the spiritual
welfare of all the people in their parishes.

Proportion of Ministers to Population

Date of Census	Total Population of Maryland	Number Parishes	Mean Parish Population	Number Ministers in Province	Mean Number of Parishioners Per Minister
1700-01	34,200	30	1,140	21	1,628
1704	36,213	30	1,207	20	1,811
1710	43,742	32	1,367	19	2,303
1712	45,733	32	1,429	25	1,829
1755	153,505	43	3,570	41	3,744
1762	164,007	43	3,814	45	3,814
1775	228,780	44	5,200	52	4,400

Proportion of Ministers to White Population

Year	White Population	Mean White Population per Parish	Mean White Population per Minister
1700	--	--	--
1704	30,614	1,020	1,531
1710	35,794	1,119	1,884
1712	37,354	1,164	1,494
1755	108,221	2,517	2,640
1762	114,313	2,658	2,540
1775	160,146	3,640	3,080

ministers. Obviously the ministers in Maryland could not possibly give
their parishioners the attention and pastoral care their English colleagues
were able to bestow on their charges. The surplus of clergymen in the
Maryland Church by the 1750s existed only insofar as the availability of
livings was concerned, for the Church never had sufficient men to truly
satisfy the needs of the laity. In 1700 the most serious and hardworking
of ministers would have been heavily burdened by the responsibilities of
establishing a caring, fatherly relationship with his Anglican congregations, exhorting the unfaithful and the unchurched, and persuading
misguided members of various sects to see their errors. By the 1770s, when
the ratio of population to ministers was almost three times more extreme,
only the ministers in the very smallest parishes could have had much
impact on the lives of the people who did not regularly turn up at worship
services.

The arrangements made by the commissioners charged with laying out
the first parishes were challenged almost as soon as the boundaries were
surveyed and registered.[1] However, several obstacles inhibited plans to
reduce the larger parishes to a more manageable size. The forty per poll
was the chief impediment. A large taxable population was needed to
generate a sufficient income for an incumbent, and in Maryland such a tax
base could be supplied only by extending the parishes over large tracts
of territory. A parish division always diminished the salary of the
incumbent (or at least that of the future incumbents if, as Baltimore
conceded in 1730, divisions took effect only after the death or removal

---

[1] In 1696 the council, prompted by Governor Nicholson, proposed to
re-divide the parishes more equally and to give them new names. The board
was particularly concerned that the small parishes could not attract
incumbents. The assembly refused to agree to the proposal, although the
delegates did announce that they would consider petitions for divisions
and new boundary arrangements when such proposals originated from the
parishioners themselves. Arch. Md., XIX, 443, 444, 447.

of the beneficiary) but the reduction of a parish during the first several decades of the establishment threatened to cut the incumbent's income to below subsistence level. "I must own," admitted Commissary Wilkinson to Bishop Gibson in 1726, "that our Parishes are generally too large, but as they [i.e., the delegates in the general assembly] go about dividing them, now either the one or both will be insufficient for our support."[1] Small parishes were usually vacant ones until well into the 1730s, and Wilkinson worried that creating new ones would simply increase the number of empty pulpits. "Lessening the revenues of the Church," he believed, would "discourage Ministers from coming over into these parts for the future."[2] The new parishes organized before the 1740s were indeed prone to chronic vacancies. St. Stephen's Parish, for instance, originally included all of Cecil County. In 1706 the inhabitants complained that the people in the northern part of the parish were unable to attend church because the Elk River virtually cut the parish in half, and the church was located south of the river. They petitioned the legislature for a division. The request was reasonable and the legislature erected North Elk Parish out of St. Stephen's the same year.[3] Unfortunately, as Wilkinson reported, there were already vacancies elsewhere in the colony, and North Elk and St. Stephen's together were "scarce a competency for one minister."[4] The new living remained empty for twelve years. Other new parishes suffered a similar fate. Queen Anne's Parish, erected in 1704

---

[1] Christopher Wilkinson to Bishop Edmund Gibson, August 1, 1726, in Perry, Collections, IV, 259.

[2] Wilkinson to Bishop Gibson, October 18, 1728, Fulham Papers, "Maryland 1696-1769," item 189.

[3] Arch. Md., XXVI, 578, 579, 624.

[4] Christopher Wilkinson to Bishop John Robinson, July 3, 1717, in Perry, Collections, IV, 88.

out of St. Paul's in Prince George's County, lacked an incumbent until
1708. St. Margaret Whitechapel in Dorchester (later Caroline) County
was a vacant living for six years after it was organized in 1725. Though
parishes formed after the 1730s usually acquired incumbents much more
speedily, the problem of maintaining sufficient salaries deterred many
necessary parish divisions until the middle decades of the century.

A second obstacle--one which hindered a division even when the parish
produced enough income for two men--was legal, rather than economic.
Incumbents held their livings as freeholds. The ministers reasoned that
an induction to any given parish bestowed on them an inalienable right to
forty pounds of tobacco from every taxable resident within the borders of
the parish as they were drawn on the day of induction. Any tampering with
the boundaries which resulted in a loss of taxables and a drop in salary
level was regarded by the incumbents as the equivalent of theft. The
legislature, on the other hand, acted on the principle that it was entitled
to restructure parishes or create new ones almost at will. In most cases
the assembly moved to interfere in the parish system only when asked to
do so. Parishioners or vestries petitioned the legislature for a division
or other boundary change, explaining their reasons for the desired
alterations.[1] Usually the petitions were addressed to the upper house,
which had the option of rejecting them or sending them down to the lower
house to be framed into bills. Sometimes commissioners were appointed by
the delegates to study the petitions. Once incorporated into a bill,
parish divisions or boundary changes were handled like any other legislative

[1] If the upper house did not think the number of parishioners in the
parish was sufficient to support two ministers, it did not hesitate to
suggest a few years' delay. See the response to the division petition
of the inhabitants of Patuxent and Collington hundreds, Prince George's
County, March 18, 1702, Arch. Md., XXIV, 211.

matter. Apparently the incumbents of the two parishes split in 1704 and

1706 were never consulted.[1] From 1706 to 1725 the legislature tampered

with some boundaries but took no action to divide any existing parishes.

Between 1725 and 1729, however, four new parishes were organized, and the

legislature also passed a bill restructuring the boundaries of five

adjacent parishes on the lower Western Shore. The incumbents were notified

of the proposed changes before all the divisions were enacted.[2] In all

but one of the cases the ministers either consented to the divisions or

thought it prudent not to object. The incumbents of the five parishes

in St. Mary's and Charles Counties, though, opposed the legislature's

proceedings, and so did Christopher Wilkinson.[3] In 1717 the commissary

wrote Bishop Robinson for advice asking whether he should try to prevent

all parish divisions which were not previously sanctioned by the bishop,

the proprietor, and the incumbent.[4] What Robinson counseled is not known,

but when the inhabitants of Wilkinson's own parish, St. Paul's in Queen

Anne's County, petitioned the legislature for a division of the parish in

1726, the commissary, pleading his "right and property," asked the assembly

---

[1] Queen Anne's Parish was formed out of St. Paul's, Prince George's County, in 1704; North Elk Parish (also called St. Mary Ann) out of St. Stephen's in Cecil County, in 1706. These were the first parishes formed after 1694.

[2] The parishes formed were: St. Margaret Whitechapel, out of Great Choptank Parish, Dorchester, in 1725; Prince George's Parish out of St. John's (also called King George's) Parish, Prince George's County, in 1726; Queen Caroline Parish out of St. Paul's, Baltimore County, All Hallow's Parish and St. Anne's Parish in Anne Arundel County, in 1728; St. Luke's Parish out of St. Paul's Parish, Queen Anne's County, 1728. The parishes involved in the 1729 reorganization of St. Mary's and Charles counties were William and Mary, King and Queen, All Faith, Durham, and Port Tobacco.

[3] Though the rectors apparently did not go so far as to complain to the legislature's Committee of Aggrievances, Henderson noted in the 1730 petition to Baltimore that they had not given their consents to the changes. "The Petition of Jacob Henderson Clerk ...," January 17, 1730, Arch. Md., XXXVIII, 442.

[4] Christopher Wilkinson to Bishop John Robinson, July 3, 1717, in Perry, Collections, IV, 88.

to put aside the division bill until the bishop of London had consented to it.[1] Stressing the undeniable necessity for a split (St. Paul's was one of the very largest parishes), the legislature overruled Wilkinson's protests and passed the bill.[2] If Wilkinson doubted the legislature's right to divide parishes without the consent of the diocesan and the incumbents, Jacob Henderson was positive that the enactment of bills which deprived ministers of their freehold rights was "extending the Legislative Authority in Maryland to greater lengths than is attempted in Parliam[en]t in Great Britain who in such cases never take away the Right of the present Incumbent during his life with[ou]t consent."[3] Henderson presented the clergy's objections to Baltimore in 1730. He not only obtained the proprietor's disallowance to the bill altering the boundaries of the lower Western Shore parishes, but secured Baltimore's assent to the principle of inviolable incumbent freehold rights.[4] After 1730 the legislature was obliged to include a clause in all division bills which guaranteed the tenancy of the incumbent. Parishes which were created out of a single original parish were generally held as a plurality of the incumbent and did not become truly independent until his death. The new ones formed out of parts of more than one parish were created piece by piece as the incumbents died or moved away. The process could take years

---

[1] Wilkinson to Bishop Edmund Gibson, August 1, 1726, in Perry, Collections, IV, 258.

[2] Because of disputes concerning the location of the boundaries the division act was not actually passed until 1728. Arch. Md., XXV, 493, 500, 501, 533; XXXVI, 22, 33, 40, 107, 290, 291; Wilkinson to Bishop Gibson, December 4, 1727, and December 10, 1728, in Perry, Collections, IV, 259-260, 269.

[3] "The Petition of Jacob Henderson Clerk ...," January 17, 1730, Arch. Md., XXXVIII, 442.

[4] Ibid.

or even decades.[1] In the meantime the parishioners received no better

pastoral service than they had before the passage of the division act.[2]

During the last twenty-odd years of the establishment period yet

another obstacle prevented the formation of needed parishes. Frederick

Calvert, the last Lord Baltimore, gave orders to Governor Sharpe to block

divisions because the proprietor wanted to preserve the large livings as

special rewards for his favorite protégés.[3] Although Sharpe personally

sympathized with the petitioners for new parishes, he dutifully ignored

them. Only Chester Parish was created during his administration.[4]

Governor Eden signed bills which would have divided two parishes on the

deaths of their incumbents, but he did so at the height of the fees and

Inspection Act controversy and the move was probably a political gesture.[5]

---

[1] St. Andrew's Parish in St. Mary's County, for instance, was authorized in a 1744 legislative session but its first vestry was not elected
until 1753, when the incumbent of one of the two parishes out of which St.
Andrew's was formed died. The parish was not entitled to a full rector
until 1764, when the other incumbent died and the parish became legally
autonomous.

[2] Ministers constantly assured the bishops of London that they were
overworked and could not meet the demands placed upon them by so many
parishioners. However, other than perhaps to hire an assistant, they were
uniformly unwilling to lighten their burden by consenting to a parish
division. Apparently they felt that their own economic needs outweighed
the spiritual needs of the parishioners. During the early decades of
the establishment, when there were too few clergymen in Maryland to
staff the available livings, the ministers really could not have remedied
the situation. By the 1760s and 1770s, though, many more parishes could
have been filled easily, and the disinclination of the clergy to divest
themselves of any taxpaying parishioners suggests they saw their parish
role in gentlemanly rather than pastoral terms.

[3] Cecilius Calvert to Horatio Sharpe, January 5, 1754, in the Sharpe
Papers, MS. 1414, MdHi. Baltimore ordered Sharpe "to prevent Divisions not
Necessary, & to preserve Particular Preferment in Value, A Reward for
Divines of Merit." Such meritorious divines included Baltimore's scoun-
drelly crony, Bennet Allen, and those like Thomas Bacon who did special
services for the proprietor.

[4] Chester was created in 1765; Sharpe's administration ran from
1753 to 1769.

[5] The bills divided All Saints' Parish in Frederick and St. John's in
Baltimore County. Since both of the incumbents survived until the
Revolution, the division acts never went into effect.

In spite of the fact that in the late 1760s and during the 1770s there were enough clergymen in the province to staff five or even up to ten new livings, only one was opened for them.

Large land areas and scattered but increasing populations remained, then, constants in the parishes of Maryland. These conditions dictated the professional life styles of the ministers. For those who took their duties seriously, life as a Maryland clergyman was one of physical hardship. Simply to accomplish the rudiments of his function--Sunday services, communion for all parishioners a few times a year, emergency baptisms, marriages, and funerals--a minister was obliged to travel interminably. The astonishing number of horses, chaises, carriages, boats, and canoes listed in the inventories of the clergymen testifies of their peripatetic lives. Travel was always exhausting, time-consuming, and dangerous, even though the road system improved during the eighteenth century. Like others who journeyed about the province, ministers fell off their horses, froze in the cold and the snow, and hazarded a swift and unpleasant death when they paddled their canoes on the creeks and rivers in springtime.[1]

How much a minister regularly traveled depended on his dedication, his physical capabilities, the size of the parish, and the location of the worship services. In Maryland public worship centered in the parish churches but was by no means limited to them. Because the parish church itself was too far away from many of the parishioners for them to attend services there, a system of secondary churches usually developed to

---

[1] Philip Reading and Alexander Williamson II have left letters noting the injuries they received while riding their rounds. Reading was also frostbitten twice. Philip Reading to the S.P.G., March 15, 1775, S.P.G. Papers, Series B, Volume 21, fol. 210ff.; Alexander Williamson II to Upton Scott, February 26, 1763, Howard Papers, MS. 469, Section 3, MdHi.

accomodate the far-flung inhabitants. In the early years of the
establishment or when new parishes were being erected, private homes or
courthouses served as auxiliary, temporary churches. As the inhabitants
became more affluent parishes built the so-called "chapels of ease" at
convenient sites. These chapels were small churches built by private
subscription or public taxes. The number of them varied from parish to
parish. Some of the smaller parishes apparently never built any, and
some of the large parishes had three or four standing by the 1770s.
Ministers usually arranged to conduct Sunday services alternately between
the parish church and the chapel or chapels.[1] Regular schedules were set
up so that the parishioners would know when the minister would preach in
their area. During the 1720s, for example, the incumbent of Great Choptank Parish in Dorchester County officiated at the parish church every
second and fourth Sunday in the month, at one chapel every first Sunday,
and at the second every third. He preached at a third chapel of ease on
the fifth Sunday of the month, if there was one, or on a weekday if
there wasn't.[2] His neighbor in Dorchester Parish served twice or three
times a month in the parish church, twice a month at the chapel, and
traveled to the islands in his parish on weekdays for worship services and
pastoral care.[3] Ministering to the parishioners in this fashion was no
easy task. One of the chapels in Great Choptank Parish was thirty-five
miles away from the parish church. Arthur Holt, rector of All Faith's Parish
in St. Mary's County, one of the smallest parishes, rode fourteen miles to

---

[1] The schedules were usually determined by a joint agreement between
the minister and his parishioners. Sometimes, though, the vestry or the
legislature established the circuit schedules.

[2] The response of Thomas Howell to the queries of Bishop Edmund Gibson,
1724, in Perry, Collections, IV, 218.

[3] The response of Thomas Thomson to the queries of Bishop Gibson,
1724, in Perry, ibid., 229-230.

officiate in one church on one Sunday and twenty-four miles to serve another on the following.[1] Every third Sunday Christopher Wilkinson rode seventeen miles to preach at one chapel and then another seven miles to officiate at a second, a performance "w[hi]ch I am not able to continue," the overstrained commissary declared, though he did.[2] Wilkinson had held a living in England for many years and thought the Maryland clergy's "dilligence & industry in the discharge of their office" was "incredible." Many of the ministers, he told the bishop of London in 1724, rode twenty miles in a morning, and in the summer preached at two different churches in one day. The commissary noted that some clerics spent one week out of every month traveling across their parishes and preaching every day to the parishioners who lived so far from the churches that they could never attend regular services. Such journeys "together with the many visits we are obliged to make on visiting & administering the Sacrament of the Lord's Supper to the sick & aged, & private Baptism to weak & young children, gives us little ease & respite," Wilkinson explained.[3]

During the early years of the Church's establishment, when vacancies were common, many incumbents added to their regular parish duties by serving outside of their living on a part-time basis. Worried about untended souls and needing the extra income desperately, ministers frequently hired themselves out to neighboring vacant parishes. They usually agreed with the vestry to preach in the vacant living once a month or every third Sunday and received in return a proportionate amount of the parish's tobacco. Serving in this fashion could increase enormously the work load

---

[1] Arthur Holt to Bishop Edmund Gibson, May 20, 1734, in Perry, Collections, IV, 315.

[2] Christopher Wilkinson to Bishop John Robinson, July 29, 1719, Fulham Papers, "Maryland 1696-1769," item 191; Wilkinson response to the queries of Bishop Gibson, June 12, 1724, in Perry, Collections, IV, 217.

[3] Wilkinson to Bishop Edmund Gibson, November 20, 1724, in Perry, Collections, IV, 247.

of a minister.[1] The practice died out as the vacancies were filled and

parishioners demanded that clergymen devote themselves to their own

territory. Even this was more than many ministers could handle. Age or

sickness reduced or destroyed their physical capacity to travel and serve.

Until about mid-century, when some private curates became available,

parishes with incapacitated incumbents simply did without religious

services.[2]

Given the circumstances, it was impossible for Maryland clergymen to

minister to their parishioners as frequently and as intimately as the

Church recommended. A large share of the church-going Anglican public

did not have the opportunity to see their minister in church more than

once every two or three weeks, if they were lucky. Children died

unbaptized or were baptized by laypersons because the ministers could not

reach them in time. Funerals took place without an attending clergyman.

Bad weather could isolate a minister from his people for days or weeks

and bring all religious observances except private devotion to a halt.

---

[1] The man who best exemplifies this was Alexander Adams I, rector of Stepney Parish in Somerset County from about 1704 to 1769. A man of incredible physical stamina, Adams served all four Somerset County parishes between 1707 and 1711 (and may have continued to do so for most of the time until 1721). The three vacant parishes plus his own contained a total of six congregations. Stepney Parish was about 30 by 16 miles in size and demanded much care from Adams. The minister, however, calculated that he traveled 200 miles per month outside of Stepney Parish proper to minister to the vacant parishes. Alexander Adams I to Bishop Henry Compton, July 2, 1711, S.P.G. Papers, Series A, Volume 6, item 108.

[2] Dedicated ministers could feel their physical infirmities as stigmas on their professional honor. John Lang, for instance, incumbent of St. James' Parish in Anne Arundel County in 1735, was so continuously ill that for long periods of time he only officiated in the church every three or four months. His people were like sheep without a shepherd, he wrote to Bishop Gibson, and to his misery they were frequenting dissenting and Catholic churches. All his work among them was going to ruin and he begged to be allowed to return to England. Unfortunately, he could not resign the parish without hope of another position because he was entirely dependent on the income to support his family. John Lang to Bishop Edmund Gibson, May 29, 1735, Fulham Papers, "Maryland 1696-1769," item 52.

Nonetheless, to a remarkable extent the Maryland ministers maintained the regular sequence of parish activities usual to the Church of England in its native location.

Though no ministers left diaries or other records depicting how and when they carried out their parish duties, the responses to the queries of Bishop Gibson provide a detailed picture of parish activities in the 1720s. Very fortunately, Gibson and other English bishops asked their own clergy the same questions at different times during the eighteenth century and so a comparison of ministerial services in England and in Maryland can be made.[1]

Services and a sermon were routinely offered every Sunday in Maryland parishes. Rarely, however, was a second afternoon sermon given or evening prayers read at the same location later in the day. Two Sunday services were normally given in British parishes at this time.[2] Some Maryland ministers preached twice on the Sabbath but they did so at two different places. The only parish which mentioned holding two Sunday services was St. Anne's, located at Annapolis. That parish, as befitted one situated in the capital city, offered more worship services on Sundays and through the week than any other in the colony. Undoubtedly the chief reason for the abandonment of the second Sunday service was that so many parishioners —and the ministers—traveled considerable distances to church and had no

---

[1] Bishop Edmund Gibson's queries to the Maryland clergy and their responses may be found in Perry, Collections, IV, 190-231. Though all the parishes apparently responded, only 23 of the 32 reports are available. Twelve are from the Western Shore, and eleven from the Eastern.

[2] Pruett ("Leicestershire Clergy," 154) found that 75% of the parishes in that county offered two Sunday services in 1718. In London in 1742, 236 out of 466 parishes (50%) held two worship services. Sykes, Church and State, 238. Sixty-seven percent of the Oxfordshire parishes (excluding those in the town of Oxford itself) held double services on Sundays in 1783. McClatchey, Oxfordshire Clergy, 80. The second Sunday service was often simply a prayer meeting.

place to stay between services and little desire or time to make the
journey twice. In the wintertime an early dusk would have made late
afternoon travel dangerous.

Services on holy days and litany readings on Wednesdays and Fridays
were less routine. Six of the twenty-three parishes do not mention holy
day observances at all (though this does not necessarily mean they were not
held) and nine of the seventeen which offered services on holy days
celebrated only the major ones. Though the Maryland ministers were not
fulfilling the letter of canon law in their relaxed observance of holy days
they were doing no differently than their British colleagues. Only about
half of the parishes in Leicestershire offered such services in 1718, and
the practice was in decline all over the country.[1] The same was true
regarding the Wednesday and Friday litany readings. In Leicestershire
about a fifth and in Yorkshire less than a third of the parishes offered
weekly prayers.[2] In Maryland such services were almost unknown. One
parish read Wednesday and Friday prayers during Lent, and the litany was
read regularly at St. Anne's, but none of the other parishes mentions them.
Several of the rectors noted they had attempted, without success, to hold
weekday services. At a visitation of the Western Shore clergy in 1721
Jacob Henderson urged the ministers to celebrate the fast days and the
festivals according to the canons, but the clergy obviously discovered
that, with the exception of the great holy days, the parishioners refused
to attend church during the week.[3]

Communion was generally offered in England only three or four times
a year except in the urban parishes. In Maryland during the mid-1720s

[1] Pruett, "Leicestershire Clergy," 154; Sykes, Church and State, 246-247.

[2] Pruett, "Leicestershire Clergy," 154; Sykes, Church and State, 247.

[3] Henderson's speech to the clergy, dated June 28, 1721 (the list of
subscribing incumbents suggests that the date was actually 1720), is
printed in Perry, Collections, IV, 134.

fully sixty-five percent of the rectors (fifteen out of twenty-three)
responding to Bishop Gibson's queries said they administered the sacraments
five or more times annually. Nine of these (thirty-nine percent)
celebrated communion at least once a month, a surprising record given the
contemporary English record.[1] Two of the parishes which offered communion
only three to four times per year explained that communicants were lacking,
and other parishes with equally low rates mention the problem of obtaining
the wine and the utensils necessary for the service. As the parishes
developed these difficulties probably disappeared.

Instruction in the catechism, Jacob Henderson throught, was "the
Groundwork of all." Anglicans thought that catechizing the children was
very important because the tenets "fixed on the memory" would "support and
maintain such knowledge in the soul."[2] Catechism gave the young people
the knowledge and the will to resist the foils of the proponents of false
religions. The canons directed the ministers to teach the catechism for
at least half an hour every week, before the evening prayers on Sundays.
In practice only a small minority of the ministers in England or in the
colony catechized the children that frequently. Three Maryland clergymen
taught the catechism regularly every Sunday, but the rest worked with the
children solely at certain times during the year. Lent was the period
favored by about a fifth of the ministers. Summer, or a combination of
spring and autumn, was when most ministers catechized. A few of them

---

[1] The rectors who served in parishes with both churches and chapels
do not always explain how they calculated the total number of communion
services listed, whether, for instance, half of the once-per-month communion services given by Christopher Wilkinson in St. Paul's Parish, Queen
Anne's County, were given in the church, the others in the chapels, or
whether he served communion twelve times annually at all the places.

[2] Henderson's speech to the clergy, June 28, 1721 [1720?], in Perry,
Collections, IV, 134.

made special trips to the county schools or to private houses to perform
this duty. Regular catechizing was difficult because parishioners were
reluctant to send their children to the church for lessons when the
weather was bad or there was work to be done on the farms and plantations.[1]

Estimating the size of the population in the average parish is a
fairly simple calculation when the figures for the total number of
inhabitants are available; judging the proportions of what one could call
the Anglican church-going public is much less so. Members of other
religious sects and denominations would naturally not have attended
Anglican services. If the ministers had any contact with them it was
privately, as friends, or in their capacity as missionaries. Nor would
most ministers have considered slaves real members of their congregations.
How many people, then, was a minister likely to see when he stood in his
pulpit and looked into the pews?

With the exception of the figures given in the 1724 responses to the
queries of Bishop Gibson, the evidence is mostly impressionistic. The
petitions to the assembly to enlarge or to build churches prove that the
congregations were growing as the population expanded. Now and again
clergymen mention the number of communicants or parishioners they served.
Samuel Skippon found that the number of people who attended his Annapolis
church in 1715 sometimes scarcely amounted to a congregation.[2] About
fifty years later, however, the church and the churchyard were insufficient
to hold all the people who crowded into St. Anne's to hear Samuel Keene

---

[1] Slaves and ignorant persons were among those who were supposed to
be catechized, too.

[2] Samuel Skippon to Bishop John Robinson, January 19, 1715, in Perry,
Collections, IV, 73. From the context of his letter it is not entirely
clear whether Skippon meant so few people attended weekday services or
whether the number of those coming to Sunday services was so small.

preach.[1] Arthur Holt was such a popular minister that parishioners were forced to listen from outside the doors and windows of his church in St. Mary's County when he officiated there in 1734.[2] Churchgoers evaluated the ministers critically, and those who preached well naturally attracted the "Gospel-greedy" into the churches.[3] A bad minister or a clumsy talker, however, could drive the people out of the church. A vestry of Shrewsbury Parish in Kent County complained to the governor in 1722 that "the bad life & Corrupt principles of thire [sic] Last Minnister they presume has been more than a Little injurious to Religion in Generall & Especially to thire parish the whole of the parishonors nott Careing to Come to divine Service during his Stay amongst them & Some others wholey leaving the Church & now constantly attend the Quakers meetings."[4] The parishioners attended the Anglican churches by choice and there were alternatives if they did not care for the minister. Congregations grew or declined on the basis of demand.

Eighteen of the thirty-two parishes sent Bishop Gibson information concerning the number of people who attended church. Ten of them reported "large" or "full" congregations. In fifty-five percent of these parishes the rector claimed that most of his parishioners attended his services. The remaining eight clergymen reported congregations which ranged in size

---

[1] Alexander Williamson II to Upton Scott, August 18, 1761, Howard Papers, MS. 469, Section 3, MdHi.

[2] Arthur Holt to Bishop Edmund Gibson, May 20, 1734, in Perry, Collections, IV, 315.

[3] The term is Alexander Williamson's. Williamson to Upton Scott, October 27, 1761, Howard Papers, MS. 469, Section 3, MdHi.

[4] The vestry of Shrewsbury Parish to the governor, Charles Calvert, September 15, 1722, in the Shrewsbury Parish (Kent County) Vestry Minutes, Volume I (1701-1730), No. 13090, MdA.

from one hundred and fifty to five hundred people and averaged 365 persons.[1]
If this average is a reasonably accurate total and is used as a basis for
calculating the number of churchgoers in the whole population during the
1720s, then something under a quarter of the white inhabitants attended
church with some regularity.[2] The number of communicants, however, was a
small fraction of the churchgoers. Some parishes had as few as ten of
them, and though other parishes contained a hundred or more communicants,
they rarely exceeded a third of the congregation. Frequently only one out
of every four or five persons who went to church accepted the Eucharist.

Church attendance also fluctuated with the seasons. Snow, ice, and
rain deterred parishioners from making their way to the churches and
increased their reluctance to sit through a sermon in an unheated building.
The temperature inside a church in the winter could be arctic: one minister
reported that on Christmas Day in 1755 "the bread provided for the cele-
bration of the Lord's Supper became frozen on the table before the Sacrament
could be administered."[3] In some parishes the vestry house, a small
building usually set apart from the church, served as a fire-heated way
station where cold parishioners could warm themselves after the ride to

---

[1] This figure refers to the congregation of the whole parish and
includes those who attended chapel services. I do not know whether the
ministers counted children as members of the congregation. The canonical
age for first confirmation was sixteen but during the eighteenth century
bishops often confirmed boys and girls at the ages of fourteen and twelve,
respectively (Sykes, Church and State, 121).

[2] The size of the average congregation as listed by the ministers
responding to Bishop Gibson's queries indicates that about 12,000 people
attended Anglican churches regularly. The population of Maryland during
the mid-1720s (obtained by multiplying the annual growth rate between the
census of 1712 and that of 1755 to the period between 1712 and 1724) was
approximately 50,000 whites. Wells, Population of the British Colonies, 147.

[3] Philip Reading to the S.P.G., March 15, 1775, S.P.G. Papers, Series
B, Volume 21, Part II, fol. 210. Reading served a church in Maryland and
a church in Delaware and he may have been speaking of either one.

church.[1] One vestry felt compelled to issue orders telling the
parishioners they were not to run back and forth to the fireplace in the
vestry house during sermons.[2] Besides making the services themselves
uncomfortable affairs, bad weather made it difficult or impossible for
ministers to travel to chapels located in the distant reaches of their
parishes. Many churchgoers must have waited for ministers who never
appeared.

In addition to their sacerdotal and pastoral duties, the clergy in
Maryland were responsible for presiding over the parish vestry. This was
a peculiar hodgepodge of an institution, partly a church building committee, partly a vice investigative group, partly an arm of the provincial
government. It was unlike the vestry organizations found in England or
in Virginia. Virginia vestries were self-perpetuating bodies of twelve
men with a decisive voice in hiring the parish incumbent. The vestries
in England were usually closed corporations concerned chiefly with enforcing
the poor laws. Maryland vestries rarely involved themselves with such
social matters and had no legal say in the appointment of permanent
ministers.[3] Though the first vestries, formed by the 1692 Establishment
Act, were closed corporations of at least six men, subsequent legislation
altered the size to six vestrymen, two churchwardens, and a presiding
minister, and made the positions elective. The freeholders in every parish
were ordered to gather every Easter Monday to unseat two vestrymen and

[1] Queen Anne's Parish, Prince George's County, petitioned for and
received funds to build a vestry house partly for this purpose. Arch.
Md., XLVI, 342, 462-463.

[2] St. James' Parish, Anne Arundel County, Vestry Minutes, d. January
4, 1737, No. 12320, MdA.

[3] Lois Green Carr found only isolated incidences of vestries caring
for the parish poor, all of them before 1705. If the vestries regularly
functioned in this capacity during the early part of the period, the
evidence is lacking. Carr, "County Government in Maryland," 360-362.

elect two replacements.[1] Churchwardens also served one year terms.[2]

The Act of 1702 stipulated that the vestry was to meet the first Tuesday

in every month. The minister, as the principal member, or two or three

vestrymen working in concert were permitted to call meetings when they

thought necessary. Vestrymen absent from meetings without an excuse were

liable for a fine of one hundred pounds of tobacco.[3]

The vestries were formed to "Promote the Execution of the good laws

of this Province ... soe farr as Concerns the Respective Parishes" and

for the "more Easey Dispatch of Parish Buisness."[4] Their chief parochial

responsibility was to maintain all church property. Vestries decided when

and where to build churches and chapels, petitioned the assembly for funds

(when needed), and hired the workmen.[5] They took possession of all gifts

given to the church and could go to court to claim them. The vestries

ordered the church ornaments and supplied the minister's surplices. If the

---

[1] The vestry records indicate that few of the freeholders bothered to attend the yearly elections. In effect the vestry became virtually self-perpetuating. A law of 1730 changed the 1702 act slightly to define the two vestrymen unseated every year as the two senior members of the group. Arch. Md., XXXVIII, 184-186.

[2] The office of churchwarden was an irksome one; churchwardens collected the fines ordered by the vestry, attended visitations, and took possession of the parish tobacco. Those elected were fined if they did not accept the office.

[3] In actuality vestries usually did not meet once a month except when business was pressing. Three or four meetings a year were most common. The ministers were excluded from fines for absenteeism; a law which would have penalized them for this passed in 1729 but was disallowed by the proprietor at Henderson's insistence. Arch. Md., XXXVI, 276-277.

[4] Arch. Md., XXIV, 266. The quotation is from the 1702 Establishment Act.

[5] When there was no incumbent in the parish the vestry received the tobacco due and used it to build or repair churches, buy land or ornaments, or to hire a temporary minister. By an act of 1698, which was incorporated into the 1702 Establishment Act, vestries could apply to the county court for an additional poll tax of up to ten pounds of tobacco per year for parish purposes. An act of 1704 gave the court authority to refuse the request but another one of 1729 required them to agree. Requests for funds over and above that sum had to be addressed to the legislature. Arch. Md., XXXVIII, 120-121; XXVI, 292-294; XXXVI, 259-260.

parish had glebe lands or a parsonage house, the vestry made sure that the minister kept them in decent condition, and the group made the arrangements to buy or sell the properties. The government further required the vestrymen to hire a registrar to keep the parish records, and obliged them to inspect the parish library at regular intervals. Not all of their duties, however, had to do with the material assets of the parish, though business of this sort took up a good proportion of the vestry's time. The vestry in Maryland was granted some authority to over-see parish morals.[1] The gentlemen served as a board of inquiry into suspected cases of unmarried cohabitation. They summoned alleged adulterers and fornicators to the vestry meeting and asked for an explanation for their unorthodox sexual behavior. If the charges seemed based on fact, the vestry admonished the offenders and ordered them to mend their ways. Couples who did not attend the vestry when called or who did not heed the admonition could be presented to the county court for trial and punishment. The vestries themselves, though, were not in any real sense of the word courts. They had no coercive powers. They could not compel offenders to appear before them nor could they administer a penalty more severe than a command to reform.[2] True, the vestry could make a return to the county court, but then anyone could lodge a complaint with the justices. The county courts in Maryland exercised the real jurisdiction over cases involving immoral behavior and the vestries served more as adjuncts to them than as separate courts in their own right. Indeed,

---

[1] The first act granting them this authority passed in 1694. Another --and a somewhat more pointed act--passed in 1712. Arch. Md., XXXVIII, 19-20, 152-154.

[2] However, in 1749 the legislature passed an act which declared that non-appearance at the vestry was an admission of guilt and deemed this sufficient evidence to convict the couple in court. Arch. Md., XLVI, 321.

although some vestries issued admonitions at a remarkable pace, other

vestries took almost no notice of illegal sexual activity in their

parishes.[1]

The government saddled the vestries with a few purely secular duties

as well. The Tobacco Act of 1728 directed the vestries to appoint the

inspectors charged with curbing tobacco production.[2] This act was dis-

allowed in 1730, but the 1747 Tobacco Inspection Act required the vestrymen

to nominate the parish tobacco inspectors.[3] Vestries performed this task

until 1770. From 1756 to 1764 vestries met in a special July meeting to

make a list of the bachelors in the parish, for the government, desperate

for war funds, had decided to tax all unmarried men over twenty-five.[4]

As the principal members the ministers were deeply involved in all

vestry activity. Governor Nicholson had made a wise move when he pushed

through the bill in 1694 which included the ministers on the board, for

otherwise the ministers would have been debarred from taking part in the

decisions which affected their professional lives. A place in the vestry

---

[1] Historians are not unanimous in their conception of the importance
of the vestry as a means of social control in Maryland. Gerald E. Hartdagen,
author of a Ph.D. thesis on the Maryland vestry, thinks that the police
powers of the vestry "were essential to the orderly processes of government
in the colony." Lois Green Carr, who wrote her dissertation on the court
system in Maryland, thinks otherwise. She maintains that the county
courts, which were functioning as ecclesiastical courts with jurisdiction
over immoral behavior before the vestries first appeared, were far more
important. Gerald E. Hartdagen, "The Vestries and Morals in Colonial
Maryland," Md. Hist. Mag., LXIII (1968), 360-378 (the quotation cited here
is from p. 360); Carr, "County Government," 221-223. The views of the
two historians, whose periods do not overlap more than twenty years, may
not be entirely irreconcilable. The act of 1749 mentioned in footnote 2,
page 176, suggests that perhaps the vestries increased their power over the
course of the century. Though I admit the possibility, I tend to agree
with Carr's interpretation that the vestries were and remained weak agents
of social control.

[2] Arch. Md., XXXVI, 266-275.

[3] Arch. Md., XLIV, 595-614.

[4] Arch. Md., LII, 503-504.

permitted ministers to air their opinions regarding the building,
situating, and outfitting of churches. The vestry debated the minister's
Sunday circuit. Problems concerning the glebe lands, the parsonages, and
the payment of the ministers' salaries were discussed at the meetings.
Not the least important advantage of a seat on the vestry was that the
ministers met regularly with some of the most influential gentlemen in the
area.[1]

Relations between the clergy and the rest of the vestry members were
not always cordial or even marginally polite. Bitter, protracted quarrels
broke out in some vestries, and in others mutual hostility disrupted
business. Many possible areas of contention were built into the relationship. Vestries were responsible for guarding the parish library, the
glebe, and other property owned by the parish but in the temporary possession
of the incumbents. Ministers sometimes developed a proprietary attitude
towards these things--after all, the clergy held them as tenants for life--
and resented vestry inspections or other interference. As collected and
reasonable a man as Christopher Wilkinson flew into a temper and boycotted

---

[1] No systematic study has yet been done on the membership of the
Maryland vestry. However, it seems reasonable to assert that a significant
proportion of the men who served on the parish boards were men of substance
and influence in the neighborhood--or belonged to families of some distinction and eminence. Lois Green Carr found that during the 1690s the vestrymen of St. John's (King George's) Parish in Prince George's County were
nearly always among the wealthiest and most powerful men in the area. Men
of smaller fortune began to enter the vestry after the 1702 Establishment
Act altered the vestries from closed corporations to bodies elected by the
freeholders. Nonetheless, some men of substance continued to serve. She
found that in neighboring Queen Anne's Parish (also in Prince George's
County) much the same process occurred. Studying the end of the period,
David Skaggs discovered a very strong correlation in vestry service and
assembly service between 1750 and 1776 in the three counties he examined
(Prince George's, Queen Anne's, and Talbot). Almost all of the delegates
were Anglicans, and the vast majority of them had vestry experience before
entering the legislature or served in both institutions concurrently.
Carr, "County Government," 669-673; David C. Skaggs, Roots of Maryland
Democracy 1753-1776 (Westport, Conn., 1973), 90-91, 217-219.

the meetings for six months when the vestry told him to make a list of the library books stored in his house.[1] Tension between the principal vestryman and his colleagues occasionally led to violence, as happened in the case of John Lang and the vestry of St. James's Parish in Anne Arundel County. In order to obtain the parish account books and the vestry minutes, vital as evidence in a court suit they had initiated against Lang, the vestrymen "in a riotous manner" broke open the minister's book closet and later smashed his front door to get at his record books.[2] Disputes concerning the apportionment of the parish tobacco soured many vestry meetings during the first decades after 1692. The Establishment Act of that year put all the tobacco collected as the forty per poll into the hands of the vestry. Vestries were to use the tobacco to build churches, and only after these had been completed could the money be granted to the minister.[3] Naturally enough, this arrangement forced some ministers to beg for a pittance. The Establishment Act of 1696 changed the distribution priorities and prohibited the vestries from withholding any of the forty per poll from an inducted incumbent for any reason whatever.[4] This act secured the clerical stipends but left one problem open: if a minister was inducted in the middle of the year, was he entitled to the proceeds of the calendar year or was he to be paid only for the time he officiated? Ministers demanded the salary

[1] St. Paul's Parish, Queen Anne's County, Vestry Minutes, 1694-1762, No. D276 (1), MdA. The entry is dated March 20, 1723.

[2] St. James's Parish, Anne Arundel County, Vestry Minutes, 1695-1793, No. 12320, MdA, dated May 20, 1735, September 7, 1740, February 3, 1741, July 7, 1741, August 3, 1742, September 7, 1742, October 11, 1742. The dispute between Lang and the vestry began when the minister reneged on a debt he owed the board. Lang had borrowed tobacco to pay for improvements to the glebe, then argued that since the improvements had benefitted the parish, he should be released from his obligations. "Case of John Lang," Dulany Papers, MS. 1265, Box 6, MdHi.

[3] Arch. Md., XIII.

[4] Arch. Md., XIX, 430.

for the whole year, regardless of when they arrived; vestries argued, gave in with reluctance, or went to court; the sheriffs, liable to suit whichever way they divided up the tobacco, dithered. Not until 1713 did the assembly (noting that the legal ambiguity had "been the Occasion of many Disputes") decide that ministers were entitled to payment only for the time they had actually served.[1] Even with this point clarified, vestries and ministers found many occasions to squabble over the apportionment of salaries.[2]

When a vestry considered the parish incumbent unfit for his office they could do almost nothing to eject him from the living. Some vestries appealed to the governor or asked the commissaries or the bishop of London for redress. Such requests were almost always in vain. The commissaries admonished a few erring clergymen during the visitation meetings, the provincial council ordered Joseph Holt to give up his parish in 1704, and Henderson deprived John Urmston (albeit with much hesitation) for drunkenness, but otherwise complaints were usually fruitless. Doomed to put up with an incumbent until his death or removal, vestries sometimes seethed with frustration and animosity.

Most vestries did not generally meet once a month for the simple reason that they did not need to. Three or four meetings a year normally sufficed to work through pending business. However, when the vestry was supervising the construction of a new church, had a suit in court, was occupied with boundary disputes, or was led by a minister anxious to obey the letter of the law, meetings were held often. Vestry meetings and

---

[1] Arch. Md., XXIX, 340.

[2] Disputes involved legal dates of clerical induction, termination dates, payment during absences from the parish, and vestry insistence on withholding the salary until debts to the board were paid.

related business (clergymen sometimes served as treasurers of the parish, directed the court suits, procured building materials, and fulfilled other similar functions) could take up a good deal of a minister's time. Although some ministers scarcely bothered to attend the sessions, others established exemplary attendance records. Samuel Skippon of St. Anne's in Annapolis missed only one recorded meeting out of the seventy which took place over a period of ten years. James Cox of St. Paul's in Queen Anne's County missed thirty-nine out of 220, and Hugh Deans of St. John's in Baltimore County was absent for twenty-five out of 189 sessions between 1742 and 1776.[1] Most ministers attended about three out of every four meetings held.[2]

Tenure

Four types of clerical tenure entitled a man to climb into the pulpit of a Maryland Anglican Church. The most common one, sought after for its permanence and security, was that of induction. Granted only by the governor or the presiding officer of the colony, an induction was a legal document, signed and sealed, which appointed a minister to a living for life. The new incumbent had only to read the induction to the vestry or the parishioners in his appointed parish, take oaths of allegiance and conformity, and he stepped into a post he could occupy until he died, retired, or resigned. From the moment that the governor signed the induction a minister had an ironclad right to the proceeds from the poll tax, held the presiding chair in the vestry, and was the tenant-for-life

---

[1] All of these examples are from the vestry records of the respective parishes.

[2] Since many of the vestry records have missing sections it is difficult to calculate attendance records. However, this rate appears to be approximately right for ministers whose attendance may be plotted with some certitude.

of the glebe. Nothing short of a commissarial decree or an order from the highest political authority in the colony could oust him from his living if he did not wish to leave.[1] Far less secure or attractive was tenure as a licensed probationary curate. This was the type of tenure invented by Governor Sharpe in the early 1750s. In this case the minister did not hold his living as a freehold but was permitted to officiate only at the discretion of the governor. Probationary curates usually received the whole of the normal salary, but they sometimes were not invited to join the vestry, and they could be removed from the living at the order of the governor. The third and fourth types of tenure were private and contractual. A vestry was permitted to hire curates when the living was vacant, using part of the forty per poll accruing during the vacancy as payment.[2] Incumbents themselves could, if they were able to afford the cost, hire any assistants they desired, provided only that the curates had the proper credentials from the bishop of London and the proprietor or his governor.

In Maryland the smooth transfer of livings from one minister to another was frequently disrupted by periods of vacancy. Empty livings were inevitable during the decades when the supply of incoming ministers failed to match the available openings. Some of the poorer parishes had difficulty attracting and retaining ministers well into the 1770s.

---

[1] As noted in Chapter II, even the proprietor did not know for certain whether or not he could deprive a minister.

[2] A council order of 1695 (Arch. Md., XX, 283) permitted the vestries to hire lay readers when the living was vacant. The 1702 Establishment Act allowed vestries to hire lay readers, but the readers had to be presented to the governor for his approval. Many vestries, however, preferred to hire a neighboring incumbent rather than a lay person. The governor was sometimes asked to authorize the hiring, though in most cases it was apparently a purely private contractual arrangement.

Vacancies of up to about two months could be excused because it took time
for the news of the opening to reach the governor and for him to procure
and dispatch a replacement.[1] Prolonged vacancies, however, were a constant
feature of the colonial Church. Two of the four types of tenure--vestry-
hired and probationary curacies--were wholly or partially designed to deal
with this chronic problem.

Only five of the first thirty parishes had incumbents when they were
formally organized. In spite of the efforts of Bray, Compton, and
Nicholson to fill the empty livings, the high death and desertion rates
for the decade of the 1690s doomed most of the parishes to long periods of
vacancy. In the year 1700, after twenty ministers had been shipped to
Maryland, sixteen parishes suffered vacancies of over two months. During
any given year of the 1690s an average of twenty-two parishes (seventy-
three percent of the total) were vacant for longer than two months. As
more ministers arrived (and fewer left as precipitously as before) the
number of persistently vacant parishes declined, and openings which
occurred due to death or resignations were filled more expeditiously.
By the 1720s the number of parishes vacant for over two months in any
given year was down to about five; only about two parishes per year
experienced a long vacancy during the 1730s. Thereafter the yearly mean
remained at around one parish.

1731 was the first year without a single prolonged vacancy on the
Western Shore. The following year the Eastern Shore parishes were also
all filled for a minimum of ten months. In 1743, for the first time
in the history of the Church in Maryland, there were no vacancies
on either shore. Though this saturation level was not maintained,

---

[1] In this paper, therefore, a vacant parish is defined as one which
lacked an incumbent or a curate for over two months in a year.

the event did mark the end of the first period of growth in the Church. After 1731 no minister could travel to Maryland and know for certain that he could step into a vacant living as soon as he introduced himself to the governor. During the 1730s and 1740s the opportunities for ministers in Maryland began to decline, and as they did, the careers of the incumbents and applicants as well as the religious lives of the parishioners were greatly affected.

Parish livings were usually empty for one of three reasons: the number of clergymen in the colony was insufficient, the parish was too small to attract an incumbent even when most of the provincial livings were filled, or the location of the parish was undesirable. Christ Church Parish, limited to the shores of Kent Island in Queen Anne's County, was the best example of a parish unable to generate a competitive clerical salary. Repeated attempts by the parishioners to persuade the government to extend the boundaries of the parish came to nothing, and Christ Church Parish remained so unappealing to clergymen that it was vacant for thirty-nine out of the eighty-four years of the establishment of the Church.[1] St. Margaret Westminster, a Lilliputian parish by Maryland standards, lacked an incumbent for about a third of the period. Small or not, parishes on the Eastern Shore were more apt to be vacant than those on the other side of the Bay.[2] Western Shore tobacco was superior in quality and brought a higher price, and the ports and rivers of that shore made transporting the tobacco an easier job than it was to the east. The Eastern Shore was also believed to be an unhealthy and uncomfortable area.

---

[1] Christ Church managed to retain only two ministers for periods exceeding 3.5 years. The thirty-nine years are cumulative, not successive, ones.

[2] Except during the first decade and a half of the establishment, when four of the five original ministers were located on the Eastern Shore. The Western Shore always included more parishes than the Eastern Shore, too.

John Eversfield arrived in the colony in the spring of 1728 to find that
all Western Shore livings were filled and that the governor contemplated
inducting him to a parish on the other shore. The young minister viewed
this appointment with consternation, declaring that he "should be
devoured by Muqittoes a dreadful kind of insects by day, and by chucks
like our bugs in England by night." Most fortunately "it pleased God to
order matters otherwise," for a Western Shore incumbent resigned his post
and Eversfield replaced him.[1] More than forty years later Jonathan Boucher
said that there were many parishes in Maryland which "Noth[ing]g sh[oul]d
tempt Me to go to, -- the Musquitoes of one Summer w[oul]d kill me."[2]

Eight parishes (eighteen percent of the forty-four) were vacant for
more than twenty cumulative years each and seven (sixteen percent) were
unstaffed from ten to twenty cumulative years. In terms of the proportion
of vacant years to total years the parish existed, eight (eighteen percent)
lacked an incumbent for more than a quarter of their lifespan. Fifteen
parishes were vacant between a tenth and a quarter of the years they
existed. Even though twenty-one parishes (forty-eight percent) were vacant
for less than a tenth of their existence, it is easy to sympathize with the
taxpayers who complained that they were forced to pay for non-existent
religious services.[3]

[1] John Eversfield to Bishop Edmund Gibson, July 4, 1728, in Perry,
Collections, IV, 261.

[2] Jonathan Boucher to the Rev. Mr. James, July 25, 1769, in "The
Letters of Jonathan Boucher," Md. Hist. Mag., VII (1913), 40.

[3] Numerous such complaints survive. Governors received some (All
Faith's Parish in St. Mary's County informed Nicholson of their dissatis-
faction as early as 1697), and taxpayers pressured the Committee of
Aggrievances to discuss the problem on at least one occasion. All Faith's
Parish, St. Mary's County, Vestry Minutes, Liber A (1692-1720), No. 12667,
MdA. The entry is dated February 21, 1697. The Committee of Aggrievances
report (d. May 6, 1700) is in Arch. Md., XXIV, 65.

Parish Vacancies in Cumulative Years per Parish
1692 - 1776

Number of Parishes	Years				
	0-4.9	5-9.9	10-14.9	15-19.9	20 and up
Western Shore	8	8	3	2	3
Eastern Shore	8	5	1	1	5
All Parishes	16	13	4	3	8
Percent of All Parishes	36%	30%	9%	7%	18%

Parish Vacancies in Percentage of Period of Parish Existence

Number of Parishes	Period of Vacancy				
	0%	0-9.9%	10-19.9%	20-29.9%	30% and up
Western Shore	5	7	8	2	2
Eastern Shore	2	7	4	2	5
All Parishes	7	14	12	4	7
Percent of All Parishes	16%	32%	27%	9%	16%

When a parish was not served by an official incumbent or a probationary curate it was not necessarily bereft of all Anglican pastoral care. The vestries of empty parishes were often anxious to negotiate with the minister of a neighboring parish for a part of his time. Occasionally a minister offered his services, but more usually it seems that vestries made the initial approach.[1] The practice of serving one parish as an incumbent and another (or several) as a hired curate was most prevalent during the early years of the period. Almost a third (thirteen out of forty-one) of the clergymen who came to Maryland before 1710 served as hired curates in parishes adjacent to their livings. The vestries of vacant parishes considered employing a clergyman to preach at the church once a month or so a poor substitution for an incumbent, but preferable to relying on lay readers alone. The ministers welcomed the extra income. Their home parishes could not object too loudly because nothing hindered the incumbent from leaving his living if they pressured him unduly. A few ministers served so many parishes that they could be considered itinerants. George Tubman, for instance, ranged through much of Charles, St. Mary's, and Prince George's counties between 1695 and his death in 1701 or 1702. Robert Owen was inducted into St. Paul's Parish in Prince George's County in 1700 and served there until 1714, but he officiated in the other parishes in the county until regular incumbents took over. Vestries hired ministers by the sermon or for a regular yearly wage proportionate to the time they spent in the parish, and the job could last anywhere from a single morning to over a

---

[1] In at least one case the governor suggested the move. John Seymour to the vestry of Shrewsbury Parish, Kent County, April 7, 1708, copied in the Shrewsbury Vestry Book, Volume 1 (1701-1730), No. 13090, MdA, under the date of May 3, 1708.

decale.[1] When they could, the vestries of vacant parishes hired more than one neighboring clergyman at the same time so that a semblance of continuing pastoral care was maintained in spite of the technical vacancy. Sometimes the ministers themselves donated their services: at least one parish, William and Mary, in St. Mary's County, was served for almost two years by a rotating group of nearby clergymen who contributed the proceeds to the orphans of other ministers.[2] With only a few exceptions, however, incumbents did not serve as hired curates in other parishes after about the first decade of the eighteenth century. The number of vacant parishes was dwindling, several ministers already served pluralities, and parishioners were loathe to permit their incumbents to officiate outside the area they were paid to care for.[3]

Some vestries initiated search programs for incumbents. During the early years of the period, when ministers arrived in groups and most livings were empty, it was important to have the ear of the governor and prudent to have representatives on hand in the capital when new clergymen were expected to disembark. St. Paul's Parish in Kent County was probably not the only parish to send off a delegation to the capital when the vestry was

---

[1] Richard Sewall, rector of St. Stephen's Parish in Cecil County from 1697 to 1723, served as curate in Shrewsbury Parish in Kent County from 1697 to 1710, at which time his own vestry refused to permit him to continue serving outside of the parish. In 1723 Sewall resigned St. Stephen's and became the incumbent of Shrewsbury, officiating until his death in 1735.

[2] Jacob Henderson described this episode but did not say how many ministers were involved, simply that "wee" served. I have assumed they officiated in rotation because this was the normal practice when more than one curate served. Jacob Henderson's answer to Bishop Edmund Gibson's query, 1723, in Perry, Collections, IV, 136. The published version of the report erroneously lists the date of the document as 1722.

[3] Multiple livings were fairly common in Maryland while the supply of ministers remained low.

informed new ministers were available.[1] Desperate parishioners petitioned
governors and the legislature, begging to be assigned a minister.[2] The
bishop of London received letters asking him for help. "We have lived here
so long without any Minister, only now and then of some neighbouring
Ministers had had few Sermons, and we and our youth grow up in ignorance,
without catechising and very little instruction in the fear of God," the
vestry of North Elk Parish wrote Bishop Robinson in 1715-1716, when the
parish had been vacant for about nine continuous years. They asked the
bishop "out of fatherly love" to send them a minister of good learning,
good life, and good conversation.[3] Unfortunately, even paternal solicitude
could not procure an incumbent for a very small and poor parish. Though
most parishes depended on the governor or the bishop of London to provide
them with ministers, one parish attempted to persuade an English curate
to immigrate to Maryland specifically for induction into its living. The
vestry of Somerset Parish in Somerset County heard that Reverend Kirby,
an acquaintance of many of the vestrymen, was considering service in the
colonies and wrote to him in the hope of inducing him to settle in Somerset.
Listing all the attractions of the living--twenty thousand pounds of
tobacco a year, plus perquisites, and possibly the mastership of the county
school--the vestrymen promised to keep the parish vacant until they
received his answer, and obligated themselves to present him to the governor

---

[1] The vestry heard that some ministers had arrived with Governor
Nicholson, and hastily dispatched two members across the Bay to St. Mary's
City to procure one of them. They were disappointed. St. Paul's Parish,
Kent County, Vestry Minutes, 1693-1726, No. 12927, MdA; the entry dates are
July 24, 1693 (an error of the clerk, for the year was 1694), and February
19, 1695.

[2] For example, see the vestry of All Faith's Parish, St. Mary's County,
to Francis Nicholson, February 21, 1697, in the Vestry Minutes, Volume I
(1692-1720), No. 12667, MdA, entered under the date of the letter.

[3] North Elk Parish (Cecil County) to Bishop John Robinson, n.d. but
1715 or 1716, in Perry, Collections, IV. 85.

if he did come. "Charity will in some measure oblige you to comply with the request," they added guilelessly.[1] Like so many other efforts to find an incumbent, this one came to nothing.

If parishioners could not always find a clergyman when they needed one, they were not always sent one they liked, either. Induction was a permanent and irrevocable form of engaging a minister, and vestries and parishioners were naturally interested in the men who were candidates for such tenure. How often the vestries participated in the selection process is unknown. Some vestrymen apparently thought they had the right to present a minister to the governor for induction, and others, knowing the law, requested governors to induct the minister of their choice as a special favor.[2] Although there was no guarantee that the governors would grant the requests, vestries were successful often enough to make the venture worthwhile. One vestry went even further and asked for permission to examine candidates for the living before induction took place--in essence, an early version of Governor Sharpe's probationary scheme. In 1734, on the death of William Hackett, rector of North Elk Parish in Cecil County, the vestry asked for and received permission from Governor Samuel Ogle to try out any

[1] The vestry of Somerset Parish, Somerset County, to Rev. [---]Kirby, June 31, 1725, and the testimonial for Rev. [---]Kirby, November 16, 1726, both in the Fulham Papers, "Maryland 1696-1769," items 206 and 109.

[2] Several examples of the latter exist. The promise that the vestry would ask the governor for an induction was a lure used to entice ministers from other colonies to take a position in Maryland and was also used to persuade unattached or roaming clergymen to settle. Both vestries and interested candidates for induction were sometimes disappointed, because the governors were under no legal obligation to pay the slightest heed to what the vestry or the parishioners thought of the men they appointed. When Sharpe initiated his probationary scheme some vestries thought it gave them the right to approve or disapprove of the eventual induction of the curate. Though governors Sharpe and Eden usually granted requests that curates be inducted into the living permanently, they did not hesitate to refuse when such an induction was inconvenient.

potential replacements. The governor inducted the man of their choice,
William Wye. When Wye died in 1744 the vestry petitioned Ogle's successor,
Thomas Bladen, "please to alow us the liberty of Chooseing or making tryal
of A minister to Supply his [i.e., Wye's] place that May be most Agreeable
to our inclanation before your Excellencey Suffers one to Come in."[1] This
time they were not successful. Bladen either received the request after
he had inducted another man into the living or he refused to consider it.
Efforts were also made to block or annul inductions which brought unpopular
ministers into the parish. The disruptions at Coventry and All Saints'
parishes during the late 1760s have already been described, and though they
were the most violent demonstrations against a governor's choice, they were
by no means the first. In 1722 the vestry of Shrewsbury Parish in Kent
County heard that Thomas Thomson was angling for an induction to their
parish. It found the prospect as distasteful as Coventry's vestry later
considered the appointments of John Rosse and Philip Hughes. The news
"created a great uneasiness in the Inhabetants of the parish in generall,"
the vestry wrote the governor, asking him not to induct a man known to be
more interested in fleecing his flock than leading it.[2] Shrewsbury's
vestry was able to avert the induction of a minister it did not want, but
it was one of the few that did. Most vestries and parishioners meekly
accepted whomever the governor was pleased to send, knowing that they had
no legal method of barring an inducted clergyman from his rightful living
or deposing him once he had arrived.

[1] North Elk Parish (St. Mary Ann's), Cecil County, Vestry Minutes,
1742-1792, M153, MdA, entry dated November 24, 1744. Vestries were not
necessarily better judges of character than governors were: William Wye
had been hounded out of the Carolinas for theft and forgery.

[2] The vestry of Shrewsbury Parish, Kent County, to Governor Charles
Calvert, entered under the date of September 15, 1722, in the Vestry
Minutes, Volume I (1701-1730), No. 13090, MdA.

Induction was the most common form of tenure in Maryland. Over
ninety percent of the clergymen who served in the colony were inducted
into a living at some point in their careers. Although inductions were
for life, it would be incorrect to suppose that incumbents usually settled
into a living and remained there until they died. Maryland ministers were
a spacially mobile group. Only fifty-nine percent (104 out of 176) of
the men who received an induction to a living in the colony remained there.
Fifty-six clergymen (thirty-two percent of those inducted) held a second
consecutive living, fourteen (eight percent) held a third, and two clergymen (one percent) were incumbents of four parishes during their Maryland
careers.[1] These moves did not just involve short jaunts to neighboring
parishes. Ministers crossed the Chesapeake Bay or moved their families
the length of the colony with surprisingly little hesitation. In the space
of five years during the 1770s John Montgomery moved from Worcester Parish
in Worcester County, at the southeasternmost tip of the Eastern Shore,
across the Bay to St. Anne's in Annapolis and then moved back to the Eastern
Shore, this time to a parish in Kent County. In one decade William West
moved from a parish in the middle of the Western Shore to one at its
southern extremity and then all the way north to Baltimore County. Even
the earliest incumbents switched shores and moved up and down the Bay with
amazing abandon.[2]

About half of the clergymen who held more than one successive
incumbency spent two years or less in their first living. To them, the

---

[1] In terms of all the ministers, inducted or not, 54% were incumbents
of one living, 29% held two, 8% held three, and 1% held four livings.

[2] Ministers arriving in Maryland before the 1730s tended to move less
frequently than their successors. Less than a quarter of the pre-1730
arrivals made a move; thereafter the decadal rate varies between a low of
48% of the incoming ministers in the 1760s and a high of 65% during the
1750s. Ministers arriving during the 1760s had, of course, less time for a
move before the disestablishment. Note that these figures refer only to
moves as incumbents and do not take into consideration moves as curates of
any type.

Number of Parishes Successively Held as Incumbent

by Decade of Arrival

Period	Total Number Incoming Clergy	Number Incoming Clergy Who Became Incumbents	Number Incumbents With One Living	Number Incumbents With Two Livings	Number Incumbents With Three Livings	Number Incumbents With Four Livings
1690–1699**	20	20	16	4		
1700–1709	21	21	18	2	1	
1710–1719	18	18	9	8	1	
1720–1729	18	18	14	2	2	
1730–1739	21	21	10	5	4	2
1740–1749	22	21	8	13		
1750–1759	17	14	5	8	1	
1760–1769	33	27	14	9	4	
1770–1776	18	11	5	5	1	2
Total	188	171	99	56	14	2
Ministers Officiating in 1692	5	5	5			
Total	193	176*	104	56	14	2

*The 17 men not on this list were curates during the entire time they were in Maryland previous to the Revolution.

**No ministers arrived between 1690 and 1692.

first living they happened to have received was less a place they intended
to settle in than a toehold on what Norman Sykes called the ecclesiastical
ladder of preferment.[1] Maryland parishes were arranged in a loose hierarchy based on income, location, and healthfulness. Ministers who came to
the colony as strangers, or those who arrived to find the parish they
wanted already occupied, took a living temporarily to bide their time and
wait for an opportunity to occur. As short-term incumbents, the ministers
could keep their pockets filled, watch the employment situation, and hope
to impress the governor with their worthiness. Though some ambitious
clergymen moved from their first to their second incumbency with such
speed that they could have had scarcely enough time to set up housekeeping,
about a fifth of them did so after an incumbency of five or more years.[2]
A few ministers changed livings after incumbencies of over fifteen years.
Richard Sewall moved to a neighboring parish after twenty-six years in his
first living. Thomas Bacon left St. Peter's in Talbot County after almost
sixteen years in the parish to accept the pulpit of All Saint's in
Frederick County, the best living in the province. A higher salary was
often the motive for the move, but clergymen did not relocate only for
economic gain. Ministers in poor health sometimes moved to smaller or
healthier parishes; others, depressed by the boredom of frontier life,
shifted to more populated and sociable areas; and some clergymen transferred
to livings in their native districts or to be near their relatives and
their property.

---

[1] Sykes, Church and State, 147.

[2] The mean year for a move following an induction was 3.4 for all
ministers. The ministers arriving in the 1760s and 1770s, though, moved
faster than their predecessors had.

Clerical mobility was augmented during the administrations of Sharpe and Eden by the prevalence of probationary curacies. An apprenticeship as a licensed curate became almost a prerequisite to full induction for ministers who arrived in Maryland without special instructions from Baltimore or who did not become private assistants. Well over half of all incoming ministers between 1754 and 1776 served as probationary curates.[1] Half of the probationers eventually received inductions to the livings in which they had served their apprenticeship, but the rest moved into incumbencies in other parishes or served more terms as curates. Some ministers were probationers in up to three different parishes before acquiring an induction, and as incumbents there was an even chance that they would move again.[2] The amount of time spent as a probationary curate varied from four months to four and a half years, averaging about one and a quarter years. How long a minister served as a licensed curate had so little correlation with his professional abilities that it seems safe to assume that curacies were less probationary than they were convenient. Licensing a man as a curate rather than as an incumbent permitted the governor to clear the move with Baltimore, fill a vacancy in a parish too small to attract an incumbent, and to employ incoming ministers while keeping his options open.

Sharpe and Eden obviously liked the probationary system. How well the clergymen and the parishioners liked it is debatable. The material

---

[1] 1754 was the year Sharpe initiated the curacies. Between that time and the Revolution 57 ministers came to Maryland, and 35 of those served as licensed curacies.

[2] All ministers did not move from probationary tenure to incumbent tenure and remain there. When an incumbent had his eye on a particular parish but could not get an induction to it, he sometimes resigned his living, moved to the desired parish as a curate, and hoped that being on the spot would help his cause.

benefits of incumbency were probably only slightly better than curacy.[1]
In many parishes curates did not attend vestry meetings. As a curate,
though, the minister had no freehold rights to the living, could be dis-
lodged if the parishioners were determined to get rid of him, and could
be moved around at the whim of the governor. Among the parishioners,
approbation and dislike must have varied from parish to parish, depending
on what kind of experiences the people had with probationary curates.
When the first licensed curate arrived in St. John's Parish, Queen Anne's
County, in 1759, the vestry was delighted. The vestry was of the opinion
that "such Measures as these shou'd be winked at rather than opposed, and
that it might be well for this irreligious Province, if all its Ministers
were held in such Suspense, and had their Livings dependant upon their
Behavior, such a Check upon them would doubtless amend their external
Conduct, and greatly obstruct such baneful Examples as many vile Wretches
of that sacred (but greatly profan'd) Order now set before the World."
Though probationary curacies were not included in the Establishment Act,
St. John's thought they were "beneficial Informalities."[2] Sharpe and
Eden, however, did not feel obliged to ask or to fall in with the vestries'
opinions of the probationers. In only one documented case did Eden specifically ask a vestry for its approval before he inducted the officiating
curate.[3] Vestries and parishioners sometimes petitioned for the induction

---

[1] Curates were paid the full incumbent salaries, sometimes minus a
nominal 100 pounds of tobacco or so to mark their lower status. It is
not completely clear whether they also automatically took over the glebes
and the parsonage houses where such existed.

[2] St. John's Parish, Caroline-Queen Anne's-Talbot counties, Vestry
Minutes, 1752-1877, No. G114, MdA, under the date of July 9, 1759.

[3] The parish was North Elk (also called St. Mary Ann's) in Cecil County
(North Elk Parish Vestry Minutes, 1742-1792, M153, MdA, dated May 10, 1773).
On the other hand, Eden refused to induct Edward Gantt into Queen Anne's
Parish in Prince George's County in 1771 when the parishioners willed it;
the governor inducted Jonathan Boucher, who was greeted with a locked church
and the threat of a stoning. Boucher, Reminiscences, 74.

of their curates but the governors were free to deny or postpone fulfilling
the request. Fifty freeholders in All Faith's Parish asked Sharpe in 1767
to induct John Stephen, who had served two and a half years as the
probationer, because "he has given us (and to the best of our knowledge)
every one of his Parishioners the utmost satisfaction & we have reason to
believe that his future conduct will be equally unexceptionable."[1] The
governor did not grant the induction for almost two years. In addition to
sometimes functioning contrary to the expectations of the parishioners, the
probationary scheme disrupted religious services in some parishes. Prior
to the Revolution eighteen of the forty-four parishes used probationary
curates. In some of the parishes two or three curates followed one another
in rapid succession, confusing parish accounts, demoralizing the parishioners, disorganizing scheduled services. A few of the smaller parishes
became in effect temporary holding areas for ministers looking for better
jobs; curates and incumbents hurried in and out of the living with
revolving-door speed.[2]

The turnover rate for government-appointed ministers naturally differed
from parish to parish. Whether a living had to be filled repeatedly
depended not only on the number of resignations tendered but on the lifespan
of the incumbents who settled there permanently. A few parishes were
perennially adjusting to new clergymen, others enjoyed generally stable
tenures, and in some parishes only one or two men officiated from the
organization of the parish until the Revolution. Several Maryland parishes
suffered from clerical tenures so short that the ministers came and went

[1] All Faith's Parish, St. Mary's County, Vestry Minutes, Liber 3
(1753-1824), No. 12669, MdA, dated September 22, 1767.

[2] One of these was St. Anne's in Annapolis. Boucher commented that
"it was usual to give it first to a candidate who was from thence promoted
to a better benefice, as they fell, and he had interest. Hence it got the
name of Gradus ad Parnassum." Boucher, Reminiscences, 54.

like so many tavern guests. St. Anne's had twenty-one incumbent or

licensed ministers during its eighty-four-year history. Some stayed for

only a few months.[1] St. Margaret Westminster, one of the original thirty

parishes, was vacant for twenty-seven cumulative years, but fit fifteen

ministers into the remainder.[2] Worcester Parish had eight rectors between

1758 and 1776.[3] Altogether seven parishes averaged less than five years'

service per incumbent and licensed curate.[4] These parishes were all at the

bottom of the Maryland parish hierarchy, too small or too remote to interest

permanent incumbents. The majority of the parishes, though, averaged

tenures between five and fifteen years.[5] The overall mean for tenure was

12.3 years, and almost half of all the parishes enjoyed—or endured—

mean tenures of ten years and up.[6] The highest average was set in Queen

Caroline Parish in Anne Arundel County. Created in 1728, the parish was

vacant for a year and a half. James MacGill was inducted in 1730 and then

served until the Revolution. His was not the only extraordinarily long

incumbency. Alexander Adams served in Stepney Parish for sixty-five years,

and MacGill's neighbor in St. Paul's Parish in Prince George's County,

John Eversfield, officiated there for almost forty-seven years.

---

[1] The average tenure for St. Anne's for 3.45 years.

[2] The mean tenure at St. Margaret's was 3.7 years.

[3] Fourteen parishes (32% of the 44) had between one and four ministers during the period the parish existed; twenty-two (50%) had five to nine ministers, six (14%) had ten to fourteen, one (2%) had fifteen, and St. Anne's (2%) had twenty-one. Both inducted ministers and licensed curates have been included here.

[4] These seven are 16% of all the parishes.

[5] Sixteen parishes (36%) averaged between five and 9.9 years; eight parishes (18%) between ten and 14.9 years.

[6] Seven parishes (16%) averaged clerical tenures of fifteen to 19.9 years; three parishes (7%) between twenty and 24.9 years, and three parishes (7%) twenty-five years and over. The tenure on the Western Shore, which boasted a series of long-lived incumbents, was 13.8 years, longer than the Eastern Shore's average of 10.6.

The fourth type of clerical tenure in Maryland was that of assistant curate. A curate of this sort was a man hired by the incumbent minister to help him in his parish duties. The arrangement was personal and contractual. The practice probably began when incumbent ministers hired their incumbent neighbors to fill in when they themselves went on trips, fearing that otherwise they would lose their livings.[1] Later the usual practice became to hire otherwise unemployed ministers rather than fellow incumbents. Apparently the first time an incumbent hired a full-time assistant was in 1727, when the aged Joseph Colbatch, rector of All Hallow's in Anne Arundel County, employed John Lang to help him with parish duties. Lang stayed with Colbatch for over a year and then accepted an incumbent position of his own.

During the 1730s at least four ministers served as assistants and four more did so during the 1740s.[2] All but one of them moved from an assistant curacy to an incumbent status. The exception, Richard Hartswell, was the first of a breed which increased with time: perpetual assistants. Hartswell never received an induction. Of the six assistant curates who came to the province during the 1750s, three of them never accomplished that goal either and left the colony to try their luck elsewhere. They were the victims of an overcrowded market. One of their more fortunate companions served two incumbents before he was granted the living he wanted. Fully a third (eleven out of thirty-three) of the incoming clergy of the 1760s

---

[1] Parishioners did not like incumbents to leave the parish for any length of time. During the entire period of the establishment, with the exception of the very beginning, ministers who traveled were expected to provide replacements.

[2] All but one of them were newcomers to the province. William Brogden resigned his parish in Dorchester County to substitute for Jacob Henderson in Queen Anne's Parish in Prince George's County when the commissary went to England in 1737. When Henderson returned, a very convenient--and possibly engineered--resignation in a nearby parish enabled Brogden to move into a living from which he neatly took over for Henderson in Queen Anne's on the latter's demise.

assisted other incumbents and almost half (eight out of eighteen) of the 1770s group did. Of these nineteen men, two served as curates while they themselves were incumbents of other parishes, nine never rose to a higher status and died or resigned as private curates, and the rest used the position as a steppingstone to other jobs.

Assistant curates moved both to probationary curacies and to full inductions. A position as an assistant curate had several advantages besides simple employment. A good curate could raise a useful following among the parishioners. Bennet Allen, for instance, was forced by parishioners to hire George Goldie, the very popular curate to the former incumbent of All Saints' in Frederick County, as his own assistant. Good recommendations from pleased parishioners influenced governors to offer preferment. In addition, serving as an assistant curate enabled some of the Maryland-born clergy to officiate in areas near their familial homes.

Assistant curates were hired and paid by the incuments, but they were not entirely beyond the reach of the vestries and the parishioners. However the curates served--whether part-time in the parish church under the direct supervision of the incumbent, or as almost autonomous ministers in the distant chapels--the parishioners were as concerned about their abilities as if they were regular incumbents. Vestries sometimes pressured incumbents into hiring curates, made all the arrangements, or forced the employers to break the contract. In 1738 the vestry of St. Peter's Parish in Talbot County obtained the consent of the incumbent, "rendered through age and Sickness unable of acting and tending his parish Church af[oresai]d as he ought," to appropriate a part of his salary to hire a curate. A letter stating the terms of employment was promptly sent off to Neil McCallum, an apparently unattached minister in a neighboring parish. McCallum accepted

the post and stayed for a year and a half. The incumbent then hired
Nathanial Whittaker as his second curate. Considering Whittaker "a person
of Immoral Life and Conversation and in no sort fitt to Discharge the
Ministerial Functions," the vestry told the incumbent that the major part
of the parishioners did not like Whittaker and did not want him to
officiate. Whittaker left.[1] In Prince George's Parish (Frederick and
Prince George's counties) the vestry was called in to arbitrate when two
curates claimed in 1759 to be the rightful assistant to the incumbent.[2]
With the permission of incumbents, vestries placed notices advertising for
curates in the _Maryland Gazette_. By the late 1760s some vestries were not
so much asking incumbents as forcing them to hire assistants. When William
West received an induction to St. George's Parish in Baltimore County in
1772 he agreed to pay a curate ₤100 a year and even presented the vestry
with a bond to that effect. The vestry was permitted to choose the curate.[3]
In 1768 Bennet Allen, unpopular rector of All Saints' in Frederick County,
swore out a contract with the vestry which obligated him to ensure that
there were three ministers in the parish at all times. Allen was given six
weeks to find curates and to have them approved by the vestry. If he failed
to do so, the bond authorized the vestry to assume the task. Allen also
promised the Lutheran and the Calvinist congregations in Frederick Town ₤25
a year each for the support of ministers who pleased them![4]

[1] St. Peter's Parish, Talbot County, Vestry Minutes, Book II (1717-1766),
M295, MdA, entries dated October 11, 1738, and April 4, 1743.

[2] The incumbent, George Murdock, was over eighty years old when the
incident occurred. He discharged his curate, Thomas Johnston, and hired
Clement Brooke instead; Johnston tried to prevent Brooke from officiating.
The vestry backed Brooke, the scion of a well-known Maryland family. Prince
George's Parish, Frederick and Prince George's counties (now Montgomery and
Prince George's counties) Vestry Book, 1719-1832, No. 12654, MdA, entries
dated December 4, 8, and 18, 1759.

[3] St. George's Spesutia Parish, Baltimore (now Harford) County, Vestry
Minutes, Volume II (1771-1850), No. 12212, MdA, entry dated June 8, 1772.

[4] Frederick County Deed Book, Liber M, fols. 39, 43, 44, all dated
October 25, 1768, in MdA.

During the eighteenth century the organizational structure of the Maryland Church became increasingly elaborate. A two-tiered system of inducted and non-inducted clergy developed which closely approximated the sub-episcopal structure of the Church in England. Competition for induction into the more lucrative parishes became very keen. Moving up the ladder of preferment demanded interest, luck, nerve, and accurate information on the health of the incumbents of the best parishes. The friendship of the proprietor or the governor and the patronage of men in high places were often critical to the acquisition of a fine parish. Bennet Allen aroused the ire of his colleagues because he came to the colony as a favorite of Lord Baltimore and was promptly elevated to the top of the hierarchy, without serving a suitable apprenticeship in the smaller parishes. Jonathan Boucher, however, who criticized him on that point, did not hesitate to accept all the help the powerful Addisons and Dulanys could give him in his own long and intricate quest for a wealthy living. Ministers who wished to end their careers as incumbents in productive parishes had to plot their moves and weigh their opportunities carefully. As the market became more complicated, the ecclesiastical duties of the governors became more burdensome. One death at the top of the parish hierarchy could engender half a dozen moves along the structure, all of them choreographed by the chief executive.

A typical sequence of removals demonstrates the complexity of the situation. In February 1742 Henry Ogle was the rector of St. John's Parish (Baltimore County), John Vaughan was the incumbent of St. Margaret Westminster Parish (Anne Arundel County), Richard Chase was at Christ Church (Calvert County), and William Maconchie was the aged incumbent of Durham and Port Tobacco parishes (both in Charles County). Maconchie died in February.

On March 1, Chase resigned Christ Church to take over Port Tobacco Parish. A newcomer, Theophilus Swift (who originated from Calvert County and was probably favored as a native) moved to Durham Parish the same day. Chase's vacant Christ Church living was filled on March 1 by Vaughan, who resigned his parish in Anne Arundel County to accept it. Hugh Deans, either new to the province or an assistant curate to someone, received Vaughan's former incumbency later in the month. In June or July Richard Chase died unexpectedly, opening the living at Port Tobacco. Henry Ogle in Baltimore County immediately resigned his parish and obtained the post at Port Tobacco by July 21. The next day, Hugh Deans, anxious to leave St. Margaret Westminster, which was a poor living, resigned and moved to St. John's in Baltimore County. Richard Harrison, just arrived in Maryland, took over Westminster in August, but left it in November to accept St. Luke's in Queen Anne's County, vacated four days before his induction by the death of the incumbent. The day he resigned, Westminster was given to Patrick Glasgow, who retained the living until a rich one opened up on the Eastern Shore the following year. This particular series of maneuvers was quite unelaborate compared to some of those orchestrated by Sharpe and Eden. The last two governors not only had to contend with the ambitions of inducted ministers, but were obliged to find places for the unprecedented throng of new ministers crowding into the province, and to appease those unsatisfied with posts as assistant or probationary curates. When Sharpe described his ecclesiastical appointments to Lord Baltimore the depictions sometimes covered pages, and they read like a general's tactical preparations for war, with clergymen scurrying back and forth across Maryland to man the parishes.

Clerical Conduct and Reputation

The Anglican ministers in Maryland never enjoyed a flattering
corporate image. "The faults & follies of some clergymen are too gross
to be excused or extenuated," Commissary Wilkinson reported in 1724, noting
that lay complaints of "the clergy's gross neglects & immoralitys" were
reaching the provincial legislature.[1] "Rascally clergy," a Philadelphian
pronounced them in 1744.[2] About a decade later, Hugh Jones and Henry
Addison, both members of the Maryland Church, concluded that they had too
many "profligate and refractory Brethren."[3] Cradock warned Governor
Sharpe in his 1753 sermon that the Church contained some extremely "worthless Creatures."[4] The general character of the clergy was "most wretchedly
bad," Thomas Chandler wrote Bishop Richard Terrick in 1767, adding that
it would "make the ears of a sober heathen tingle to hear the stories that
were told me by many serious people."[5]

Contemporaries of unimpeachable personal character left scathing
indictments of the clergy. The assembly made recurrent attempts to regulate
them. Some clergymen were accused murderers, some were thieves, drunkards,
or adulterers. Unquestionably a case can be made for depicting the
Maryland ministers as a tribe of rogues and scoundrels (infiltrated, of

[1] Christopher Wilkinson to Bishop Edmund Gibson, November 20, 1724,
in Perry, Collections, IV, 246-247.

[2] Comment of Mrs. Cume (somewhat prejudiced as a Presbyterian) to
Dr. Alexander Hamilton, quoted by Hamilton in Carl Bridenbaugh, ed.,
Gentleman's Progress: The Itinerarium of Dr. Alexander Hamilton (Chapel
Hill, N.D., 1948), 27.

[3] Hugh Jones and Henry Addison to Bishop Thomas Sherlock, August 27,
1753, in Perry, Collections, IV, 27.

[4] Skaggs, ed., "Thomas Cradock's Sermon," WMQ, 3d. Ser., XXVII,
(1970), 640.

[5] Thomas B. Chandler to Bishop Richard Terrick, October 21, 1767,
in Perry, Collections, IV, 335.

course, by a few worthy men.)[1] However, it is both simplistic and unjust
to cite the complaints against the clergy without examining the
motives of the accusers or any contradictory evidence. All of the opinions
listed above, for instance, are ones which are usually quoted when the topic
of clerical morality in Maryland arises, and they are rarely qualified
Christopher Wilkinson much admired the conscientiousness of most ministers
and thought that the profligates were relatively few.[2] The critics--Jones,
Addison, Cradock, and Chandler--were men who ardently desired the institution of an American bishop and were not above exaggerating for a good cause.
Chandler based his opinions on a two-week journey to the lower Eastern
Shore, the heart of Maryland Presbyterianism, during the height of the
Coventry affair.[3] As for evidence affirming the basic decency or
adequacy of the clergy, approbative statements were made by laymen and
clergy, too. The Maryland Church also included men whose characters and
abilities would have made them outstanding in any of the religious
communities of Britain or the colonies. Furthermore, the social context
in which the Maryland clergy functioned must be taken into account, and so
should the overall reputation of the ministers serving in the Church in
England during the same period. The ministers in the colony were members of
a crude, rough, often loose society addicted to drinking, swearing, and
gaming, and the failings of which they have been accused were often as much
sins of the times as sins of the man. Immigrant clergy, plunged as very
young men into such a setting, sometimes lost their heads and forgot they
were supposed to set an example for conduct, not to follow the prevailing

---

[1] For an example of this sort of treatment, see Charles Barker, The
Background of the Revolution in Maryland (New Haven, 1940), 47-51.

[2] Christopher Wilkinson to Bishop Edmund Gibson, November 20, 1724,
in Perry, Collections, IV, 246-247.

[3] For the Coventry affair, see pp. 69-74.

modes. Native clergy occasionally conducted themselves more as the

gentlemen they were born than the priests they became. Furthermore,

if many colonials held the profession in low esteem, a good many Britons

felt the same about their parish clergy. The prestige of the Anglican

Church in general was low during much of the eighteenth century. If a

special vehemence marks the complaints against the Maryland clergy, it

may be attributable partially to despair. In Britain, ministers who

disgusted or irritated their parishioners could, if necessary, be

cashiered; in Maryland, they had to be endured.

In all, thirty-five Maryland clergymen--about one in six--acted in

a manner which prompted complaints about their unsuitable behavior. The

failings of the ministers fell into two categories: character or morals,

and learning or professional negligence.

Immorality and lack of integrity were the weaknesses most often

associated with the provincial ministry. Charges of this type range in

gravity from outright criminal activity to tippling at weddings. The most

serious accusation was that of homicide, leveled against three ministers

and probably justified in the case of two of them.[1] Eight ministers were

---

[1] An anonymous list of the Maryland clergy, written in c. 1722, notes
that Thomas Phillips was tried for his life in Virginia for shooting a man.
Phillips traveled a great deal through the colonies between 1707 and 1719,
when he settled in Maryland, but no source I can find indicates that he was
ever in Virginia. Jacob Henderson and Christopher Wilkinson, who probably
would have transmitted such a report to London, say nothing. The list, "A
Character of the Clergy in Maryland," is printed in Perry, Collections, IV,
128-129.

The two other cases were reported by Governor Sharpe. In 1753
George Cooke, rector of a parish in Calvert County, was jailed for the
murder of a woman. He was acquitted at his trial, but according to Thomas
Cradock, there were "shrewd Circumstances against him" that "had fix'd in
the minds of many such Prejudices of his Guilt, that even Charity labours
hitherto in vain to root them out." Guilty or not, Cooke's trial let loose
"scandalous reflections on the whole Order of the Clergy," to the great
embarrassment of his colleagues. See Horatio Sharpe to Cecilius Calvert,

denounced for the sexual improprieties of adultery and fornication. Four

of these men were probably innocent, and the evidence against a fifth is

inconclusive. George Tubman, Joseph Holt, and Hamilton Bell were, however,

guilty of some sexual misconduct. George Tubman, accused of bigamy in 1698,

was actually guilty of pre-marital sexual relations and breach of promise,

and was suspended by Governor Nicholson. Joseph Holt was deprived by the

council in 1704 on the grounds of adultery and negligence.[1] Hamilton Bell

was not officially censured, for his affair with a married woman had

occurred before he had received orders.[2] Undoubtedly, ministers other than

these three carried on liaisons, but we know nothing of them because they

were either very discreet or because no written accusations have survived.

February 10, 1754, Arch. Md., VI, 39, and Skaggs, ed., "Thomas Cradock's
Sermon," WMQ, 3d. Ser., XXVII (1970), 639. The Calvert County court records
for this period have been burned.

In 1768 Richard Brown, incumbent of King and Queen Parish in St. Mary's
County, faced prosecution for murdering a slave. Reportedly his own son
was the only witness to the killing, and when Brown was accused of the crime
he fled with the boy to Virginia, shipped him to Scotland, and returned to
Maryland to attend an inquest at which nothing could be proved. Sharpe
said his parishioners refused to attend services at the church, "about which
indeed he is said to be extremely indifferent." Whether under pressure
from his parishioners or as a conciliatory gesture, Brown hired a curate
and withdrew into retirement. Horatio Sharpe to Hugh Hammersley, June 22,
1768, Arch. Md., XIV, 507.

[1] The cases of George Tubman and Joseph Holt have been discussed in
Chapter I, pp. 19-20, 27, 30-31.

[2] As a student at the Presbyterian Log College in Pennsylvania during
the early 1740s, Bell had been involved in a liaison which led to a presby-
tery hearing and trial. He later converted to Anglicanism, married the
widow of his predecessor at Somerset Parish, and settled down to what seems
to have been a quiet and unexceptional career. No evidence indicates that
his parishioners knew of his disreputable past, but that area of Maryland
was inhabited by many Presbyterians and they probably learned of it. See
Leonard J. Trinterud, The Forming of an American Tradition: A Re-Examination
of Colonial Presbyterianism (Philadelphia, 1946), 142, 333-334.

The high proportion of unsubstantiated or erroneous charges, however,
indicates one of the inherent dangers in pastoral work. Living in public,
unmarried or widowed ministers were natural targets for scandalmongers, and
some of the disreputable gossip bruited about the province was patently
false. Ministers could hardly hope to appear saintly to everyone, and
circumspect behavior in public was sometimes not enough to prevent
embarrassing rumors from circulating. When Alexander Williamson II lived
in a boarding house in Annapolis, for instance, the presence of young
females there gave rise to such opprobrious speculation that he afterwards
avoided living near unattached women and even refrained from bringing white
women to the plantation he subsequently bought.[1] Marriage vows were not
much protection against slander, either. Francis Lauder was the married
incumbent of St. Andrew's Parish in St. Mary's County in 1765 when a
parishioner accused him of fathering her illegitimate child. The
authorities discovered later that the mother and the real father had lied
about the paternity of the child, hoping to force the minister to shoulder
the blame. Although Lauder's parishioners had "so high & [sic] Opinion of
the moral Recktude of their Pastor that nothing less than Demonstration
would avail against him," as another minister reported, the affair was an
ordeal for Lauder. Humiliated, he took the trouble to write to some of
his fellow clergymen to protest "the Dreadful Injury offered to his

---

[1] Alexander Williamson II to Upton Scott, n.d. but c. May–June 1761,
Howard Papers, MS. 469, Section 3, MdHi.

Character as a Clergyman married Man &c."[1]

Two men received livings in Maryland although they had previously been accused of theft and forgery. William Wye wormed his way into the S.P.G. on false credentials, and in 1717 received an appointment to North Carolina. He hired a horse and chaise to fetch his wife and to travel to the port, then sold the horse to a stagecoachman and blithely packed the chaise on board ship. Wye lost his parish when news of the robbery reached North Carolina, but he was able to acquire a living in Virginia and then one in Maryland.[2]
Matthias Harris displayed less panache. A prominent planter, assembly delegate, and the son of a former speaker of the lower house, Harris frittered away a large inheritance and found himself in financial straits. Always interested in religion, he went to London in 1752 or 1753 to take orders, and while there forged a bill of exchange. An outcry against him

---

[1] Alexander Williamson II related the incident in letters to Upton Scott, dated May 4 and July 1, 1765, now in the Howard Papers, MS. 469, Section 3, MdHi.

The men accused of sexual misconduct whose cases are not discussed above were Thomas Phillips, Andrew Lendrum, and Bennet Allen. In 1726 some of the vestrymen and parishioners of Christ Church Parish in Queen Anne's County wrote Bishop Gibson that Phillips was cohabiting with a transported convict and was suspected of having a child by her. The petitioners did not substantiate the accusation and the validity of the charge remains in doubt. Vestry and parishioners of Kent Island (Christ Church Parish, Queen Anne's County) to Bishop Edmund Gibson, July 1726, in Perry, Collections, IV, 257. The slur against Andrew Lendrum originates with Governor Sharpe, who mentioned in 1768 that a Reverend Lendrum was said to live in adultery. The governor probably confused Lendrum with Lauder and erred on the details of the case. See Horatio Sharpe to Hugh Hammersley, June 22, 1768, Arch. Md., XIV, 507. The rumors concerning Bennet Allen and his sister have been mention in Chapter II, p. 76. They were completely false, for the lady who lived with the minister was indeed his blood sister, Elizabeth Allen.

[2] "The Humble Petition of John Smart to the Bishop of London," n.d. but c. 1717, S.P.G. Papers, Series A, Volume 12, item 16.

led Sharpe to refuse him an induction, but Governor Eden eventually gave him a parish.[1]

Twenty-five ministers were charged with drunkenness, swearing, fighting, gaming, or other unspecified obnoxious behavior. Because most of the cases were never officially scrutinized by the government or the commissaries, evaluating the veracity of the accusations is difficult. Many of these clergymen have reputations blackened solely on the grounds of gossipy remarks or heresay reports recorded by an individual correspondent. The standards by which different people judge the presence or the extent of vice vary from person to person and the documented complaints are rarely detailed; a minister said to drink could be a man who indulged himself with a glass of wine at dinner or a habitual alcoholic. Furthermore, counting the number of "scandalous" ministers and then comparing them with the total number of officiating clergy is a rather unreliable index of clerical irregularities. The list of very gross offenders is probably quite complete, for they would have been the men the commissaries discussed with their superiors or the governors with the proprietors. The sins of a large number of pettier offenders, however, may never have been documented. Many parishioners who were unhappy with their minister's conduct could not write, and others must have seen little use in complaining to the authorities. Very likely at least some ministers earned disgraceful reputations which did not long survive them.

Drunkenness was the most common character fault of the Maryland clergy, if the number of reported cases approximates the truth. Seventeen of the twenty-five clergymen cited for deviance from their professional code were

---

[1] The representations against Harris have been discussed in Chapter II, pp. 62. See also Horatio Sharpe to Cecilius Calvert, September 14, 1753, and Calvert to Sharpe, January 5, 1754, in Arch. Md., VI, 6, 30. Information concerning Harris's financial troubles before his ordination may be found in the Lloyd Papers, Subsection "Matthias Harris Papers, 1747-1752," MS. 2001, MdHi.

said to be imbibers. Excessive drinking was a very worrisome problem. It
made the drinker appear ridiculous to some parishioners and disgusting to
others, increased the minister's tendency to fight or swear, and induced
him to neglect his pastoral duties. About seven ministers (circa four percent
of the entire clergy) are known to have imbibed so heavily that they were
unable to fulfill their offices. Intemperate drinking was probably one of
the charges which prompted the council to deprive Joseph Holt in 1704.
John Urmston, the only Maryland minister deprived by authority of the Church,
was often intoxicated on Sundays, constantly drunk on other days, and "in
his drunkeness guilty of many brutal actions," according to his parishioners.
He burned to death when he fell into a fire during a drunken fit.[1] Had he
dared to, Henderson would have liked to remove William Tibbs and Nathaniel
Morrell ("the most absolute Sott in Nature") for negligence and immoral
behavior resulting from chronic intoxication.[2] In a regular episcopal
diocese in England, men such as Thomas Baylie (cited by Wilkinson in 1718
for excessive drinking, quarreling, and swearing), Nathaniel Whittaker, and

---

[1] Urmston also appeared at a 1730 visitation in a drunken condition.
"A Visitation of the Clergy of the Eastern Shore....," June 25, 1730, in
Perry, Collections, IV, 296; see also Jacob Henderson to Bishop Edmund Gibson,
March 13, 1732, in Perry, ibid., 302. The quotation cited here is taken
from a report by Henderson to Bishop Gibson, August 7, 1731, in Perry,
ibid., 308.

[2] Henderson to Bishop Gibson, April 25, 1735, Fulham Papers, "Maryland
1696-1769," item 75. Morrell arrived in Maryland in 1734 with the blessings
of the proprietor but without a license from the bishop of London. Henderson,
effectively in retirement as commissary, did not attempt to dislodge him.
In 1746, though, the vestry and churchwardens of Morrell's Charles County
parish petitioned the upper house, complaining of "many Irregularities"
committed by Morrell. They were probably drink-related. The upper house
ordered Morrell to attend an inquiry, which apparently was never actually
held. Arch. Md., XLIV, 291. William Tibbs, Henderson's long-time nemesis,
drank in addition to several other failings. His vestry certified in 1715
that he became drunk on the sacramental wine so quickly that it could hardly
"be supposed that the bread and Wine is digested in his Stomach." "The
Case against Tibbs," Fulham Papers, "Maryland 1696-1769," item 133. See
also the vestry of St. Paul's Parish, Baltimore County, to Jacob Henderson,
September 10, 1731, in Perry, Collections, IV, 309.

Neil McCallum (described by Governor Sharpe in 1768 as one of the worst

of ministers, who "by reason of his Sottishness" had "for many years been

absolutely unable to officiate in the Church or to discharge any part of

his Duty") would have been disciplined for their drinking problem.[1]

About ten other ministers drank too much to suit some parishioners

but not enough to qualify them as chronic alcoholics.[2] For three of these,

indeed, incidents of excessive drinking were probably aberrations from

their usual behavior.[3] The other seven were clergy whose appreciation of

liquor was only part of a general character considered scandalous by their

parishioners or fellow clergy. These seven, plus perhaps another five men

not specifically cited for drinking,[4] were ministers whose proclivities for

brawling, gaming, litigation, or rabblerousing brought opprobrium on the

Church. Though most of these twelve were simply public nuisances, a few

---

[1] Wilkinson's dealings with Baylie are noted in Christopher Wilkinson to Bishop John Robinson, May 26, 1718, in Perry, Collections, IV, 107. Baylie left the country shortly after the citation. Whittaker's character has been described in Chapter II, p. 69. Sharpe described McCallum (who served in Dorchester Parish, Dorchester County, from 1740 until 1772) in a letter to Hugh Hammersley, June 22, 1768, Arch. Md., XIV, 507.

[2] These men were Bennet Allen, Walter Chalmers, James Colgreve (or Cosgreve), John Donaldson, Henry Hall, Thomas Johnston, Andrew Lendrum, John Lillingston, William Maconchie, and James Williamson.

[3] Walter Chalmers, Henry Hall, and John Lillingston. Chalmers inbibed at weddings (Deposition of Katharine Jacques, Montgomery County Land Records, Liber C, fols. 326-331; I am grateful to Allan Kulikoff for bringing this source to my attention). Henry Hall was charged with only one bout of drinking and the charges originated in spite. John Lillingston apparently lead a drinking party at Talbot County courthouse in February 1692, but he was acquitted when the case came before the provincial council, and in other respects his behavior and reputation were exemplary. For Hall, see the articles against him, filed February 25, 1718, by Jacob Henderson, in the Fulham Papers, "Maryland 1696-1769," item 131. For Lillingston, see Arch. Md., VIII, 213, 371-375, 378.

[4] Theodore Esdras Edzard, Thomas Chase, Thomas Howell, Thomas Thomson, and Nathaniel Whittaker.

were true rogues, a type described by a shocked fellow cleric in 1724 as
"carrying on the interest of the Devil & his Dominion with all their
might."[1] James Williamson, for instance, once characterized as a man
"notorious & consummate in villainy," was depicted by the vestry of
Shrewsbury Parish in Kent County as a person of "bad life & Corrupt
principles." The vestry complained that he had driven worshippers from
the church, who had declared that "there can be littell Religion in the
man who preaches ag[ainst]t a Sin on the Sunday w[hi]ch he Soo often
practices the rest of the Week."[2] Williamson apparently reformed later in
life and lived to see his son Alexander enter the ministry. Nathaniel
Whittaker, on the other hand, died a despised man. Quick-tempered and
mean, his reputation was such that when he received an induction into
Coventry Parish in Somerset County in 1748 the parishioners locked him out
of the church. Daniel Dulany described him as "a Man not only unfit for
the Station in which he was placed, but so infamously profligate that it
would have been a discredit to any Person of Character to admit him to the
Regard and notice of a common acquaintance."[3] A litigious man, his

---

[1] Giles Rainsford to [the S.P.G.?], April 10, 1724, in Perry,
Collections, IV, 233.

[2] Giles Rainsford to the Secretary of the S.P.G., August 16, 1724, in
Perry, ibid., 241; Shrewsbury Parish vestry to Governor Charles Calvert,
September 15, 1722, in the Shrewsbury Parish, Kent County, Vestry Minutes,
Volume I (1701-1730), No. 13090, MdA, entered under the date of the letter.

[3] The episode of the locked church and the description of Whittaker
are from Daniel Dulany's opinion written for Philip Hughes during the Coventry
Parish affair of the late 1760s. See Arch. Md., XXXII, 225. The parish sued
Whittaker for breaking the peace when he forced his way into the locked
building, but lost the case because the minister could prove he had a right
to enter the church. The vestry then questioned his ordination and withheld
his salary for a time. Before gaining the induction to Coventy in 1748,
Whittaker had served as curate to Daniel Maynadier at St. Peter's Parish in
Talbot County and had been ordered to leave the parish by the vestry in 1743
on the grounds that he was "a person of Immoral Life and Conversation and in
no sort fitt to Discharge the Ministerial Functions." (St. Peter's Parish,
Talbot County, Vestry Minutes, Volume II [1717-1766], M295, MdA, dated
April 4, 1743.) He then served five years in St. Margaret Westminister in
Anne Arundel County.

parishioners noted after his death that he had been "in some One of the Goals the greatest part" of his incumbency for debt, libel, assault and battery, and other unclerical charges.[1] Once, when he took a woman to court for whipping him with a hickory switch, the court fined her only one penny, "it being imagined by the Court that he well deserved it."[2] The rest of the clergy in Maryland were very aware of the damage Whittaker did to their professional reputations; Alexander Williamson II swore that if he could prosecute unworthy brethren he would "shew no Quarter to the Whitacres."[3]

A few ministers were charged with faults of a more pastoral nature. Their offenses included demanding special fees for private baptismal or communion services, permitting clerks to read the devotions, absenting themselves from their parishes, failing to maintain the confidentiality of private consultations, administering the sacraments too infrequently, and refusing to perform funerals and other rites under adverse conditions.[4]

The number of ministers Maryland parishioners considered heterodox or deficiently educated cannot be determined from the extant evidence. Clerical ignorance was not a complaint which would warrant any intervention by the government, the court, or the Church authorities, and scarcely any specific protests were ever lodged. Heterodoxy, a punishable crime according to canon law, was extremely difficult to prove. All the reports of heretical ministers in the province are unsubstantiated and most are simply hearsay.

---

[1] The vestry of Coventry Parish, Somerset County, to Philip Hughes, n.d., Arch. Md., XXXII, 229.

[2] Maryland Gazette, June 16, 1747.

[3] Alexander Williamson II to Upton Scott, June 15, 1761, Howard Papers, MS. 469, Section 13, Box 21, MdHi.

[4] All the ministers charged with pastoral delinquency were also men accused of engaging in objectionable activities when not wearing a gown and surplice.

People generally doubted the sincerity of the clergymen who had converted
to Anglicanism from Presbyterianism, but apparently only three men were
actually accused of holding heretical, deistic, or schismatic views.[1]

Of the thirty-five clergymen known to have been accused of various
types of unclerical behavior perhaps six were innocent of all charges.
About twenty-nine men, or circa fifteen percent of the entire ministry,
probably deserved disciplining for at least one count of irregular
activity. The full number of immoral or negligent ministers can only be
guessed at. The condition of the clergy was discussed in regular written
reports only during the years when Wilkinson and Henderson functioned as
commissaries. Few vestries or groups of parishioners wrote down whatever
complaints they might have had against their local ministers. With the
exceptions of Sharpe and Nicholson, the Maryland governors did not try to
keep the proprietors or the English ecclesiastical establishment informed
about the type of man who served by their leave. In England specific,
verifiable grievances against ministers surfaced in the ecclesiastical
courts or were reported in the bishops' visitation inquiry answers. In
Virginia, protests would have come to the attention of the commissaries.
However, the lack of an arbitrating agency in Maryland meant that some

---

[1] These three were Richard Chase, Archibald Spencer, and William
McClenaghan. Jacob Henderson wrote to Bishop Edmund Gibson in 1735 that
Chase was "a person of much Levity, no Learning and Supposed to be a
Freethinker or Deist; he gives himself great Liberties in ridiculeing
religion." Henderson to Bishop Gibson, April 25, 1735, Fulham Papers,
"Maryland 1696-1769," item 75. William Robinson, a Virginia minister,
tried to block Spencer's ordination by sending word to London in 1748
that the man had openly declared himself a deist. Robinson to the bishop
of London, July 27, 1748, Fulham Papers, "Virginia," Box 2, item 50.
McClenaghan apparently was drawn to New Light Presbyterianism during the
late 1750s while serving as the assistant pastor of a Philadelphia S.P.G.-
funded church. In 1760 he left the church to set up a private conventicle
in Philadelphia. He came to Maryland in 1766. See the "Minutes of the
Committee," n.d. but June 1760, and William Smith to Archbishop Thomas
Secker, July 1, 1760, both in Perry, Collections, II, 305-311, 319-324.

instances of parochial dissatisfaction must have remained verbal and undocumented. The colonists may have detested ministers who have no official black mark against their names. We probably know about the worst cases of irregular behavior among the clergy and many of the less serious ones, but the contempt with which the body of the clergy was sometimes treated suggests strongly that more men irritated their parishioners than those mentioned in the documents.

Without question the Maryland Church employed ministers whose moral degeneracy and professional incompetence sickened laymen and clergy alike. Though the incorrigible misfits were only a small group of men, easily equalled in proportions by the number of fine or even superlative ministers who served concurrently, men such as Whittaker and Tibbs incalculably damaged the prestige of the Church. As their fellow ministers saw it, the Church was an infant institution surrounded by cunning and malicious enemies--Catholics, dissenters, deists, and atheists--who delighted in using the existence of such incompetents to vilify the Church and the faith.[1] When bad ministers drove parishioners out of the true Church the number of people who did not receive religious services in return for their poll taxes expanded, compounding the danger to the always-fragile financial settlement of the Church. Parishioners with good ministers could never feel completely secure so long as men of low caliber were granted livings in Maryland, for the death or resignation of a decent incumbent always meant that a man such as Whittaker could ensconce himself in their living for the next several decades.

---

[1] See, for instance, Peregrine Coney, John Lillingston et al. to Bishop Henry Compton, May 18, 1698; "Dr. Bray's Memorial, shewing the Necessity of one to superintend the Church and Clergy in Maryland ...," n.d. but c. 1700; Jacob Henderson to Bishop John Robinson, September 1, 1715; Hugh Jones and Henry Addison to Bishop Thomas Sherlock, August 27, 1753; all in Perry, Collections, IV, 11-12, 51, 80, 331.

In all fairness to the ministers, serving well in Maryland demanded much more work and a greater measure of integrity than many of them could have imagined when they volunteered. The colonists themselves (particularly during the early years of the establishment period) were immoral to a degree which shocked many of the immigrant clergy, who exclaimed at the amount of alcohol routinely consumed and the prevalence of sexual sins.[1] The temptation to do as their neighbors did overwhelmed some ministers, who forgot that parishioners expect priests to act according to a higher standard of behavior than other mortals. The ministers found the common people grossly ignorant regarding religious matters and often distressingly indifferent to spiritual exhortations.[2] The Catholics, Presbyterians, Quakers, and later the evangelicals were, many ministers felt, like packs of wolves lying in wait to seize wavering members of the flock.[3] Countering their attacks, perceived as more virulent and more vicious than those assailing Anglican ministers elsewhere, required more intellectual resources or persuasiveness than some ministers could command. Failure bred hopelessness and apathy. The everyday workload was in itself debilitating. Aside from the rigors of their professional duties, the conditions under which many ministers were forced to live contributed to delinquency. Men accustomed to living close to the company of other people found themselves condemned to the loneliness of frontier parishes. The natives as well as the immigrants were dismayed by the exigencies of country life. As late as 1761 Alexander Williamson, moving from Annapolis to a parish in Prince

---

[1] One of the many examples of such declarations may be found in Samuel Skippon to Bishop John Robinson, January 19, 1715, in Perry, Collections, IV, 73.

[2] See Samuel Skippon to Bishop John Robinson, January 19, 1715, and Thomas Bacon to the Secretary of the S.P.G., August 4, 1750, in Perry, ibid., IV, 73, 324-325.

[3] As an example, see Hugh Jones to the Secretary of the S.P.G., July 30, 1739, in Perry, ibid., 321-322.

George's and Frederick counties, was depressed to discover that the nearest family he could socialize with lived ten miles away. "I cannot," he wrote friends in Annapolis, "as yet prevail with myself to think I shall ever be able, with all the Philosophy I now am or ever can be possessed of, to spend my Life in so retired a Place as this is."[1] Williamson longed for the people, the entertainment, and the culture of Annapolis. Earlier, a good many ministers had to wait for years before their salaries sufficed to support a wife or children. The isolation of their lives must have been intolerable. Educated and cultured clergymen yearning for stimulating conversation too often found the colony an intellectural desert. If they lacked witty or learned companions, they could not always find solace in books, either, for books were expensive, often unavailable, and--where they existed at all--the parish libraries were small and frequently in rotting condition. Furthermore, the ministers were, by virtue of their offices, public men, subject to the scrutiny of parishioners who could be less than charitable when it came to judging their appointed shepherds. The ministers were prime topics of conversation, and some of what was said was malicious gossip which injured them as men and as priests.

---

[1] Alexander Williamson II to Upton Scott, May 8, 1761, Howard Papers, MS. 469, Box 21, Section 13, MdHi.

Chapter V

Wealth

Unlike some religious institutions, the Church of England did not
encourage its clergy to live penuriously. Most Churchmen did not consider
poverty a mark of individual grace, nor did they think that the presence of
numerous indigent clergy was a sign of healthy otherworldliness in the
ranks. In fact, the Anglican Church regarded poor clergymen as an embarrassment. During the course of the Reformation the Church abandoned the
medieval concept of the priest--chaste, poor, obedient, and agent necessary
to the miracle of transubstantiation--and consequently forfeited much of
the traditional mystique and prestige of priesthood. Customarily, priests
had been considered an order quite apart from the rest of society, a group
of men whose social status was (theoretically, at least) not derived from
breeding, wealth, or life style. They were in effect exempt from the
prevailing rules of social classification. Following the break with Rome,
ministers in the English national church could no longer expect that
members of an increasingly secularized society would treat them with the
deference and partiality most inhabitants had once accorded Catholic
priests. Like any of their parishioners, the ministers had to find a place
for themselves on the social ladder. Anxious for public respect and honor,
the Church therefore insisted that the act of ordination entitled ministers
to gentle status. It fully recognized, however, that theoretical gentility
needed to be manifested by the usual outward trappings of such a rank, and
hence was extremely concerned when clerical incomes fell short of social
pretensions.

The poverty of a large proportion of the Anglican ministry was a
problem which was much discussed during the seventeenth and eighteenth
centuries. John Eachard, who published a book on "The Grounds & Occasions
of the Contempt of the Clergy and Religion" in 1670, spoke for many when
he declared that the "mean condition" of so many of the clergy was one of
the main reasons "their sacred Profession is much disparaged, and their
Doctrines undervalued."[1] The labors of poor clergymen, noted Robert Nelson,
"have no Influence upon the Minds of Men, except it be those very few that
are able to distinguish their Characters from their Circumstances."[2]
Augmenting the support of the ministers was not a simple project. Clergymen
in the Church of England received most of their incomes as incumbents in
tithes and by renting the glebes and parsonages. The method of paying
tithes had become highly idiosyncratic through the years: in many parishes
tithes had been commuted into fixed money fees, they had been leased out
or sold, or custom and contracts had otherwise altered the original arrangement. Each living was worth a different sum and was likely to be paid off
in a special manner.[3] The intricacies of the system fostered fraud and
evasion. The Church could not meliorate the incomes of the poorer clergy
without exhaustive research into the financial underpinnings of thousands of
parishes and without infringing on the rights and sensibilities of patrons
and tithepayers. Nothing was done to help the indigent clergy until 1704,
when Queen Anne waived the Crown's right to first-fruits and tenths
(respectively, taxes paid upon entry into a benefice and an annual tax on

---

[1] John Eachard, The Grounds and Occasions of the Contempt of the Clergy
and Religion, 9th ed. (London, 1685), 100.

[2] Robert Nelson, "Address to Persons of Quality and Estate," in
Works....all compendiously methodized for the Use of Families (London, 1715),
264.

[3] For a description of the different tithing arrangements in one
county, see Pruett, "Leicestershire Clergy," 100-115.

the living) and turned the proceeds over to a commission to distribute
to ministers with insufficient incomes. Queen Anne's Bounty, as the
measure was known, very gradually raised the stipends of the poorest clergy
by systematically allotting funds to the parishes in order of need.[1]

In 1692 the Maryland legislators chose a method of providing for the
clergy which was far removed from the English tithe system. A poll tax was
a rather novel means of raising ecclesiastical revenues, but it was the
method used in the colony for levying most civil taxes and was convenient
and practical. The legislators dismissed the notion of instituting tithing
because "the present Constitution of this Province being in its Infancy
will not admitt of raising a Maintenance for Ministers by way of Tyths as
in England and other places by time brought to perfection."[2] The legislative
journals do not record whether or not the delegates discussed adopting the
fixed salary system used in Virginia. If they did, the Virginia method may
have struck the legislature as both too cumbersome and too inequitable for
the denizens of the sparsely populated frontier regions, who would have had
to pay higher dues to their ministers to make up for the lack in numbers.

The first Maryland Establishment Act did not actually promise a
minister the full forty pounds of tobacco from every taxable in
his parish. The county sheriff, who collected the tax "in manner and form
as the publick or County Levies" were gathered, was entitled to keep five
percent of the total as his own fee.[3] The act directed that the remainder
be turned over to the vestry and used to build a church or chapel. Only
after the construction was completed was the residue--if any--of the forty

---

[1] For a discussion of the Bounty, see Best, Temporal Pillars, 78-136.

[2] This statement appears in the Establishment Act of 1696. Arch. Md.,
XIX, 426.

[3] Arch. Md., XIII, 429.

per poll to be appropriated for "the use and benefit of the Minister of that Parrish if any Minister [be] Inducted into the same."[1] This injunction led to bitter wrangling between ministers and vestries during the years it remained in effect. The act of 1696, noting that the vestries had already had three years to build churches ("which is thought to be Sufficient for that end and purpose"), forbade the vestries "under Colour and pretext of finishing the said Church or keeping the same in repaire" to withhold or detain any part of the forty per poll due to a legally inducted minister.[2] The same act, though, required all ministers to appoint a parish clerk and to pay him a thousand pounds of tobacco per year out of their own incomes.[3] The deductions for sheriffs' fees and clerks' salaries were incorporated into the final settlement.[4]

The salaries which the legislators voted the Anglican clergy were probably not intended to be more than minimally sufficient.[5] The delegates who granted the forty per poll in 1692 did not know, of course, exactly how many parishes would be formed. However, they were presumably aware that the taxable population in Maryland was over 9,500 and that, given the extent of the territory, at least twenty-five or thirty parishes were needed. They probably estimated that the average parish salary would range fairly

---

[1] Arch. Md., XIII, 429.

[2] Arch. Md., XIX, 430.

[3] Arch. Md., XIX, 428.

[4] The Establishment Act of 1700 ordered both deductions; the act of 1702 omitted to mention sheriffs' fees, but this mistake was rectified in an amendment passed in 1704. Arch. Md., XXIV, 92-93, 421.

[5] They might, however, have been far less. During the debates in the assembly over the passage of the 1692 act a vote was taken on whether to permit the ministers twenty or forty pounds per poll. The majority voted for forty pounds. Considering the scanty population in Maryland, a stipend based on a poll tax of twenty pounds would have been insufficient to attract any ministers to the province. Arch. Md., XIII, 396.

close to the 13,333 pounds of tobacco permitted to the ministers in Virginia, and that the mean sterling value of the parishes would be between ₤40 and ₤45 sterling after deductions.[1] In 1696, when the legislature again voted on clerical salaries, the knowledge that there were thirty parishes in Maryland and that a census of the previous year had listed 10,390 taxables would have enabled the legislators to compute the average parish living at a minimum of 12,160 pounds of tobacco after deductions, or about ₤43 sterling.[2] By 1702 the taxable population in Maryland was known to be over 12,214 persons, raising the mean parish living to at least 14,402 pounds minus the standard deductions, and the price of tobacco had improved to a point where the legislators could have anticipated that the average parish incumbent would receive about ₤60 sterling.[3]

---

[1] All figures for mean annual price of Maryland tobacco used in this chapter are from the U.S. Bureau of the Census, Historical Statistics of the United States, Colonial Times to 1957 (Washington, D.C., 1975), 1198. The mean price of farm tobacco in 1692 was 0.80 pence sterling per pound. The taxable population in Maryland in 1692 was actually over 10,000, but I have presumed that the legislators would not have known the exact figures. Menard, "Economy and Society," 456.

[2] The mean price of a pound of farm tobacco was 0.85 pence sterling in 1696. Historical Statistics, 1198. The census of 1695, plus one of 1696 which lists 10,381 taxables, are in Arch. Md., XXV, 255. The act of 1696, it should be noted, also required ministers to pay 1,000 pounds of tobacco to a clerk, and this deduction has been calculated into these figures.

[3] In 1701 Governor Blakiston reported 12,214 taxables in Maryland for the previous year. Arch. Md., XXV, 255. This figure is used for the calculations here. However, as Menard has pointed out ("Economy and Society," 436, 456) several errors were made in the census. He estimates the number of taxables in 1700 at 12,973. The population figures bandied about in London by proponents and opponents of the bills of 1700 and 1702 varied considerably from the truth and from each other. Quaker Joseph Wyeth, in his tract An Answer to a Letter from Dr. Bray (London, 1700), claimed there were 24,000 taxables in Maryland and that the Church was costing them ₤4,000 a year. Bray replied in A Memorial Representing the present Case of the Church in Maryland with relation to its establishment by Law (London ?, n.d.) that he had it on the best authority (presumably Francis Nicholson) that the number of taxables did not reach 12,000. He thought there were about 11,000. Both of these tracts are reprinted in Bernard C. Steiner, ed., Reverend Thomas Bray: His Life and Selected Works Relating to Maryland (Baltimore, 1901), Maryland Historical Society Fund Publication No. 37. In this volume the information noted above may be found on pp. 188-189, 216-217.

By English standards a salary of £60 a year was a middling income for a clergyman. In 1696 Gregory King estimated that of the ten thousand ministers in England, eight thousand averaged £45 a year and the rest about £60.[1] When Queen Anne's Bounty was established early in the eighteenth century, over half of the ten thousand livings in England and Wales were worth less than £50.[2] In Leicestershire in 1706-1707 salaries ranged from £5 or £6 to about £400, with about a third of the livings worth less than £50, a third worth from £50 to £100, and a third worth over £100.[3]

To their cost, many of the ministers who sailed for Maryland during the early years of the establishment believed the comparatively rosy figures quoted to them as prospective salary levels. Filled with anger, dismay, and rue, their letters back to London and their complaints to the Maryland authorities indicate how often their incomes failed to live up to their expectations. Their tobacco did not fetch the price they had reckoned on, the cost of living was much higher than it was at home, some of them had evidently not been warned about the deductions, insolvent inhabitants reduced the tax base, and the incomes of many parishes fell far short of the average. Unquestionably, the high rate of resignation and outmigration among clergymen during the first two decades of the settlement was due to disappointment with their salaries.

The original thirty parishes had not been laid out with any consideration of keeping them roughly equal in population. From the very beginning the number of taxables in the parishes--the major variable in Maryland salaries-- had differed immensely. The first reports of parish taxables date to 1693, when three parishes listed their taxable populations at 265, 315 and 629

---

[1] King's report is reprinted in Charles Wilson, England's Apprenticeship, 1603-1763 (London, 1965), 239.

[2] Sykes, Church and State, 212.

[3] Pruett, "Leicestershire Clergy," 100.

persons.[1] Minus the sheriffs' fees, the incomes generated in these parishes were 10,070 pounds, 11,970 pounds, and 23,902 pounds of tobacco. St. Paul's Parish in Queen Anne's County, which reported the largest taxable population of the three, was probably the most lucrative parish in 1693 as it was in 1698, when the Maryland ministers sent the bishop of London a list of taxables and salaries for all but one of the parishes.[2] By 1698, according to the ministers, St. Paul's Parish included almost five times the number of taxables found in St. John's Parish in Baltimore County, the smallest parish in terms of taxable inhabitants.[3] The net salary of the incumbent of St. Paul's was almost six times that of the minister at St. John's (22,028 pounds to 3,864 pounds of tobacco).[4] The average salary came to 12,625 pounds. Fully sixty percent (nineteen out of thirty) of the parishes were valued at less than the 16,000 pounds offered to all incumbents in Virginia.

---

[1] In order, the parishes are: All Faith's in St. Mary's County, St. Paul's in Kent County, and St. Paul's in Queen Anne's County. In these three instances and in most instances noted hereafter information on the number of taxables in a parish is taken from the parish vestry or account books, in the MdA. For the sake of brevity, and because the records are not usually paginated, detailed references will be omitted in footnotes except when the information is not derived from the parish records in Annapolis.

[2] The exception was St. John's Parish (also called King George's) in Prince George's County. The list (in the Fulham Papers, "Maryland 1696-1769," item 127) was apparently appended to a letter sent to Bishop Compton in the spring of 1698. The Fulham Papers list gives the taxable population and salary rates for only 28 parishes; a 29th parish is added in "An Account of the several Parishes within this Province," a document signed by the clerk of the Maryland upper house, which otherwise duplicates the figures given in the Fulham list. "An account...." is in Perry, Collections, IV, 13-20. Ideally, the figures for taxables on these two lists would have been the returns made by the county sheriffs in late 1697 or early 1698. However, when the Fulham figures are compared with those given in the vestry minutes of five parishes which record taxables for 1698 or earlier years, it is clear that the returns noted in the Fulham lists may in many cases actually be the rates for years between 1694 and 1697.

[3] The taxable population in St. John's is listed as 128, and St. Paul's at 606. The vestry minutes of St. Paul's lists 616 taxables in 1697 and 647 taxables in 1698.

[4] The salaries for the clerks and the fees for the sheriffs have been deducted from these figures.

Parish Incomes c. 1698*

in Tobacco

	0-4,999 lbs.	5,000-9,999 lbs.	10,000-14,999 lbs.	15,000-19,999 lbs.	20,000 and up lbs.
Number Parishes	3	6	10	9	1
Percent of 29 Parishes	10.4	20.7	34.5	31.0	3.4

* These figures are the incomes remaining after deductions for sheriffs' fees and clerks' salaries. The list includes 29 of the 30 parishes. As explained in note 2 on the previous page, the distribution is approximate only.

Figured at the 1698 mean farm price of tobacco, a penny sterling per pound, St. Paul's in Queen Anne's County was theoretically worth about ₤91 and St. John's in Baltimore County, ₤16.[1] The average stipend should have come to roughly ₤52. The ministers, however, were not paid in prime tobacco. The quality of the plant was not regulated until the Tobacco Inspection Act went into effect in 1748. Previous to that year the planters, anxious to spend as little as possible, sensibly reserved the worst of their crop for taxes and customs. The tobacco the clergy received was usually poor or even trash, discolored, stalky, and worth a fraction of the tobacco the planters freighted for Europe.[2] The ministers informed the bishop of London in 1698 that the merchants in Maryland would very rarely allow them

---

[1] These figures are the net sums due to the clergymen after the standard deductions.

[2] Testimonials to the poor quality of the tobacco received by the ministers abound in the Fulham and S.P.C. papers. See, for instance, "The Case of Robert Keith sent Missionary," and "The Memorial of Robert Keith," both n.d. but c. 1707, in the S.P.G. Papers in the Lambeth Palace Library, "Maryland," Volume XII, fols. 53-55, and the "Testimonial of Residents of Somerset County," and "An Account of Trotter's Mission," in the same source, fols. 7, 73-74. Christopher Wilkinson disparaged the quality of the tobacco almost two decades after these early complaints. See Christopher Wilkinson to Bishop Edmund Gibson, September 9, 1724, and December 4, 1727, in Perry, Collections, IV, 245, 260.

goods at the going rate of a penny per pound, and sometimes gave them only a halfpenny or a farthing.[1] A note appended to the list of parish incomes of that year stated that fifty shillings per thousandweight (0.60 pence per pound) was the usual price of public tobacco.[2] When tobacco sold generally for a good price the reduced value of their public tobacco was a disappointment to the ministers, but when the market slumped the value of their incomes dropped to virtually nothing.[3] "Not one shirt to be had for Tobacco this Year in all our County," Alexander Adams wrote Bishop Compton from Somerset County in July 1711, "and poor ten shillings is all the Money I have received by my Ministry & perquisites since Oct[obe]r last."[4] The cost of shipping (high during war years), the poor quality of the tobacco, and the difficulties experienced by some ministers in transporting their tobacco to a Chesapeake port discouraged many of them from attempting to freight the tobacco to England themselves, forcing them to accept the prices offered to them by local merchants.[5] Immigrant ministers, unfamiliar with

---

[1] Peregrine Coney, John Lillingston et al. to Bishop Henry Compton, May 18, 1698, in Perry, Collections, IV, 10. Moreover, the merchants disliked accepting the ministers' notes for the tobacco because "it is generally very troublesome for them to get it paid in any reasonable time, and that often they cannot get it at all, wholly losing their time and labour in going from place to place to demand it of those Planters to whom the Sheriffs send them."

[2] Fulham Papers, "Maryland 1696-1769," item 127.

[3] Previous to the Tobacco Inspection Act, "bust" periods in the tobacco market were roughly 1681-1697, 1705-1718, 1727-1733, 1740-1749. Earle, Tidewater Settlement System, 18.

[4] Alexander Adams to Bishop Compton, July 2, 1711, S.P.G. Papers, Series A, Volume 6, item CVII.

[5] The ministers mention their fear of the cost of shipping in Peregrine Coney, John Lillingston et al. to Bishop Henry Compton, May 18, 1698, in Perry, Collections, IV, 10. In 1724 Christopher Wilkinson wondered whether the king could be persuaded to grant the clergy the right to send a ton or two to England minus the customary dues (Wilkinson to Bishop Edmund Gibson, September 9, 1724, in Perry, ibid., 245). Alexander Adams told the S.P.G. in 1711 that there was "neither ship nor store in or near our County for purchasing tobacco." Alexander Adams to the Secretary of the S.P.G., July 2, 1711, S.P.G. Papers, Series A, Volume 6, item CXXVIII. He was speaking of Somerset County, and other such complaints regarding the lower Eastern Shore were sent by other ministers as well.

Parish Incomes, c. 1698[*]

at 1.0 Pence Sterling Per Pound of Tobacco[**]

N = 29

	£ 0-19.9	£ 20-39.9	£ 40-59.9	£ 60-79.9
Number of Parishes	3	6	9	11
Number of Parishes as Percentage of N	10	21	31	38

at 5 Shillings per Hundredweight of Tobacco[***]

(0.60 pence per pound)

	£ 0-19.9	£ 20-39.9	£ 40-59.9	£ 60-79.9
Number of Parishes	6	13	10	0
Number of Parishes as Percentage of N	21	45	34	0

[*] Fees for sheriffs and salaries for clerks have been deducted.

[**] 1.0 pence sterling per pound was the mean farm price of tobacco in 1698.

[***] 0.60 pence sterling per pound was the price the ministers claimed to receive for their tobacco in 1698.

the complexities of a cash crop economy, found it a strain to adjust to incomes which not only fluctuated in response to the international tobacco market but were almost always substantially lower than they had initially anticipated.[1]

Ministers could only be disappointed by the return for their tobacco if they had managed to acquire a title to it in the first place, and during the first two decades or so of the establishment they sometimes worked far harder to collect tobacco than to get rid of it. Until 1696 incumbents were entitled to no portion of the forty per poll but that which the vestries chose to give them. Salaries, consequently, varied greatly depending on whether the vestry had paid for the construction of the parish church and whether it was inclined to provide the incumbent with a minimal wage in the meantime. After the act of 1696 ministers should have received the full forty per poll except for the standard deductions, but there is evidence that recalcitrant sheriffs and highhanded vestries continued in some cases to manipulate the payment of the salaries. George Trotter, who arrived in Maryland in 1698, was a victim of such illegal meddling. Inducted into both

---

[1] Robert Keith, to cite one example, calculated that his salary from Coventry and All Hallows Parish should have been worth ₤120 a year at a penny sterling a pound just after the beginning of the century. He was shocked to find it was really worth only ₤60. The merchants, he claimed, deducted a third off the price of his tobacco before they would change it into a bill or money. "The Memorial of Robert Keith," and "The Case of Robert Keith sent Missionary," in the S.P.G. Papers in the Lambeth Palace Library, "Maryland," Volume XII, fols. 53-55.

The testimony of reputable clergymen makes it apparent that the tax tobacco was of an inferior sort, but it is unclear how much the price of such tobacco regularly lagged below the mean price of tobacco in general. When inventories list public tobacco due to a minister I have compared the price given for it with the mean price of tobacco listed in Historical Statistics, p. 1198, and find that this tobacco is usually at or very near the mean price.

Using the rate given by the ministers as a fair price for public tobacco in 1698, though, the income of St. Paul's Parish in Queen Anne's County is reduced to ₤55 sterling, while St. John's in Baltimore is a beggarly ₤10. The average for that year is merely ₤31 at 0.60 pence per pound. At that rate, a fifth of the parishes are worth under ₤20.

Somerset and Stepney parishes in Somerset County, Trotter was informed by
the vestries that he would have to be content with a small allowance
because neither parish had completely paid for its church--a pronouncement
which clearly violated the 1696 law. For his second year of service,
Trotter received the full forty per poll from Somerset only on the condition
that he pay off the workmen for finishing the church, and he continued to
receive only a small allowance from Stepney. When the churches were finally
paid for, the vestry of Somerset refused to carry out the formality of
issuing the sheriff an order to pay Trotter. The sheriff, accordingly,
declined to give Trotter his tobacco. Deciding that the sheriff and
the vestry were conspiring against him, Trotter went to Annapolis to obtain
an executive order for the tobacco and to resign his parishes. Though he
granted the order, he was never able to use the tobacco because the
shipping season was by that time over, and the people to whom he entrusted
the tobacco squandered it over the next year. In 1703 he moved to
All Faith's Parish in St. Mary's County. The sheriffs of that parish
usually did not pay him in time for him to freight his tobacco with the
fleet, and sometimes they did not pay him at all. Trotter decided he had
had enough in 1706 and returned home, as impoverished as he had been when
he sailed to Maryland.[1] His experience was probably extreme but not
particularly atypical. Sheriffs sometimes dallied and hedged--the vestry
of Shrewsbury Parish, for instance, was obliged in 1715 to issue a stern
warning to the sheriff to desist his "insufferable" habit of detaining the
minister's tobacco in years of high prices and paying it off when prices
were low--and could, through negligence, malice, or indecision prevent a

---

[1] "An Account of Trotter's Mission," S.P.G. Papers in the Lambeth
Palace Library, "Maryland," Volume XII, fols. 73-74.

minister from obtaining his salary.[1] Vestries, too, could effectively impound a minister's salary by pressuring sheriffs to withhold payment or by tying up the tobacco in litigation. During the first two decades of the establishment delays and disputes were not uncommon; the system was novel, and the rights of both the vestries and the ministers were not always clearly defined.[2]

Through the early 1720s many Maryland ministers were very hard pressed to support themselves and their families on their parish incomes. Tales of distress and woe abound from this period. The men found the price of living distressingly high. In 1698 they claimed that the cost of board and keeping a horse used up a quarter of the incomes from the best parishes, and the remaining funds, they declared, "will hardly find us with Clothes and other necessaries." They did not dare to bring their wives from England.[3] Those who did have families risked the experience of Gabriel D'Emilliane, who told the council in 1702 that although he held two parishes "the said Revenue is not Sufficient to supply him with necessarys whereby he hath been obliged to Run in debt thirty three Pounds in one year tho he was Reduced next to a starving condition with his Family the last Summer."[4] To supplement their

---

[1] Shrewsbury Parish, Kent County, Vestry Book, Volume I (1701-1730), No. 13090, MdA, entry dated May 3, 1715. Sheriffs were sometimes caught in the middle of quarrels between clergy and vestry over salaries and responded to contradictory demands from both sides by simply detaining the tobacco.

[2] Until the legislature decided the matter in 1713 a chief point of contention was the question of who owned tobacco which accumulated in the parish during vacancies. Ministers usually argued that the next incumbent was entitled to the whole, while the vestries felt that the income should be used to benefit the parish. The legislature decided that ministers were entitled to payment only from the day of induction to the day of death or resignation. Arch. Md., XXIX, 340.

[3] Peregrine Coney, John Lillingston et al. to Bishop Compton, May 18, 1698, in Perry, Collections, IV, 10. Jacob Henderson said in 1723 that because the merchants marked up English imports at over 100% the cost of living was reckoned at double what it was in England. Reply to Bishop Gibson's queries, n.d. but 1724, in Perry, ibid., 138.

[4] Arch. Md., XXV, 133.

incomes, ministers opened schools, hired themselves out to neighboring

parishes, accepted pluralities, served as chaplains to the assembly, and

begged the S.P.G. for allowances. Acquiring a second living could be the

fastest means of increasing income, but parishioners intensely opposed

the constitution of pluralities and relatively few were granted. In any

case, as D'Emilliane learned, the incomes from two small parishes sometimes

did not suffice either. During the first two decades of the establishment

a good proportion of the ministers earned additional wages by contracting

with the vestries of vacant parishes for individual sermons or for part-

time service on a regular basis. Some vestries paid four or five hundred

pounds of tobacco per sermon, and many of them paid the ministers a

proportion of the forty per poll corresponding to the amount of time the

ministers served in their parishes. Though extra-parochial service

disappeared as the parishes were filled, it unquestionably enabled many of

the ministers to survive the very lean early years. Applying to the

S.P.G. for a subsidy was usually a less successful means of supplementing

incomes. Dr. Bray, the bishop of London, and the S.P.G. all were concerned

with the financial troubles of the Maryland clergy. Bray obtained S.P.G.

subsidies (which were generally set at ₤50 a year) for some of the

Maryland-bound clergy if they were intended for very poor livings.[1]

---

[1] See Thomas Bray to the Secretary of the S.P.G., March 24, 1705, in
Perry, Collections, IV, 55-56, and the two memorials of Robert Keith in the
S.P.G. Papers in the Lambeth Palace Library, "Maryland," Volume XII, fols.
53-57. Keith's memorials suggest that the S.P.G. refused to subsidize
parishes worth more than 10,000 pounds of tobacco a year. Bray's letter
indicates that Bray occasionally promised subsidies without first obtaining
the approval of the S.P.G., or it may be interpreted to mean that he was
granting allowances out of his own funds.

With some hyperbole, Thomas Bray described the forty per poll in 1701
as "mean a support, as I believe is given to the Clergy in any Establish'd
Church in the Christian World." A Memorial Representing the present Case of
the Church in Maryland, reprinted in Steiner, ed., Thomas Bray, 188. In
1700, Bray admitted that the high price of tobacco during the past several

Bishop Compton sometimes asked the S.P.G. to grant allowances to specific

ministers either inducted into or headed for the more impoverished

Maryland livings.[1] He also recommended on several occasions that the

S.P.G. subsidize "the meaner Parishes in Maryland w[hi]ch have as much need

as any part of North America" due to "the deadness of the Tobacco trade in

those parts."[2] The S.P.G., however, preferred to support ministers in the

colonies where the Church was not established. Certainly less than ten and

perhaps less than half a dozen Maryland clergymen received S.P.G. allowances

at any time, and none of them seems to have held them for more than a few

years at most. The majority of the clergy had to make do with what they

told Governor John Hart in 1714 was "but a very bare Competency."[3]

Besides their salaries, ministers also received fees for conducting

marriages, funerals, and other religious ceremonies. By the establishment

acts of 1700 and 1702 they were permitted to charge five shillings sterling

for performing marriages, providing that the ceremony was conducted at the

church during regular hours of worship.[4] An act of 1704 set the rate at

one hundred pounds of tobacco, and one of 1717 altered the fees to ten

shillings for marriages performed by license and one hundred pounds of

years had raised the income of a few parishes to £80, "tho' that is higher
than they can promise themselves the same for the future," but noted that
at least twelve of the parishes were not worth more than a third of that
sum. A Memorial Representing the Present State of Religion on the Continent
of North-America (London, 1700), reprinted in Steiner, ed., Thomas Bray, 160.

[1] Bishop Henry Compton to the Secretary of the S.P.G., February 24,
1705, S.P.G. Papers, Series A, Volume 2, item LIX; Compton to the Secretary,
November 19, 1711, S.P.G. Papers, Series A, Volume 6, item CXLV.

[2] Bishop Henry Compton to the Secretary of the S.P.G., November 15,
1706, and October 14, 1707, S.P.G. Papers, Series A, Volume 3, items XIV,
CXX. Compton was especially concerned that the ministers in Maryland were
too poor to buy books for themselves if they were situated in parishes
which lacked S.P.G. libraries. See W. Hall to the Secretary of the S.P.G.,
October 10, 1712, S.P.G. Papers, Series A, Volume 7, item XL.

[3] "The Humble Representation of the Clergy of Maryland ...," Arch. Md.,
XXIX, 362.

[4] Arch. Md., XXIV, 92, 266.

tobacco (or six shillings eight pence currency) for weddings celebrated
after the posting of the banns.[1] Accounts kept by ministers suggest that
when weddings were held outside of the canonical hours or in places other
than churches or parsonages the clergymen customarily received a somewhat
larger fee.[2] Charges for a funeral also varied. Four or five hundred
pounds of tobacco were the most common remuneration for a funeral sermon
(as opposed to simply a burial service) during the early decades.[3] When
ministers conducted long, elaborate funerals for dignitaries and prominent
citizens they expected a larger sum, and for a plain reading of the burial
service they may have received nothing or only a nominal fee. Fees due
for other pastoral functions were probably regulated by local custom. How
much such fees boosted the yearly income of the average minister is
difficult to say. All the reliable accounts of income from fees date to
the years just preceding the Revolution. In 1776 Thomas Chase's marriage
services brought him about ₤75 currency (₤45 or ₤56 sterling, depending on
the exchange rate used), equivalent to about a fifth of his regular income.[4]

---

[1] Arch. Md., XXVI, 356; XXXIII, 114-115.

[2] The best surviving list of marriage fees was kept by Thomas Chase in
St. Paul's Parish, Baltimore County, during 1776. He usually received ten
shillings for the ceremony, but sometimes earned up to ₤4. See St. Paul's
Parish, Baltimore County, Register, 1710-1789, Volume II, MdDL.

[3] The accounts sent to the courts by estate administrators sometimes
list the cost of a funeral sermon as a debt against the estate of the
deceased. From 1692 to about 1710 most of the accounts list the figures
given here as the cost of a funeral service, though there is some variation
both above and below them. I have not checked the accounts after 1710
carefully, but a cursory look suggests that ₤2 current money was a
usual fee by the 1740s. Probate material is in the MdA.

[4] St. Paul's Parish, Baltimore County, Register, 1710-1789, Volume II,
MdDL. Chase's account, which apparently runs from January 1 to December 12,
1776, lists earnings through that date at ₤73 18s. 0d. I have expanded the
sum slightly to compensate for the remaining weeks in the year. ₤45 sterling is the equivalent of ₤75 current money at an exchange rate of 1: 1.66;
₤56 sterling is the equivalent at 1: 1.33.

William Edmiston of St. Thomas's Parish in Baltimore County informed the
British Audit Office commissioners that his fees came to ₤75 sterling a
year, equal to about a quarter of his regular income.[1] However, David Love
told the commissioners that in 1775 or 1776 he had received surplice fees
of only ₤8 in addition to a salary of ₤228 sterling, and Henry Addison
thought that fees added no more than ₤20 a year to his ₤436 sterling
income.[2] Clearly, ministers who lived in parishes with large Anglican
populations benefitted financially because they conducted more fee-
producing ceremonies than their colleagues in small or denominationally
diverse parishes. A fairly well-to-do minister of the 1770s did not regard
fees as a critically important addition to his regular salary, but during
the early years of the eighteenth century some ministers verging on
bankruptcy or starvation must have viewed the timely death or marriage
of a parishioner as a godsend.

Few Maryland ministers enjoyed the traditional clerical perquisites
of glebe lands and a parsonage before about the third decade of the
establishment. In England clergymen customarily held plots of land, called
glebes, as life tenants during their incumbencies, and were usually granted

---

[1] British Audit Office Papers, American Loyalist Transcripts, A.O.
13.61, Microfilm 1093, fols. 71-72, DLC. Edmiston figured his salary
according to the act of 1773, at 32 pounds of tobacco or 4 shillings
currency per poll; he used an exchange rate of 1.66 currency to 1.0 sterling.

[2] British Audit Office Papers, ibid., fol. 111. Love calculated the
income from his parish inaccurately, though this does not affect the
absolute figure of ₤8 for fees. He figured that each of his 1,100 taxables
would pay 40 pounds of tobacco although the rate had changed in 1773. The
information on Henry Addison is from the Addison Papers, MS. 3, Box 1,
MdHi. The document is a copy of his deposition to the Audit Office comis-
sioners. Addison did not explain how he calculated his income, but he
probably also put the poll tax at forty pounds of tobacco.

a parsonage of some sort as well. Virginia followed this tradition and
in 1727 legally entitled all incumbents to a glebe of at least two hundred
acres.[1] About thirty out of the forty-four Maryland parishes contained
glebes by the Revolution, but they were a rarity at the beginning of the
period.[2] Apparently only a single glebe (which may have shortly included
a parsonage) existed in 1694 and by 1700 there is evidence of only three
more.[3] Although Governor Copley's instructions ordered him to see that "a
convenient house be built at the common charge for each Minister," the
clause was not incorporated into the Establishment Act of 1692 nor any of
the subsequent settlement legislation.[4] Governor Nicholson tried to prod
the legislature into providing glebes and parsonages for all the ministers--
"according to his Maj[es]ties Instructions"--but was told that the matter
would not be considered until the establishment was more settled.[5]
Actually, the legislature never took any action of the expansive kind
Nicholson hoped for, and was content to pass bills securing the parishes'

---

[1] Gundersen, "The Anglican Ministry in Virginia," 9. The parish was
also obliged to furnish a manse and outbuildings on the glebe.

[2] Parishes acquired glebes by bequest and by purchase. During the
period when vacancies were common vestries sometimes used the accumulated
tobacco to buy glebes or to build parsonages, which were then used to attract
unattached ministers. Later it was more common for the vestry to petition
the assembly for a special poll tax in order to buy land.

[3] The first glebe, in St. Mary's County (probably William and Mary
Parish) was listed at 300 acres renting for 2,000 pounds of tobacco a year
in 1694 (Arch. Md., XX, 106). A parsonage in St. Mary's County--the only
one in the province--was noted by the ministers in 1698; Benjamin Nobbes,
who took over William and Mary, moved into it with his wife. Peregrine
Coney, John Lillingston et al. to Bishop Henry Compton, May 18, 1698,
in Perry, Collections, IV, 10.

[4] Arch. Md., VIII, 276.

[5] Arch. Md., XIX, 35. Nicholson even told the upper house that if a
way could be found to build a parsonage in every parish he himself would
give ₤5 sterling for each house begun under his administration. The
secretary of state, Thomas Lawrence, promised he would donate 1,000 pounds
of tobacco per parsonage.

right to bequeathed property and outlining the method by which vestries could buy land if they so desired.[1] The parishes gradually acquired property in a piecemeal and haphazard fashion which frustrated many of the early ministers.[2] Arriving in the colony for the most part poor and single, they discovered that they were obliged to board with parishioners or at ordinaries for long periods of time. This recourse was not only undignified, it was expensive, and renting or building a house for themselves was also costly. Without glebes, the ministers lost proceeds they could have received as rent, and were prevented from putting in crops or raising livestock until they could lease or buy land of their own.

In 1723 Bishop Gibson asked the clergy to describe their financial situation. By this time the very lean years were drawing to a close, and though some parishes were still worth very little, the steadily rising population was enabling more of the ministers to live in some comfort. Five of the twenty-three who responded to the query admitted that when tobacco sold at a good price they could count on salaries which reached or exceeded ₤100 sterling.[3] They were the rich men of the profession, for a quarter of the respondents still lived on less than ₤50 a year. The gap between ministers doing well and those struggling along was very pronounced. Jacob Henderson's income in a good year reached ₤200, while the incumbent

---

[1] Arch. Md., XIX, 589-591; XXVI, 302-303.

[2] Not only were the ministers sometimes incorrectly informed regarding existence or the condition of land and living quarters in their intended parishes, but vestries broke promises to build parsonages or buy land which they made to incoming ministers. See, for example, Gabriel D'Emilliane's account of how he was "sadly disappointed" in Durham Parish, in Arch. Md., XXV, 133-134.

[3] In 1723-1724 there were 32 parishes in Maryland. Twenty-two ministers responded to the query, but one man held a plurality; I have counted him as two men and have also divided his income by two. The query answers may be found in Perry, Collections, IV, 191-231. The answers of the ministers cannot be set in a table or graph because they did not calculate their incomes by a uniform standard; the figures given above must be regarded, therefore, only as rough indications of wealth.

of Christ Church Parish in Queen Anne's County, the smallest parish in the province, reported making £30 at most. (Thomas Thomson, rector of Dorchester Parish in Dorchester County, grumbled that his £35 salary was a small one considering his "trouble and pain.")[1] Almost all of the ministers reminded Gibson that since they were paid in tobacco their income fluctuated from year to year depending on the price they could obtain for it. A third of them even refused to speculate on what the sterling value of their parishes in recent years came to, and others sent figures to illustrate the unpredictability of their incomes. Henderson's parish could be worth anywhere from £60 to £200, Christopher Wilkinson's parish from £60 to £120, and Richard Sewell's, £30 to £60, all without substantial alteration in the number of taxables.[2] Not only the changes in the annual market price of tobacco but the general quality of the local product was of importance in determining how much a clergyman could receive for his tobacco. By common agreement tobacco produced on the Eastern Shore was inferior to that of the Western Shore, and the tobacco grown in the lower Western Shore region was the finest of all. Two Somerset County ministers mention that merchants gave them only four shillings sterling per hundred pounds of tobacco (0.48 pence per pound) at a time when the mean price of tobacco from the middle or lower Western Shore was much closer to a penny per pound.[3] Indeed, during good years, Jacob Henderson's parish in Prince George's County produced more income than Christopher Wilkinson's parish in Queen Anne's County,

---

[1] The response of Thomas Thomson, n.d. but c. 1724, in Perry, Collections, IV, 230.

[2] Henderson was incumbent of Queen Anne Parish, Prince George's County; Wilkinson of St. Paul's, Queen Anne's County, and Sewell of Shrewsbury Parish, Kent County.

[3] The response of Alexander Adams, and the response of James Robertson, both n.d., but c. 1724, in Perry, Collections, IV, 212, 221; Historical Statistics, 1198. The index for the price of Maryland tobacco from 1711 to 1775 was compiled by Carville V. Earle, who based his series on probate records from Anne Arundel and Prince George's counties.

although Henderson had some 250 fewer taxables in 1723.[1] Henderson's

trash tobacco was obviously better trash than Wilkinson's.

Evidence based on parish tax records strengthens the impression that

by the mid-1720s most of the ministers could survive on their salaries

without undue hardship. In 1698 the average parish salary was just over

12,500 pounds a year; in 1715 Governor John Hart estimated that it was

about 18,000 pounds, and by the middle of the 1720s it was over 28,000

pounds.[2] Had the ministers been able to sell the tobacco at the mean market

price of a penny a pound, the average minister would have been making in

the neighborhood of ₤115 in 1725. Given the poor quality of parish tobacco,

however, an average of between ₤90 and ₤100 is more likely.

Since the 1690s, moreover, many of the parishes had acquired glebes

and some had even built parsonages for the ministers. By 1725 at least

sixty percent of the parishes (nineteen out of thirty-two) had glebes of

some sort.[3] They ranged in size from about a hundred acres to four hundred,

though two hundred acres was the most usual dimension. The quality of the

[1] According to vestry accounts, Queen Anne's Parish had 1,065 taxables
in 1722 and 1,025 in 1724; St. Paul's had 1,321 in 1723.

[2] For 1698, see this chapter, p. 225; for 1715, "An Account of the
Sev[e]r[a]ll Offices within the Province of Maryland," Arch. Md., XXV, 322.
Hart gave a figure of 20,000 pounds as the average and I have subtracted
the standard deductions. The average for the 1720s is based on information
(derived in all but one case from vestry accounts) regarding parish taxables
in fifteen parishes between 1722 and 1725. When the information was available, I have used the taxable rate for 1724; otherwise, I have used the
statistic for the year closest to 1724. The 15 parishes, just less than
half of the total, include the richest and the poorest parishes and, all in
all, should be representative of the whole. Though it is impossible to
calculate the average salary precisely, 28,000 pounds of tobacco should not
be far off for the period.

[3] Responses to Bishop Edmund Gibson's queries, in Perry, Collections,
IV, 191-231. In addition to the 17 glebes noted in the replies to the
query, there were glebes in All Hallow's, Worcester County, and St. George's,
Baltimore County, by 1724. Since the incumbent did not do so, I have not
counted the lots owned by the parish of St. Anne's in Annapolis as a glebe,
although they were leased out and the rector received the rent.

glebes differed considerably from parish to parish. According to what the
ministers told the bishop of London a number of the glebes were virtually
worthless, for the land was so poor or unimproved that they could neither
live on it themselves nor rent it out.[1] In fairness it should be said that
the ministers themselves, reckless farmers or indifferent landlords, were
sometimes responsible for ruining the land for their successors.[2] Some
parishes really provided quite well for their incumbents. All Hallow's
Parish in Somerset (later Worcester) County promised any minister who could
be persuaded to accept the living "a Glebe of near 400 acres of rich land,
with a good dwelling-house an apple orchard and peach orchard of 1,000
trees" in 1719.[3] Inventory accounts demonstrate that ministers did in fact
grow crops on some glebes, though many of them preferred to lease out the
land and concentrate on exploiting and improving their own properties.[4]

---

[1] Five of the ministers said their glebes were unlivable, unrentable
or very indifferent, and another noted his was still forest.

[2] For example, the vestry of St. George's Parish in Baltimore County
reprimanded incumbent Stephen Wilkinson because "it appeareth to the Vestry
that the Improvements on the Glebe Land are gone to decay by the Negligence
or Sufferance of the Rev[eren]d Stephen Wilkinson, which must undoubtedly
prejudice his next Successor or Lay the Parish under a Great Expense to
repair them if the Land & Plantation be left by Mr Wilkinson in its present
Condition." The vestry of All Faith's Parish in St. Mary's County ordered
the clerk to note in the minutes that Robert Scott, the deceased incumbent,
had neglected the glebe and that the land had "gon to Ruing." St. George's
Spesutia Parish, Baltimore County, Vestry Minutes, Volume I (1718-1771),
No. 12211, MdA, entry dated February 1, 1743; All Faith's Parish, St. Mary's
County, Vestry Minutes, Liber 2 (1720-1752), No. 12668, MdA, entry dated
April 12, 1734.

[3] The vestry of All Hallow's Parish to Bishop John Robinson, August 1,
1719, in Perry, Collections, IV, 116. At least one of the glebes, that in
William and Mary Parish in Charles County, was stocked with cattle and hogs
for the use of the minister by 1750. Arch. Md., XLVI, 340. Scattered but
unverifiable evidence suggests that some of the parishes may have been
provided with slaves at various points during the establishment period.

[4] For an example of crops at the glebes, see the account of the estate
of Esdras Theodore Edzard (actually, Theodore Esdras Edzard) in Accounts,
Liber 14, fol. 466, MdA, dated January 13, 1736, which lists a crop of
tobacco at the glebe in the amount of 1,678 pounds.

Most of them also rented or built houses of their own, for no more than a third of the clergy had parsonages by the mid-1720s, many of them described as small, unfit to live in, or even ruinous.[1]

Shortly after the report to Bishop Gibson in 1724, the Maryland ministers found their growing financial well-being threatened by the legislature's insistence on altering the Church's financial settlement in conjunction with tobacco regulation. Having complained for three decades about the quality of their tobacco the clergy might have been expected to applaud the scheme, but not only did some of them doubt that regulation would drive the price up, they felt that any rise in price would not benefit them anyway, because the regulation act of 1728 gave taxables the option of paying their dues as a fixed sum of money as well as in a reduced amount of tobacco.[2] The people would pay the tax in whatever medium was cheapest in any particular year. The clergy could not see how the act might make them better off than they were, and that consideration, plus a concern to maintain the inviolability of the Establishment Act, drove them to seek the annulment of the act. Less successful in destroying the regulation act of 1730, which permitted taxables to pay a quarter of the dues in grain, the ministers were obliged to put up with it for the two years during which its provisions were in effect.[3]

---

[1] These descriptions are taken from the answers of the ministers to Bishop Gibson's queries, in Perry, Collections, IV, 191-231. The 23 respondents list seven parsonages. One more existed at the time in All Hallow's Parish, Worcester County, and perhaps another at St. Stephen's Parish in Cecil. The ministers complained that most of them were required to maintain the houses themselves.

[2] "An Act for Improving the Staple of Tobacco ...," Arch. Md., XXXVI, 266-275.

[3] "An Act for Improving the Staple of Tobacco ...," Arch. Md., XXXVII, 138-151. In fact, the price of tobacco was so low during the early 1730s that some ministers may have been secretly glad to receive as part of their salary a product more edible than tobacco.

During this same period the quarrel between the ministers and the legislature regarding parish divisions erupted. Salaries were again at the root of the disagreement. The clergy were just emerging from a long term of generally depressed circumstances and were looking forward to more prosperous times as the population continued to rise. They sympathized with the desire of the public for smaller parishes and a larger number of ministers, but were reluctant to give up a third or half of their salaries to implement that wish. Until the mid-1720s the incomes produced by the parishes had been so small that the legislature usually acknowledged the folly of dividing them. Only two parishes were created between the first provincial division and 1725, and both of them suffered a long stretch of vacancy before ministers consented to move in.[1] Dividing an underpopulated though territorially large parish was apt to result in two vacant parishes, and when inhabitants pressed the legislature for a division they were prudently told to wait until the income sufficed for two ministers.[2] By the mid to late 1720s the assembly thought that several of the larger parishes had reached that point, and, in the space of four years, carved out four new parishes.[3] The clergy objected to this action for two reasons: first, they thought it was illegal to deprive an incumbent of any part of his income, and secondly, they did not agree with the assembly's definition of a "suitable competency" for a minister.

---

[1] Queen Anne's Parish, created out of St. Paul's Parish in Prince George's County in 1704, remained vacant until 1708. North Elk Parish in Cecil County, created in 1706, remained vacant until about 1718.

[2] Arch. Md., XXIV, 211.

[3] The parishes were: St. Mary Whitechapel out of Great Choptank, Dorchester (later Caroline) County; Prince George's Parish out of King George's, Prince George's County; Queen Caroline Parish out of St. Paul's, Baltimore County, All Hallow's and St. Anne's in Anne Arundel County; St. Luke's out of St. Paul's, Queen Anne's County. Whitechapel was formed in December 1725 and St. Luke's in October 1728.

How much did a minister need to earn to live up to his station with dignity? Great Choptank was divided when the living was worth about 41,900 pounds of tobacco, King George's when worth about 49,800, and St. Paul's when valued at about 67,400 pounds.[1] Christopher Wilkinson of St. Paul's, thinking of his large family and the poor quality of the tobacoo, wailed that his 67,400 pounds was "but a scanty maintenance for one Minister," but the assembly met all objections to the division with the curt observation that the 40,000 pounds apportioned to Wilkinson after the cut was a sum "which we take to be a very handsome maintenance for a Minister."[2] A year later, in 1728, the legislature wrote Governor Benedict Leonard Calvert that under the provisions of the tobacco regulation act the average clerical salary would be about 30,000 pounds, worth ₤150 currency (about ₤112 sterling), and intimated that this amount was sufficient.

As in the past, Jacob Henderson became the spokesman for the clergy. In a published letter to Daniel Dulany, who had supported the divisions and the changes in the Church's financial settlement, Henderson lashed out at those who considered the clergy's income sufficient if not liberal.[4] He

---

[1] These figures are for salaries minus the standard deductions. Great Choptank had 1,128 taxables in 1725; King George's Parish had 1,336 taxables in 1726 and was left with 791 after the division (29,058 pounds after deductions); St. Paul's 1,800 taxables were split into groupings of 1,000 and 800.

[2] Christopher Wilkinson to Bishop Edmund Gibson, December 4, 1727, in Perry, Collections, IV, 260; Arch. Md., XXXVI, 33. The sum of 40,000 used by the legislature is the residue still inclusive of deductions; minus these, it becomes 37,000.

[3] Arch. Md., XXXVI, 169-170. The legislature calculated the money value of the salaries at the conversion rate set in the act, 10 shillings currency per hundredweight.

[4] The Rev. Mr. Jacob Henderson's Fifth Letter to Daniel Dulany, Esq; In Relation to the Case and Petition of the Clergy of Maryland (Philadelphia, 1732). If the rest of the correspondence was published, nothing else seems to have survived.

denied that any of the divided parishes had exceeded a "reasonable
Subsistence."[1] Even Wilkinson, he declared, who was "as prudent,
industrious and saving a Man, as well could be" did not "exceed in the
Provision made for his Family (tho' he injoyed that Parish many Years)
before his death."[2] Henderson most emphatically did not think that 40,000
pounds a year was more than a reasonable maintenance and he laughed at
Dulany's assertion that 32,000 pounds (what remained after the division
at King George's Parish) was a handsome, ample, and liberal support for a
clergyman. "I do not think it exceeds half a Subsistence," Henderson said
flatly, and asked Dulany why the lawyer-politician himself was not content
with double that amount.[3] Henderson defined a reasonable subsistence as a
sum which "would maintain a Clergyman and his Family, in a comfortable
decent Manner, in every Thing suitable to his Station; would inable him to
educate and provide for his Children in a rational way, if he had any; to
use Hospitality, to do acts of Charity, and in case of Old-age, Sickness and
Infirmity to provide him an Assistant."[4] Henderson believed it was fair to
ask the community to provide ministers with a salary to cover these
expenditures because clergymen were dissuaded by reason of their profession
from engaging in activities (such as trading for profit) by which other
people enhanced their financial situations.[5]

---

[1] Henderson, Fifth Letter to Dulany, 10.

[2] Henderson, ibid.

[3] Henderson, ibid., 9, 10.

[4] Henderson, ibid., 11.

[5] Henderson, ibid., 23. Dulany said that Henderson lied when he
declared that ministers did not engage in trade because Henderson himself
traded. Henderson replied that he had always refrained from trading to
the extent that he made any advantage from it. The minister denied that
any Maryland clergyman's salary was sufficient to improve his fortune
beyond a "bare supply of Provision" for his family. Henderson, ibid.,
23, 24.

The discussions between Henderson and Dulany reveal a sharp difference
in the way the minister and the layman viewed the obligations of the people
towards their religious leaders. Henderson saw the ministers as the care-
takers of the precious souls of the parishioners, heirs to a very ancient
tradition, professional men, honorable men, gentlemen. The incomes due to
the ministers belonged to them by no less than divine right,[1] and considering
the importance of the service they provided to the community, he expected
them to be recompensed amply and cheerfully. Dulany, less impressed with the
dignity of the profession, viewed the poll tax as a sort of benevolent
charity: it was decent and right to support the clergy, but he disliked
any hint of greediness on their part, he did not want the tax to be a drain
on the people, and he did not approve of ministers becoming wealthy through
the labors of other men. That Dulany's views were shared by many would
become apparent in the growing volume of petitions to split parishes and
by the hostility against the established church, including its clergy,
which would emerge during the late 1760s and early 1770s, a time of
unprecedented prosperity for the ministers.

If Henderson considered the Maryland clergy underpaid in 1732 he still
had to admit that they were probably better supported than in any other
British colony.[2] The average Maryland salary had already outstripped the
16,000 pounds offered by Virginia parishes to such a degree that the
disadvantages of uninspected tobacco were fully offset. Migration into
Maryland picked up as ministers from the north abandoned their ₤50 S.P.G.
stipends and southern ministers left their fixed allowances. True, there
were still parishes in Maryland with incomes so small that no one would

---

[1] Henderson, Fifth Letter to Dulany, includes a disquisition on the divine origin of tithing, pp. 13-21.

[2] Henderson, ibid., 30.

accept the livings except as a last resort, but anyone could see that the trend was for the incomes to increase steadily with time.

How much the Tobacco Inspection Act of 1747 affected clerical incomes as a whole is uncertain. In effect from 1748 through October 1770, the act cut the poll tax to thirty pounds of inspected tobacco or 3s. 9d. currency, depending on whether or not the taxable planted tobacco for sale.[1] The legislature intended the two media to be roughly at par, but they did not remain so. By the late 1760s the booming tobacco market had pushed the value leaf several times above the conversion rate of 1747.[2] Since the currency equivalent of the thirty per poll was a fair price for the late 1740s, clerical incomes in the non-tobacco growing areas presumably fell off at most a quarter (supposing that all taxables paid in money), while incomes from parishes in the tobacco producing regions also dropped a quarter for a brief period and then regained or surpassed their pre-1748 level as the increased price of tobacco made up for the loss of ten pounds per poll.[3]

Maryland in the 1750s was the best spot in America for Anglican clergymen who longed to improve their fortunes. During the 1760s the colony became nothing less than a magnet, drawing ministers in such numbers that the Church could not provide livings for them all. The good price of tobacco (after 1750 the mean price of farm tobacco on the Western Shore

---

[1] Arch. Md., XLIV, 604-605. In 1748 sterling was exchanged at 100% above currency, so the poll tax in sterling would have been 1s. 10 1/2d.

[2] Historical Statistics, 1198.

[3] Unfortunately, from 1748 to the Revolution little information exists as to how individual parishes paid the ministers--in leaf, currency, or a combination of the two. Thus salaries cannot be computed without guessing the medium of payment and hence the final total. Though one can postulate that the parishes in the middle and lower Western Shore, prime tobacco country, were supported mainly in tobacco, that the parishes to the northwest and northeast paid a large proportion of the salaries in currency, and that the parishes on the lower Eastern Shore probably paid in both mediums, no reasonably accurate tables can be set up.

only once dropped below a penny sterling per pound) combined with a rising

population to make even the medium-sized Maryland parishes the envy of the

profession.[1] The incomes produced in the larger parishes were awe-inspiring

to men in a profession which made few people wealthy. Jonathan Boucher,

plodding along on his 16,000 pounds of tobacco in Virginia, was dazzled to

hear of Maryland salaries reaching the unbelievable heights of 70,000 or

even 100,000 pounds at a time when tobacco exceeded 1.5 pence per pound,

and he could hardly curb his impatience to move across the border.[2] A

report forwarded to the bishop of London, which lists the sterling value

of all of the Maryland parishes in 1767, demonstrates the magnitude of the

increase in Maryland salaries since the 1690s.[3] Only seven parishes (three

of which were parishes recently divided or created) had less than a thousand

taxables and the average parish consisted of a taxable population of

1,379 persons.[4] In terms of taxables, parishes in 1767 were four times

larger than they had been in 1694--and this even though there were almost

---

[1] The price of tobacco may be found in Historical Statistics, 1198.

[2] Jonathan Boucher to Rev. M. James, March 9, 1767, in "Letters of Jonathan Boucher, " Md. Hist. Mag., VII (1912), 340. Boucher heard that All Saints' in Frederick County was worth 100,000 pounds and he was not far off the mark; interpolation from the list of 1767, described in the following footnote, places the salary at All Saints' at 96,330 if all taxables paid in tobacco. However, Boucher's estimation that Henry Addison's King George's Parish in Prince George's County was worth 70,000 is about 15,000 pounds too high.

[3] "List of the Parishes in Maryland and their Annual Value, as returned in the year 1767," in Perry, Collections, IV, 336-337. The anonymous author of this enumeration listed sterling values for the parishes without explaining where he acquired his information. By comparing his result with the known number of taxables in several parishes in 1767 and adjacent years, I have determined that he calculated the sterling value of the parishes based on a poll tax in money (3s. 9d. currency per poll, or 2s. 9 3/4d. sterling at the rate of 1: 1.33). Using this information, I have then calculated the number of taxables in the parishes. Since the author may have used figures two or three years out of date, the average given here is approximate.

[4] Interpolation from the list produced a figure of 60,712 taxables for Maryland; there were 44 parishes.

half again as many parishes.[1] Computed in tobacco, the average parish was
three times as well subsidized as it had been seventy-odd years before.[2] In
sterling value, of course, the average parish income had risen considerably
more than three times the 1694 level. At 0.75 pence sterling per pound of
tobacco, the average salary in 1694 would have been worth about ₤41, which
is a generous estimation because it is unlikely that the ministers would
have been able to sell their public tobacco at that rate. The average salary
by the 1767 inventory was ₤184 sterling. This list, though, was calculated
on the assumption that all Maryland taxables contributed equally at the
fixed rate of 3s. 9d. currency (2s. 9 3/4d. sterling) each. Actually, that
rate was legally only applicable to persons who did not produce tobacco for
sale, for the Inspection Act of 1747 ordered tobacco producers to pay the
clergy in leaf. The salaries given on the list are therefore really the very
minimum required by law. They are not reflective of the fact that many
ministers, and perhaps most of them, received the major portions of their
salaries in tobacco. Since the value of thirty pounds of tobacco at this time
was higher than 2s. 9 3/4d. sterling, these clergymen were actually making
a good deal more money than the list indicates. How much the individual
salaries differed from the minimum depended on what proportion of the
taxables had paid in tobacco and how much the price of tobacco deviated
from 1.125 pence per pound (2s. 9 3/4d. divided by 30). The difference
could be considerable. Figured in currency, to take one example, Henry
Addison's 1,895 taxables in King George's Parish in Prince George's

---

[1] Menard ("Economy and Society," 456) estimates a taxable population
in 1694 at 10,365 persons, or an average of 345.5 per parish.

[2] Minus the deductions, the average income in 1694 (based on population alone) would have been 13,129 pounds of tobacco; the figure for 1767
is 38,301. The figure for 1767 would have been 51,402 had the tobacco
tax remained at 40 pounds per poll.

Salaries According to "List of the Parishes in Maryland and Their Annual

Value, as Returned in the Year 1767"

in £ Sterling[*]

N = 44

	50-99	100-149	150-199	200-249	250-299	300-349	350-399	400-449	450 and up
Number Parishes	2	10	14	13	2	0	2	0	1
Percent Parishes	4.5	22.8	31.8	29.6	4.5	0	4.5	0	2.3

[*] The source of this list, and the reservations with which it must be viewed, are explained in the text, pages 247-248.

County would have provided him with a salary of about ₤245 sterling after deductions.[1] Had half of his taxables paid in tobacco and had Addison sold it at the mean price (1.63 pence sterling per pound) his income would have increased to ₤302, and it would have been ₤360 had all paid in tobacco.[2] Because King George's Parish was in a tobacco region, Addison's real salary must have been closer to ₤360 than it was to ₤245. If half the provincial taxables paid in tobacco in 1767--as they almost certainly did--the mean salary after deductions would have been ₤219 sterling. In any case, by 1767 under a third of all parishes could have been valued at less than ₤150 and at least forty percent (and probably well over half) exceeded ₤200 sterling in value. By the standards of their time and their profession the Maryland ministers were indeed enjoying a handsome maintenance.

Between 1767 and 1770 clerical salaries paid in tobacco peaked as the tobacco market boomed. The mean price of tobacco on the Western Shore in 1770 was 2.06 pence sterling per pound, up twenty-six percent from 1767, and exported tobacco could sell for 3 pence per pound.[3] As the planters congratulated themselves on their good fortune the clergy watched the market with equal delight. Unfortunately for both groups, the tobacco boom was over by mid-1772 and prices quickly sank back to the level of 1766 or 1767.[4] Even worse for the ministers, the Tobacco Inspection Act expired in October 1770, and left the validity of the poll tax in doubt.

---

[1] The number of taxables is calculated from the 1767 list in the manner previously explained.

[2] The salary for the clerk, which is one of the deductions, was figured at the mean price of tobacco for 1767.

[3] Historical Statistics, 1198.

[4] Ibid.

The pamphleteers debated and the clergy dithered; the sheriffs, responsible for collecting the tax, had to decide what to do at the risk of being sued by the ministers for neglecting their duty or being sued by the parishioners for illegal seizure of property. Individual sheriffs reached their own decisions. In some parishes the sheriffs declined to collect any taxes at all, while in others the taxpayers paid what and when they wished to sheriffs who hesitated to pressure them.[1] On the other hand, there were sheriffs who continued to collect the poll tax at the rate set by the Tobacco Inspection Act and some who did so using the old standard of the forty per poll.[2] Though there is really little evidence to go on, reports from various ministers imply that during the three-year hiatus between the lapse of the Inspection Act and the enactment of the last clerical support bill in December 1773, salaries in general deteriorated sharply.

The "Act for the Support of the Clergy" of 1773 set the poll tax at thirty pounds of inspected tobacco or four shillings currency per taxable and for the first time permitted the taxable to pay in the medium he chose.[3] For the ministers the act marked the end of the era in which salaries escalated in conjunction with the price of tobacco. From that

---

[1] Jonathan Boucher told a correspondent in November 1773 that he had not received a penny for two years. Jonathan Boucher to Rev. M. James, November 16, 1773, "The Letters of Jonathan Boucher," Md. Hist. Mag., VIII (1913), 183.

[2] Sheriff Richard Lee, Jr., of Charles County, arrested a local taxpayer after the expiration of the Inspection Act for not paying the forty per poll. See Vivian, "Poll Tax Controversy," Md. Hist. Mag., LXXI (1970), 167-169. Sheriff John Clapham of Anne Arundel County advertised in the Maryland Gazette beginning March 7, 1771, that he would accept either currency or leaf at the Inspection Act rates. David Love, rector of All Hallows in Anne Arundel County, was paid the value of forty per poll in currency at 12s. 6d. per hundred by some of his parishioners for two years. David Love to Horatio Sharpe, May 23, 1774, in High, "Letters from Love," HMPEC, XIX (1950), 362.

[3] The act may be found in Arch. Md., LXIV, 254-256.

point onward people would pay ministers in tobacco when leaf sold under 12s. 6d. currency per hundred pounds (1.5 pence currency per pound, or 1.125 pence sterling) and in currency when tobacco sold at a higher price.[1] The clergymen who had been paid primarily in tobacco lost market advantages and suffered a cut in their income. Jonathan Boucher told the commissioners of the British Audit Office that his preferment dropped by half after the passage of the act, but he was probably among the ministers most affected.[2] The clergy accustomed to money payments gained a bit by the act because the poll tax was set at 4s. rather than 3s. 9d. currency per poll.[3] "I suppose about half of the Clergy gains by this new regulation, the rest of us will be considerable losers," David Love remarked at the time.[4] However much the clergy mourned the descent from the heights, the act of 1773 did not exactly beggar anyone. Only two or three parishes produced less than £100 sterling after 1773, the average parish was still worth over £200, and All Saints' Parish in Frederick County, the most lucrative parish in Maryland, furnished an income of between £850 and £1000

---

[1] The currency to sterling conversion is computed at 1.33 currency to 1 sterling. In 1772 and 1773, though, two conversion rates existed, 1.33:1 and 1.66:1. Since the conversion rate in 1774 and 1775 was 1.33:1, I have used the lower figure.

[2] "The Memorial of Jonathan Boucher," British Audit Office, A.O.13.39, American Loyalists, Series II, Number 39, Claims, Maryland, A-D, DLC Microfilm.

[3] Converted at 1.33:1, 4s. currency is 3s. sterling.

[4] David Love to Horatio Sharpe, May 23, 1774, in High, ed., "Letters from Love," HMPEC, XIX (1950), 361.

sterling.[1]

During the very last years of the establishment, then, Maryland

clerical salaries were not always what they had been during the bonanza

years. By British and colonial standards they remained substantial. The

golden era, however, had undoubtedly passed, and even if the Maryland

Declaration of Rights of 1776 had not abolished the settlement of the Church,

the trend in clerical incomes would most probably have been to decline.

The perquisites of the profession, such as glebes and parsonages, may well

have become more common, but the number of parish taxables in the average

parish would have fallen. The perpetuation of very large parishes was no

longer defensible on the grounds of clerical need. In 1770 the legislature

had already arranged for the break up of two of the biggest parishes (All

---

[1] "A conjectural estimate of the amount of the annual Incomes of all
the Church Livings in Maryland, as they now are and as they were before the
passing of the late Law," is found in the Fulham Papers (reprinted in Perry,
Collections, IV, 343-344). Based on a taxable population of 74,300, the
list concludes that the post-1773 average income was ₤338 currency or ₤203
sterling at 1.66:1 (at 1.33 to 1, the mean was ₤253 sterling). According
to the anonymous compiler, the average parish after deductions was worth
₤171 sterling at 1.66:1 (at 1.33:1, ₤213 sterling), but he includes
insolvencies in his deductions, which I have not. I find that at 1.66:1
the average post deduction salary in about 1775 was (using his population
figures, which are admittedly rough) ₤184 sterling at 1.66:1, and ₤232
sterling at the exchange rate of 1.33:1, which was valid in 1774 and 1775.

Interestingly, the 1775 list also notes conjectural incomes before
the 1773 law and puts the mean at ₤240 sterling. According to parish
figures given, 55% of the parishes were cut by less than 20% in salary and
16% actually made gains. Although these figures are not exact and should
not be taken at face value, they do give some idea of the impact of the
act.

My statement that two or three parishes alone were worth less than
₤100 sterling is not based on the 1775 list but on interpolation from the
list of 1767 and comparison with any exact figures I have for parish
taxables in the mid-1770s.

All Saints' Parish had 6,114 taxables in 1770 (Arch. Md., LXII, 450)
and Bennet Allen, the last rector, declared to the Audit Office that his
salary in 1775 was ₤1,069 4s. sterling. Bennet Allen to the Earl of Bathurst,
July 18, 1814, photostat in the Revolutionary Collection, MS. 1814, MdHi.

Saints', Frederick County, and St. John's, Baltimore County) on the deaths
of the incumbents, and unquestionably more division acts would have
followed.[1] The public wanted more intimate pastoral care, and given the
availability of un-beneficed ministers, the legislature had every reason
and opportunity to open up new livings. The formation of new livings
automatically created smaller salaries. Moreover, after 1773 the poll tax
itself was no longer particularly secure. The settlement of 1773 was due
to expire in twelve years and the legislature would have been free in 1785
to arrange a diminished poll tax or even to allow the settlement to lapse
quietly.[2]

***

Land records and probate records may be used to supplement annual
income as indicators of clerical wealth. As individual measures of wealth
both of these sources are flawed and difficult to interpret. They cannot
be glibly transformed into precise tabulations of clerical wealth at
successive points in time. Next to annual income, however, land and
probate records are the best hard evidence available on the economic standing of the Anglican clergy. If they cannot be used to measure the exact
degree of change over time, they do demonstrate the general progress of
ministerial wealth.

---

[1] Arch. Md., LXII, 333-334, 450-451.

[2] In 1773 the Assembly had thought £200 currency (plus a glebe) a sufficient income for the ministers. Arch. Md., LXIII, 365. Jonathan Boucher
expressed the belief that the future outlook for the clergy was gloomy when
he wrote Dr. William Smith in 1774 that incomes would decrease because of a
rise in the cost of living and a decline in the value of currency, "added to
this that by thus being subjected to new-modelling and Reformation it ceases
to be an Establishment which, to me, seems to imply something fixed and
permanent." Boucher to Rev. Dr. William Smith, February 14, 1774, in
"Letters of Jonathan Boucher," Md. Hist. Mag., VIII (1913), 236.

Land was at once a producer, a product, and a symbol of wealth in
Maryland. Broad acres of good soil meant large crops of tobacco or grain,
meant ships filled with hogsheads, and, when the return was satisfactory,
meant a graceful, genteel life style. Maryland ministers, less dependent
on land for their immediate needs, were as charmed by this vision as anyone
else. They bought land for the same reasons, if perhaps not with the same
urgency, as other people did: to farm, as a speculative venture or an
investment, to bequeath to their children. Some clergymen, indeed, threw
themselves into estate building with such determination that one suspects
that their parishioners eventually respected them far more as successful
planters than as clergymen. Just over half of all the ministers owned land
in Maryland at some point in their careers.[1] As owners their control over
land was much more complete than it was as life tenants of the glebes.
Land held in fee simple could be carefully selected, sold at will, settled
on children, and, if suitable, embellished with buildings, fences, paths,
mills, and other improvements.[2] Glebes, even if large, did not seem to

---

[1] One hundred three ministers (and perhaps three more) are known to have
held land in Maryland.

The chief sources of information on landholding are the rent and debt
books (accounts kept to compute quitrents and other dues to the proprietor),
patent and warrant papers, chancery records, county and provincial court
deed books, and occasionally wills and other probate records. None of these
sources was kept perfectly nor have they all survived intact. They may all
be found in the MdA. For a description of the holdings of the archives,
consult Elizabeth Hartsook and Gust Skordas, Land Office and Prerogative
Records of Colonial Maryland (Baltimore, 1946).

[2] The greatest problem in dealing with the land records is that none of
the sources regularly gives information on the quality of the land or the
improvements on it. This omission is crucial. If a minister owned, for
example, 300 acres of prime tobacco land, complete with a gracious mansion,
numerous outhouses, and well-pruned orchards, how is his landholding to be
compared with that of a minister who owns 900 or 1,000 acres of marsh or
uncleared forest? Total acreage alone cannot categorize a minister as a
pauper or a rich man, though generally speaking a man with a thousand-acre
estate tended to be wealthier--enjoying a larger stipend, dying with a richer
inventory--than one with 300 or 400 acres.

enhance a minister's social status because everyone knew the acres did not
really belong to him, but land owned privately could and did raise a
clergyman's standing among his neighbors.

When ministers arrived in Maryland directly from Great Britain they
tended to be single and in depressed circumstances. The early immigrants
in particular were downright poor. Lacking liquid funds, they had to
borrow from the vestries in order to buy a horse or pay their board until
their salaries became due.[1] Starting out in debt, often confronting a
terrible tobacco market, many of them simply could not accumulate the
capital or secure the loans to invest rapidly in land, if at all. Only
eight of the immigrants of the 1690s are known to have acquired land
(forty percent of the group) and at least a third of these did not buy
property until they had been in the colony ten or more years.[2] Money was
not the only hindrance. Throughout the establishment period a minister
bought land as an act of settling down. Very rarely did a clergyman buy
land and then accept a living in another parish. Those who hoped or
intended to move to another living did not bother to encumber themselves
with real estate when they had the option of leasing.[3] The early ministers,
many of whom left the province in short order, obviously hesitated to invest

---

[1] Loans from vestries are noted in vestry records. See, for instance,
All Faith's Parish, St. Mary's County, Vestry Minutes, Liber A (1692-1720),
No. 12667, MdA, entry dated September 29, 1694, and St. George's Spesutia,
Baltimore County, Vestry Minutes, Volume I, (1718-1771), No. 12212, MdA,
entry dated June 21, 1726.

Ministers sometimes had to wait a long time before they received their
first salaries. The sheriff noted the number of taxables for the county
court held in November, informed the minister of the tobacco due in February,
and began paying it off at that time. If a minister arrived in a parish in,
say, January 1698, he might have had to wait until spring of 1699 for his
first payment.

[2] Dates or periods of first land acquisition are known for 73 out of
the 103 landowners.

[3] Because leasing agreements were rarely entered into deed books, the
extent of tenancy among the clergy cannot be established.

in land before they had made a firm commitment to stay in the area.

After 1700 a larger proportion of the ministers became landowners and they began to acquire the property in a shorter period of time. From 1700 through the 1750s between half and three-quarters of the men arriving each decade procured real estate. Most of them owned land within ten years of their arrival in Maryland and a substantial proportion of these acquired the land within five years after their arrival.[1] The ministers who came to Maryland in the 1760s and 1770s were less inclined than their predecessors to buy land soon after their disembarkation. Although the turbulent times may have had something to do with their reluctance to invest in real estate, a more likely explanation is that the ministers who had to spend years acting as curates and probationers because of the tight employment market did not want to buy land before they had achieved an induction into the living of their choice. Then, too, the land market in Maryland was tighter by the 1760s and 1770s than it was earlier.

Buying land, of course, was not the only means of acquiring it, though that method was the most common. Land could be inherited and it could be received as a dowry payment or as a gift. About ten of the Maryland native ministers appear to have inherited land from relations and the properties were usually large, most commonly about five hundred acres. Henry Addison is the prime example of a minister whose inheritance alone made him a land-rich man, for his father, Colonel Thomas Addison, left his third son 2,136 acres of fine land in Prince George's and Frederick counties. Scions of other distinguished or wealthy families, such as Thomas John Claggett, Matthias Harris, and Jeremiah Berry, received less impressive but no less

---

[1] The date or period of first land acquisition is known for 66 men out of the 96 who bought land after 1700. Thirty of these became landowners in under five years; 21 more between five and ten years. The rapidity with which land was acquired appears to have changed greatly in the 1720s--witness to the escalating incomes which permitted such expenditures.

useful bequests from their parents. Advantageous marriages, though,
facilitated estate-building for a larger number of ministers. Maryland
wives sometimes brought land into the marriage as a dowry or as personally-
owned property, and this land was occasionally supplemented by subsequent
family inheritances and gifts. The nature of the Maryland land records and
complicated genealogical lines inhibit research into the question of how
often marriages brought land endowments, but it is unquestionably true
that such endowments were not infrequent and that they were sometimes large.
A good marriage to a propertied woman was a splendid means of starting to
build an estate or extending a small one. Jacob Henderson and Henry Hall,
for instance, two of the most land-wealthy ministers in the province,
married a widow and a widowed daughter, respectively, of planter Mareen
Duvall of Prince George's County during the early decades of the eighteenth
century. Henderson's wife, twice-widowed, brought 811 acres into the
marriage (her bridegroom apparently did not own land), and Hall's wife
brought him 450 acres.[1] Both of these men eventually accumulated estates
of over three thousand acres. As did the ministers who bought land, those
who became landowners through inheritance or marriage tended to remain in
the area in which the property was located. If they held livings outside
the vicinity of the land they received, clergymen pressured the governor
for a transfer or accepted curacies near their property while awaiting a
fortuitous vacancy.

Of the 103 known landowners, seven clergymen managed to put together

---

[1] These figures are compiled from deed, debt, and rent books. Hall's
wife may have brought only 350 acres instead of 450; the information is
ambiguous.

estates of over two thousand acres.[1]   At least three of these men owed

their initial success to land received by way of inheritance or judicious

marriage.[2]   Length of tenure was also a factor, for none of these men

served less than twenty years in the colony and almost all of them took

that long to build their estates out to their widest extent. Geograph-

cally, the very large clerical estates tended to be located on the

Western Shore in Prince George's, Frederick, and Anne Arundel counties. The

land-rich ministers did not belong to any particular generation of

immigrants; one (at most two) future land magnates arrived just about every

decade from the beginning through the 1740s.[3]

A fifth of the landholding clergy (twenty-two men, or about eleven

percent of the entire ministry) were substantial landowners whose estates

peaked at between a thousand and two thousand acres. Typically, these men

were the aging aristocrats of the profession, men who had served at least

ten years in Maryland, generally in the better parishes. Another fifth

(twenty-three men, or about twelve percent of the whole) acquired estates

of five hundred to a thousand acres. A full half of the landholders (about

twenty-seven percent of all ministers) owned more modest holdings of up to

five hundred acres. These were not necessarily clergy who could not afford

to buy more property. The group includes ministers who preferred to live

---

[1] The figures given here and later for total acreage are for the
estates measured at the time they extended most widely, not for acreage at
death. In the vast majority of cases the total acreage at death was the
same as at the time of widest extent.

The land-rich ministers were: Henry Hall (3,263 acres plus lots),
Jacob Henderson (412 acres at death; 4,170 acres at his peak), James
Robertson (2,663 acres), Alexander Adams (2,192 acres at death; 4,229 acres
at his peak), John Urquehart (3,065 acres), Henry Addison (5,090 acres plus
lots at the Revolution), and John Eversfield, worth 1,346 acres at the
Revolution but a man who had bought at least 4,110 acres and had given the
bulk to his children.

[2] Addison, Henderson, Hall.

[3] The ministers who arrived in the 1750s, 1760s, and 1770s did not
include any men with 2,000 acres or more previous to the Revolution.

Landownership
at Death, Removal Out of Maryland, or the Revolution

Period	Number of Ministers	Total Known Landowners	ACRES						Landowner, but Acreage Unknown
			1-99	100-499	500-999	1,000-1,499	1,500-1,999	2,000 and up	
1690-1699	10	2		1	1				
1700-1709	17	6		4	1	1			
1710-1719	12	5	1	2					2
1720-1729	10	5		2	1	1		1	
1730-1739	17	9	2	5	2				
1740-1749	21	12		3	4	3	1	1	
1750-1759	14	6		1	3	2			
1760-1769	24	17		8	2	4		2	1
1770-1776	68	39	2	16	10	10		1	
Total	193	101*	5	42	24	21	1	5	3

Landownership
at Death, Removal Out of Maryland, or the Revolution
by Decade of Arrival in the Province

Period	Total Arrivals	Total Known Landowners	ACRES						Landowner, but Acreage Unknown
			1-99	100-499	500-999	1,000-1,499	1,500-1,999	2,000 and up	
Pre-1690	5	3		1	1	1			
1690-1699	20	6		3	1	1		1	
1700-1709	21	13	1	6	2	1		1	2
1710-1719	18	10		5	3	2			
1720-1729	18	12	2	1	3	4	1	1	
1730-1739	21	12		6	3	2		1	
1740-1749	22	15		4	6	4		1	
1750-1759	17	11		7	2	1			1
1760-1769	33	15	2	8	1	4			
1770-1776	18	4		1	2	1			
Total	193	101*	5	42	24	21	1	5	3

*Two ministers who were landowners are not included in this table because they lost their land prior to death. They both came to Maryland during the 1690s.

in towns and those who had no interest in running a farm or a plantation.[1]

The probate records underscore the same trends evinced by the annual income rates and the land papers: a great range in wealth right from the beginning of the establishment, and impressive financial gains by the late 1720s and the 1730s which continued until the end of the period.[2]

---

[1] These figures include only estates in Maryland. Several of the ministers owned land outside of the province which, added to their Maryland estates, would have raised them into a higher category of landownership; I have chosen to ignore extra-provincial holdings since in too many cases the extent of ownership cannot be ascertained.

Except for the year 1775, I have not tried to establish annual clerical landholding in order to find out if the mean estate grew with time. I think, though, that without question it did. In 1775, 27 of the 49 ministers owned land and the average estate was 858 acres (minus Addison's enormous holdings, the mean drops to 696 acres). The median was 725 acres. Nine of the 27 owned over a thousand acres.

[2] The probate records used in this section include inventories, estate accounts, and balances of payment records, all of them available at the Hall of Records in Annapolis, Md. Inventories were taken of estates shortly after an owner's death by two court-appointed assessors, a relative of the deceased, and the chief creditor. A list was made of all moveable property owned by the deceased and the value of each item was estimated at what it would bring at a forced sale. Most inventories were followed by accounts and/or balances, in which the estate administrators explained to the county court how the estate had been settled: what debts had been paid out, what debtors to the deceased had paid in, and how much was left to distribute to the heirs. There are problems in dealing with these records. First, estates which do not include an account or a balance sheet, listing the debts (if any) of the deceased, cannot be used as I have done the calculations here; the figures listed in this study for estate values are the totals remaining after deductions for debts and claims. Secondly, there is the problem of determining how representative inventoried and accounted estates are of the whole decedent group. One hundred seventeen ministers altogether died in Maryland from 1692 through 1775; usable records for only 67 of them (57%) are available. (Note: only one of the 13 men who died during the 1770s left a usable estate record. If these 13 are excluded from the total of 117, the rate of inventoried and accounted estates as part of the whole decedent population jumps to 63%.) Because the uninventoried estates seem to be those of men who cannot be expected to have been among the wealthier clergy (this impression is based on the land records, income estimates and tenure rates) the results noted here may well be biased upwards. Thirdly, there is the problem of dealing with comparison of estate values over time. Somehow inflation must be taken into account. The St. Mary's City Commission, in Annapolis, Maryland, is currently working on this problem and I have made notes when I have used information supplied by the Commission. I am grateful to Lois Carr in particular for her help.

For information on the problems in dealing with probate material, see

More than a fifth of the inventoried decedents died in debt, owning
little moveable property not only because their salaries were low but because
they did not live very long. Average length of tenure at death for the
inventoried decedents from 1700 to 1710 was 6.5 years, and the mean was 7.7
years the following decade. Not surprisingly, the richer ministers tended
to be those who survived longest. Still, the sheer range in ministerial
wealth is notable. The richest minister (who also was the decedent with
the longest tenure) for this period was worth £522 at death, and the poorest
died after four years in Maryland in debt to the tune of £216.[1]

In 1722 Henry Hall died after twenty-four years in Maryland, the first
of the ministers to be worth in excess of £1,000 after his debts were paid.
Not only was he a rich man (his estate came to approximately £1,520), but
he was one of the very largest clerical landholders, owning 3,263 acres.[2]
Hall was a member of the premier group of Maryland clergy, the top five or
six percent who combined landholdings of over a thousand acres with

Gloria Lund Main, "Measuring Wealth and Welfare: Explorations in the Use
of Probate Records from Colonial Maryland and Massachusetts, 1650-1750,"
(Ph.D. diss., Columbia University, 1973). For Maryland studies which have
used probate material to study wealth distribution, see Russell R. Menard,
P.M.G. Harris, and Lois Green Carr, "Opportunity and Inequality: The
Distribution of Wealth on the Lower Western Shore of Maryland, 1638-1705,"
Md. Hist. Mag., LXIX (1974), 169-184; Aubrey C. Land, "Economic Base and
Social Structure: The Northern Chesapeake in the Eighteenth Century,"
Journal of Economic History, XXV (1965), 639-654; and Land, "Economic
Behavior in a Planting Society: The Eighteenth Century Chesapeake,"
Journal of Southern History, XXXIII (1967), 469-485.

[1] John Lillingston, who had served in Maryland as a minister for some
time before the establishment, died in 1709 worth £521. He also owned at
least a thousand acres of land. The poorest minister was Robert Baron.
The average estate of 1700-1710 (using eight inventoried estates out of a
possible eleven decedents) was £122, though excluding Lillingston's estate
the mean drops to £65. The mean value for the 1710s (9 out of 12 reporting)
was £33. The ministers did not exaggerate in their reports to London.

[2] Though a final balances of distribution for Hall's estate is not
extant (which is why the estate is not included on the table on the following page), the available material does indicate that charges against the
estate would not have exceeded a third of the original inventory value.

moveable estates of over £1,000. Large personalty estates almost without exception went with large landed estates, though the reverse was not so unexceptionally true. These very wealthy decedents had several traits in common: they usually owned land in the lower or middle Western Shore, and in almost all cases they had served in Maryland for twenty years or more.[1]

Although most ministers were not nearly as wealthy as the small group at the top, the estate accounts from the 1720s on indicate that the clergy were becoming progressively better off. The mean estate of the 1730s was worth £210, that of the 1750s, £779, and during the 1760s, the mean value of the thirteen inventoried estates (out of twenty-two decedents) was an incredible £1,177. Even taking into consideration the fact that if the values of the uninventoried estates were known the averages would in all liklihood be quite a bit lower, the contrast between the 1760s--when six decedents were worth over £1,000--and the early years of the establishment is striking. When the mean for the 1760s is deflated to allow for the rise in the cost of living, the result (£726) is still almost six times higher than the mean for the 1700s.[2]

Bondservants and slaves were major property items. All told, seventy-four ministers (thirty-eight percent of the entire clergy and seventy-two percent of inventoried estates) are known to have owned slaves at one time

[1] The men who combined landed estates of over 1,000 acres with inventory evaluations of over £1,000 numbered about 12, or 6% of all the clergy (10% total decedents). Due to the gaps in the probate and the land records an exact count is not possible; there may be about five more of them, at a guess. Estates of over £1,000 constituted 16% of the inventoried estates.

[2] Deflated to a base of 1722, the mean for the 1730s was £167, for the 1750s, £496, and for the 1760s, £726. A mean for the 1770s cannot be calculated because almost all estates from these years lack accounts and/or balances. These figures are in Maryland currency. The deflated means are calculated using an index computed for the lower Western Shore by the St. Mary's City Commission, furnished to me by Lois Green Carr. Any errors which may have been made in the calculations are, though, my own.

Inventoried Estates

by Decade of Death*

Decade of Death	Total Deaths	Usable Inventories	INVENTORIED ESTATE £				Mean Tenure at Death, in Years
			Highest Valued Estate of Period	Lowest Valued Estate of Period	Mean Value	Real Mean Value**	
1690–1699	5	1	--	--	--	--	--
1700–1709	11	8	521	-7	122	122	6.5
1710–1719	12	9	230	-216	33	33	7.7
1720–1729	7	5	705	-0.5	542	531	19.4
1730–1739	14	11	1,200	-53	210	167	16.7
1740–1749	21	11	1,985	-250	443	307	13.5
1750–1759	12	8	2,497	-13	779	496	15.4
1760–1769	22	13	5,543	-41	1,177	726	21.7
1770–1776	13	1	--	--	--	--	--

*The figures are in sterling until 1720, in currency thereafter. Debts and charges against the estates have been deducted.

**The real values of the estates are deflated to a base of 1722, using an inflation index computed for the lower Western Shore.

during their residence in Maryland.[1] Thirty-two clergymen had bondservants working for them at the time of their deaths or the Revolution, and of these, twenty-four were also slaveholders. Almost half of the slaveowning clergy (thirty-five out of seventy-three) had five or fewer slaves; approximately sixteen percent of them held six to ten slaves, eleven percent held eleven to fifteen, and eighteen percent owned more than fifteen slaves.[2]

Over time both the incidence of slaveholding among the decedents and the average number of slaves held by such men increased. Only a third of the estates inventoried from 1700-1709 contained slaves at all, and these estates averaged 3.3 slaves each. From the 1710s on, routinely sixty to eighty percent of the inventoried decedents owned slaves and the number of slaves per slaveowning decedent climbed and remained high: to 13.7 slaves each during the 1740s, and 11.8 slaves during the 1760s. Bondservants, on the other hand, were much more common before the 1740s than they were afterwards.

Financially, the Maryland Church became enormously successful. The evolution of an affluent clergy was an important development--perhaps the decisive one--in the history of the Church. The salaries available to provincial ministers influenced to a considerable extent who and how many joined the institution. Employment opportunities were largely determined

---

[1] Seventy-two percent of the inventoried ministers owned slaves. I have included in the total number of slaveowners (74 men) all those men who mention slaves in their wills, their correspondence, deeds, and in their reports to the British Audit Office. The actual number of slaveholders was undoubtedly larger than the figure given here, for there must have been uninventoried clergymen who owned slaves and many of those alive at the Revolution owned them, too, but left no record of ownership.

[2] Of the 74 slaveowners, five men are known to have held some slaves but the tallies are not known.

by the remuneration offered to ministers at any given time, contracting as salaries rose. The organizational structure of the Church was affected by clerical wealth, for the generation of all three types of curacies was a result of or was made possible by economic conditions within the ministry. The financial status of the clergy at different periods influenced their social standing and, of course, their style of living. Parochial relations were affected by clerical wealth, too, and so were relations between the Church and the state. Ultimately, the disestablishment of the Church was received with the approbation of the general public not only for ideological or political reasons, but because it abolished the burdensome poll tax and because it eliminated the possibility that ministers would continue to grow rich at the expense of other, poorer men.

Chapter VI

The Clergy in Society

Families

"The Clergy generally come single into the Province," Jacob Henderson

observed in 1731, noting one of the most conspicuous demographic traits of

the group.[1] As a former bachelor immigrant himself, the commissary could

have testified from experience that youth and modest financial circumstances

were the primary reasons for the unmarried condition of so many of the

incoming clergy.[2] Ministers who elected to serve in Maryland were typically

young men in their twenties who had been ordained only a short period before

they set sail for America.[3] Many were recent university students or had

served in menial positions as tutors, clerks, or deacons, occupations

without sufficient remuneration to have encouraged them to contemplate

marriage. Ministers who came to Maryland at a more advanced age were more

likely to have wives and children, but here again a remarkable proportion of

them seem to have been men who never married or were widowers.[4] The objections

---

[1] Henderson, Fifth Letter to Dulany, 24.

[2] Because information on dates of marriage is sparse, the exact number of
ministers who arrived in Maryland as bachelors cannot be ascertained. Using
all the information available, I estimate that not many more than 20 men
(about 10% of the whole group) had living wives when they came to Maryland.

[3] Canon law prohibited ordination before the age of 24, and although
some clergy were ordained at a younger age (particularly during the early
decades) most men were at least 24 when they came to Maryland. The approximate birthdates for about 84% (162) of all the clergy can be determined.
Over half of these, and perhaps about two-thirds of all 193 ministers, were
under 30 years of age when they arrived in the colony.

[4] Of the 162 ministers whose birthdates may be reasonably gauged, 54
(33%) were in their thirties at the time of their arrival. I think that
something over a quarter of all ministers were in this age bracket when they
came. Ten percent of the 162 ministers, and probably about the same proportion of the whole group, were over 40 when they took their first living
in Maryland.

of their wives, concern for the safety of their families, and the high
cost of moving must have deterred most married ministers from deciding
to make the trip to Maryland.[1] Native men thinking of going to England
for ordination had to consider what would happen to their families should
they themselves die during the long voyage. Some men accepted the risks,
but most applicants for Maryland parishes came or returned unmarried.[2]

The majority of the ministers eventually acquired wives.[3] Prying,
prattling neighbors could make life awkward for a bachelor minister, and
besides, a proper wife was a professional and social asset. Clergymen were
well-advised to marry respectably and to marry brilliantly if they could.
The wife of the minister was a highly visible figure in the community: she
sat in the minister's special pew on Sundays, entertained her husband's
friends and colleagues, and lent her house for church-related social
gatherings such as weddings and vestry meetings. Whether she was the
mistress of a tiny parsonage or a substantial plantation, it was important
for her husband's career that she be worthy of the respect of his congregation. Marriage with a woman from a good family, moreover, was one of the
fastest, surest means of moving ahead socially. However much ministers

---

[1] The problems ministers encountered persuading their wives to come
with them have been discussed in Chapter III, p. 113-114.

[2] Some of the early clergymen left their wives and families in Britain,
either planning to return to Britain after a few years or hoping to bring
them to Maryland after they had been given a parish and could provide a
place to live. How many ministers did this is unknown, but they were
probably only a few and in all likelihood they were S.P.G. ministers who
could leave their families part of their ₤50 stipend. The best documented
case of this sort is that of Robert Keith (see his memorials in the S.P.G.
Papers in the Lambeth Palace Library, "Maryland," Volume XII, fols. 52-59).

[3] Using admittedly incomplete information, roughly about 15% of the
clergy did not have wives at any time during the period they served in Maryland. These men were primarily those among the early arrivals who died quickl
or left the colony in short order, and those who came around the period
of the Revolution and who did not marry prior to November 1776.

claimed that the act of ordination raised all of them--regardless of
their individual origin, education, or character--to the rank of gentlemen,
they knew very well that the right to wear an unusual collar did not
guarantee that their parishioners would regard them in that light. Too
many incompetents and profligates were in the Church, too many critical
dissenters, deists, and skeptics were outside. Marriage into a family with
breeding, money, and connections helped a minister to skirt the touchy
question of clerical gentility by enabling him to support his claim with
evidence more convincing to most people than an episcopalian ceremony. To
a minister in humble circumstances a good marriage was a quick boost up
the social ladder; to one who was in his own right a member of the gentry,
a fine match provided, at the very least, useful in-laws.

From the first a share of the Anglican clergy married into the
families who composed the upper class in Maryland. Drawing their wealth
primarily from their estates or their mercantile activities, these gentry
families dominated the economic and political hierarchies in the counties.
With time they became increasingly exclusive and inbred.[1] Some ministers,
however, still managed to marry women from prominent families. At the
very least about fifteen percent of all the ministers did so.[2] Early

---

[1] A discussion of social class in Maryland may be found in Aubrey C.
Land, "Economic Behavior in a Planting Society: The Eighteenth-Century
Chesapeake," Journal of Southern History, XXXIII (1967), 469-485; Land,
"Economic Base and Social Structure: The Northern Chesapeake in the
Eighteenth Century," Journal of Economic History, XXV (1965), 639-654; the
changes in the society of one county are explored by Allan Kulikoff,
"Tobacco and Slaves: Population, Economy, and Society in Eighteenth
Century Prince George's County, Maryland," (Ph.D. diss., 1976, Brandeis
University).

[2] Twenty-five clergymen are known to have married into families whose
wealth, prominence, and service to the colony indicate that they were
members of the gentry class. Since genealogical records in Maryland are
disappointingly few it is probable that there were a good many more
ministers who made fine matches--perhaps up to a quarter of the total.
The percentage of prominent marriages among the clergy would have been
higher had the Revolution not disrupted the Church.

clergymen married into the Duvalls, the Tylers, the Hynsons, the Claggetts.
Their successors became relatives of the Addisons, the Dulanys, the
Goldsboroughs, the Hoopers. By no means were the men who married well-
connected and sometimes wealthy women themselves necessarily members of the
social or economic elite of the clergy. In many instances immigrant
clergymen of undistinguished parentage, mediocre fortunes, and limited
prospects married women greatly above their own stations. The contrasts
between the relative social and economic positions of husband and wife were
particularly apparent during the early decades of the establishment. As
the fortunes and the prospects of the ministers improved during later years
the differences became less pronounced, and as native gentry entered the
ministry, more marriages with upper class women were unions between social
equals. Nonetheless, right up to the Revolution immigrant and lower class
ministers, unlike most of their non-clerical cohorts, were able to marry
women from the very pinnacle of Maryland society.[1]

Who the ministers married when they did not take well-connected wives
is not really known.[2] Several of them married the widows or the children
of other clergymen, some married the daughters of doctors, lawyers, or
merchants. Most of them, however, probably married the daughters of their

---

[1] Jonathan Boucher, for instance, the son of an alehousekeeper and
schoolmaster, married Eleanor Addison, daughter of John Addison and a
relative of Walter Dulany, in 1772. Boucher estimated her fortune at £2,500
sterling, two and a half times his own. Boucher, Reminiscences, 77, 91.
His contemporary John Montgomery, before ordination a poor tutor in Pennsylvania, married a daughter of Walter Dulany at about the same time, and
Hugh Neill, who had also tutored for his living before ordination, married
Henrietta Hooper, daughter of the speaker of the general assembly, during
the 1760s.

[2] Though parish clerks were supposed to keep accurate birth, death,
and marriage records for all local inhabitants, many of them were very lax.
A large percentage of the vital records has been lost. The genealogies of
the most prominent families, of course, are the ones most thoroughly
researched, but when ministers married outside of the upper gentry class
usually nothing or very little is known about their wives.

most ubiquitous neighbors, the small or medium-sized planters and farmers.[1]

When the first ministers came to Maryland the only ties they had to one another were those of profession and sometimes of friendship. Within twenty years ties of blood and marriage connected a few families. Within fifty years family ties crisscrossed the parishes, and by the Revolution, after two or even three generations of intermarriage and inbreeding, complex kinship relationships bound many clerical families. Of all the ministers who served in Maryland during the 1760s and 1770s, almost a third (twenty-eight out of eighty-seven) were related to at least one other living clergy-man.[2] Though ministers occasionally married widows of other Maryland clergy (four did so), and sometimes the daughters of their colleagues (at least another four), kinship between immigrant clergy generally came through the families of their wives or through the marriages of their respective offspring. Many native clergy were related to each other by both blood and marriage. Maryland-born ministers were usually the ones with the most extensive links to other clergymen. Thomas John Claggett, to cite a some-what extraordinary example, was a second generation clergyman who could claim kinship with at least eight living ministers in the years just prior to the Revolution.[3] Two or three relations in the profession were the more

---

[1] Thomas Chase and Thomas Fletcher married daughters of Thomas Walker, who kept an ordinary in Somerset County, but they are the only ministers known positively to have married into a family of that class. Walker, though, was a prosperous man.

[2] That is, a clergyman who was alive during some portion of the other's tenure.

[3] Claggett was related to natives Richard Brown, Samuel Keene, Jeremiah Berry, John Scott (from Virginia), and Edward Gantt, and to immigrants Isaac Campbell, John Eversfield, and Joseph Threlkild.

usual number.[1] Had the Revolution not occurred it is quite conceivable
that the livings in some areas would have become the prerogatives of a
small circle of related, clergy-producing gentry families.[2]

Like most of their contemporaries ministers tended to produce large
families. Five to eight children were not an unusual total.[3] What became
of these children depended to a considerable extent on the status and
wealth of their parents, for during the eighteenth century Maryland society
became increasingly stratified and access to the upper class more difficult.[4]
Like their parents, the children of clergymen were not uniformly of one
social class or economic bracket. Well-born ministers, ministers who
married prominent gentlewomen, and those who made fortunes enabled their
children to take a place in the upper ranks of society. Clergymen who
failed to provide their offspring with estates or useful relations were

---

[1] The genealogical ties between ministers were unbelievably complex;
English lacks the terms to describe some of the relationships. Multiple
marriages were not unusual (about 12% of the clergy--24 men--are known to
have married at least twice previous to the Revolution, and this figure is
probably far short of the actual count) and they often married once, twice,
and even three times widowed women, thus providing themselves with a
gallery of relations in up to dozens of families. Their households were
sometimes filled with children sporting three or four last names. Tangled
and extensive kinship connections were not, of course, peculiar to the
ministers but were a phenomenon of the period engendered by a variety of
demographic, social, and economic causes. These have been discussed in
Kulikoff, "Tobacco and Slaves," Chapter 10. Because the gentry class, at
least in the lower counties of the Western Shore, was very tightly knit
by mid-century, immigrant clergy who married into it could be quickly
integrated into their neighborhood society.

[2] By the 1770s this development is already perceptible in a few
counties, particularly those on the lower Western Shore.

[3] Kulikoff estimates 7 to 7.5 children per marriage on the average for
the lower Western Shore during the eighteenth century. Kulikoff, "Tobacco
and Slaves," Chapter 3. I have obtained information on the minimum number
of children produced by 79 ministers and find that of these, 30 produced
5 or more children. This information is given here only to bolster the
statement made in the text and should not be regarded as a hard statistic.

[4] The decline in opportunity in Maryland is a major theme in Kulikoff,
"Tobacco and Slaves," and is also dealt with in Menard, "Economy and
Society," 415-449.

likely to condemn the males to lives as poor planters, tenant farmers,
tradesmen, or teachers, while their daughters could hardly hope to marry
any better.[1] The plight of underaged, fatherless (sometimes orphaned)
children of impoverished ministers, forced to evacuate the parsonage or
glebe, was extreme.[2] Such distress, however, was more common during the
early part of the century than it was later on. By mid-century most
children could count on some patrimony, whether lands, slaves, or money,
and many of those who had reached their majority or had married had already
been given part of their inheritance. What they received from their fathers
made a few of the sons large landowners and wealthy men, but more often
the division of the estate reduced the holdings of the children to a more
modest size.

Few of the children of the Anglican clergy sought an education more
advanced or more specialized than they could receive at home from their
fathers. Only about ten percent of the clergy are known to have sent a
son into one of the professions.[3]

In general the ministers were more prominent in the communities than

---

[1] The children of deceased clergymen could, though, receive a boost
if their mothers remarried wisely.

[2] The arrangements made by some clergy to ameliorate one such case is
mentioned on p. 188. During 1769 and 1770 the clergy discussed forming an
incorporated society for the support of the widows and children of deceased
clergymen. Such an organization already existed in England, and Anglican
ministers in other colonies were interested in the same project. By this
time, though, the clergy in Maryland needed it less than any of their
colleagues.

Some widows and children--the number is not known--returned to
Britain.

[3] Most of these sons became clergymen themselves. I have not systematically researched what became of the numerous children of so many clergy,
although I have noted the fates of those who turned up in the course of my
research. Most of the children seem to have remained on their paternal
estates as planters. What became of those who had nothing to inherit is
frankly not known. A mariner, a hatter, a grocer, and at least one draper
were sons of ministers with small or mediocre fortunes.

their sons were. The exceptions were those sons who combined landholding
and/or a profession with public officeholding. Thirteen sons of twelve
ministers became legislators in the Maryland general assembly before the
end of the Revolution. Some, such as Henry Hall, Alexander Williamson,
and Samuel Chase, were important men on a province-wide scale. Williamson
became speaker of the house, in fact. Sons of clergymen became quorum
justices, justices of the peace, sheriffs, vestrymen, county clerks, tobacco
inspectors, and coroners.[1] In the best gentry tradition a few held multiple
posts, such as Jeremiah and Jonathan Nichols, sons of Henry Nichols, who
were justices and high sheriffs for Talbot and Queen Anne's counties,
respectively, or James Hindman's son, Jacob, a legislator and high sheriff
of Talbot County.[2]

Parochial Relations

Ministers encountered the bulk of their parishioners most regularly
during worship services held in the local churches and chapels.[3] Scheduled
at intervals ranging from a week to a month, depending on the parish, these
meetings were both social and religious gatherings. Often several hundred

[1] Under the directorship of Edward C. Papenfuse, the Legislative History
Project in Annapolis, Maryland, has collected the names of the colonial
legislators of that province. These have been published in Edward Papenfuse,
David W. Jordan, Carol P. Tilles, Directory of Maryland Legislators 1635-1789
(1974). The staff has also researched the genealogies of the delegates,
and Dr. Papenfuse kindly permitted me to use their files. Archivists in
the Hall of Records in Annapolis are currently compiling a list of civil
officeholders in Maryland ("Master Index to the Personnel of Provincial,
State, and Local Government"). I was given permission to see the list, for
which I am grateful. It is not complete, with the result that my own list
of ministers' sons who held office is also incomplete. I have found, however,
18 sons of 15 ministers who held an office of public trust.

[2] The examples offered here for sons who held several offices do not
by any means exhaust the list.

[3] For reasons of necessity or convenience services were sometimes held
in courthouses, private homes, and in the open air, but services in the
buildings built for that purpose were most common.

people crowded into the pews and galleries and even spilled out the front door into the churchyard. Dressed traditionally in their best, they came to preen, to gossip, and to chat with their neighbors as well as to take communion and to hear a sermon.[1] Genial and prudent ministers did not waste the chance to mingle, either. From the point of view of a conscientious worshipper, though, socializing at the church was of secondary importance. The primary reasons for meeting together were religious ones: to praise God with prayer and song in the fellowship of other Christians, to reaffirm the faith by participating in its rituals and ceremonies, and to be instructed and enlightened by means of lessons and sermons. In all of these activities the ministers were the organizers, directors, and chief actors.[2] For a few hours every week they commanded the bodies if not the attention of the people given into their charge.

Except when periodic sacramental celebrations were performed, the sermon was the central event during a service. As set down in the Book of Common Prayer the episcopal litany prescribed much of what was ordinarily said and done in the churches, and the sermon was the main vehicle of clerical individuality. It was also by far the most popular part of the meeting. Ministers built their reputations on the caliber of their preaching. Most, after all, could be relied on to perform the rites and to read the litany with some competence and dignity, but the man who could preach with eloquence and persuasiveness and love was the one who became, as one

---

[1] The government recognized that the meetings provided an excellent opportunity for dispensing news and information of general interest. The legislature often ordered public announcements nailed to the church doors (see, for instance, Arch. Md., XIX, 305), and ministers were ordered to read proclamations and new laws.

[2] Some ministers, however, permitted lay readers or the parish clerk to read the Scripture lessons and the homilies.

congregation put it, "the darling of his flock."[1] For many parishioners
sermons were the most accessible form of intellectual stimulation and it
seems that quite a few were highly critical listeners. Correspondents
discussed the style and the content of the sermons they heard, evaluating
the merit of the work and the author.[2] The outstanding sermons of popular
preachers were sometimes published at the request of their parishioners or
the legislature.[3] Ministers who wrote well-received works on matters of
immediate or general interest, and those who made a specialty of preaching
on a particular topic, were invited to deliver sermons to congregations
outside of their own parishes. Dull, obtuse, and unlettered clergymen, on
the other hand, were liable to drive their congregations into the churches
of a neighboring parish, or, what was far worse, into the churches of a
different sect.

Sermons composed by approximately seventeen ministers are still available.[4] All but one of them date after 1749. Even though these are but a

---

[1] From the tombstone of Leigh Massey, at the Poplar Hill Church in
William and Mary Parish in St. Mary's County.

[2] An example of this type of commentary may be found in letters from
Stephen Bordley to Matthias Harris, September 3, 1740, and October 18,
1740, in the Stephen Bordley Letterbooks, Volume II, MS. 81, MdHi.

[3] When the legislature ordered a sermon printed it was generally one
which had been preached to them by their chaplain, who was usually the
incumbent of St. Anne's in Annapolis.

[4] The majority of the sermons which have survived are kept in the
Vertical File of the MdDL. The collection of sermons by Thomas Cradock
is extensive--about 100 pieces--and will be the subject of a forthcoming
book by David C. Skaggs. Aside from Cradock, about ten sermons by Thomas
Chase are available and less than twenty represent the work of the other
ministers. Since the authors of some of the sermons are in doubt, the
exact number of contributors cannot be determined. A list of almost all
the known published sermons may be found in Lawrence C. Wroth, A History
of Printing in Colonial Maryland 1696-1776 (Baltimore, 1922). Few of
them have survived.

poor indication of what was said in the pulpits across Maryland, they suffice to suggest some common themes and concerns. Since the collection includes sermons in a range of styles and quality, furthermore, it affords a glimpse of the professional abilities of the men who staffed the Anglican Church towards the end of the colonial era.

When a minister stepped up to his pulpit, sermon in hand, his congregation could anticipate a lecture which normally lasted for about an hour.[1] In most cases the sermon was read verbatim from a prepared text.[2] The Anglican clergy, fond of strictly organized sermons replete with Scriptural quotations and punctuated with references to classical authors and orthodox divines, apparently scorned to speak extemporaneously from the pulpit--a practice they probably would have thought reeked of enthusiasm. All the extant sermons were composed by the ministers themselves, though there is evidence that some clergymen occasionally read published works.[3] Almost every one of the manuscript sermons includes a memo noting the date and the place it was delivered. Many of them were preached again and again, sometimes in different locations but often in the same church. Thomas Chase, for one, had a repertoire of sermons which he periodically worked through in St. Paul's in Baltimore County.

---

[1] Thomas Cradock wrote many sermons of under ten handwritten, half-quarto sized pages, but the other sermons are usually between 15 and 25 pages in length. Sermons could reach up to 50 printed pages.

[2] Some ministers may, of course, have memorized their sermons or spoken from notes. However, the length of the available manuscripts, the care with which they were usually transcribed, the fact that many sermons were sewn together to form books, easily portable, and the condition of the MSS., indicate that they were read.

[3] Reading published sermons was not an unusual practice in the English Church. Many Maryland clergy avidly collected published lectures, and Jonathan Boucher (Reminiscences, 120) specifically notes he thought his curate copied a sermon by Benjamin Hoadly.

Robert Reade was so fond of his Good Friday lecture that he gave it
repeatedly to one congregation, and other ministers considered their efforts
worth several hearings.[1] As sermons were often written in cycles around a
collective topic, congregations served by clergymen who preferred not to
overtax their own ingenuity must have been able to predict the topic of
many a Sunday's sermon.[2]

The sermons preached by the Anglicans in Maryland during the third
quarter of the eighteenth century were typical of the period and characteristic of the church of the "via media," the cherished "middle way."[3]
Intellectually very conservative for most of the century, the Church was
not receptive to criticism from within, and ministers were not encouraged
to be innovative thinkers. Complacency (a characteristic of the Hanoverian
church) and a reluctance to precipitate religious controversy stifled
theological creativity. Taught to embellish accepted doctrine rather than
to examine it, the clergy produced sermons which copied the themes and
arguments put forward in the readily-available books and pamphlets of the
Church's leading theologians. The Maryland ministers did the same.
Generally trained in Britain or by Britons, the colonial clergy remained

---

[1] Chase read some of his sermons over a period of thirty years. His
sermons and that of Robert Reade may be found in the Vertical File, MdDL.

[2] The ministers were not always free to choose their own subject
matter. The ecclesiastical calendar, with its round of feast days and
celebrations, indicated appropriate topics for certain seasonal services.
At times the Maryland government ordered the clergy to observe special
occasions, such as fast days, thanksgiving days, or important national
anniversaries, with suitable lectures. Sermons aimed at distinctive groups,
the assembly or the Freemasons, for instance, were written to fit the
audience.

[3] For Anglican theology during the 18th century, see Norman Sykes,
From Sheldon to Secker: Aspects of English Church History 1660-1768
(Cambridge, 1959), 140-187; Sykes, Church and State, 231-283; Roland N.
Stromberg, Religious Liberalism in Eighteenth-Century England (London,
1954): C. R. Cragg, From Puritanism to the Age of Reason (Cambridge, 1950);
and G. R. Cragg, The Church and the Age of Reason (New York, 1961).

curiously unaffected by what was, for most of them, a novel and alien environment. In style and content the sermons preached from the Maryland pulpits were almost indistinguishable from those read to audiences in England and Ireland.

Optimistic rationalism and Latitudinarianism were the major intellectual trends in Anglicanism at this time, and they are unmistakably present in the sermons composed in Maryland. Rationalism, with roots in Locke's empiricism, Newton's scientific discoveries, and the works of the Cambridge Platonists, stressed the perfect compatibility of reason and religion. Far from challenging religious tenets, reason was held to be the best defender of them. Rationalists thought that man was endowed with the ability to discern from natural phenomena that the universe was an orderly structure designed by a benevolent diety. If God's revelation of himself in the Bible sometimes transcended nature, most of what was declared in Scriptures could be proved by right reason. Men were invited to examine the teachings of the faith themselves, for, as Thomas Cradock assured his Maryland congregation, truth would bear up to scrutiny.[1] The clergy were convinced that their particular variety of Christianity was best because it above all others could stand proof against a rational investigation. While urging parishioners to analyze the Bible and Anglicanism with the full force of their intelligences, the ministers, in the spirit of Latitudinarianism, were prepared to allow differences of opinion on points of theology not central to Christianity. Latitudinarians insisted that the really important teachings of Christianity--the existence of God, the sacrifice of Christ, the authority of the Scriptures, life after death--were few in

---

[1] Thomas Cradock, Sermon on Matthew 11:5, preached Christmas, 1754, in the Cradock Collection, MdDC.

number, and they were not disposed to demand uniformity on debatable
doctrinal minutiae. Anxious to prevent theological controversy and to
forestall possible schisms, they preached the virtues of practical toleration. Thomas Cradock spoke for many clergy when he declared that "when
the Fundamentals of Religion are well secur'd; then to be overtenacious in
matters of l[e]ss Moment is not to Serve the Causes of God & Truth, but
our own Passions and Prejudices & private Interests."[1] The Maryland Church
could not afford internal strife.

Whenever possible the ministers avoided doctrinal exposition and
concentrated on teaching their parishioners to behave rationally in an
ordered world. Rational behavior was, of course, highly moral behavior.
Man was a creature filled with appetites and passions which, uncontrolled
by the "superior light of Reason," led headlong to disaster.[2] A rational
man was modest, charitable, honest, temperate, loving, and hardworking
because he knew that to be otherwise disrupted not only his own internal
harmony but that of society. Unhappily, reason was often too frail to
counter innate drives. The result of yielding to one's animal nature was
vice, superstition, and ultimately slavery. The Maryland clergy were
convinced that the colony offered an unusually large array of temptations,
and that the ignorance of the people rendered them particularly vulnerable.
Inculcating moral precepts and training the parishioners to combat their
lusts and passions with reason were the principal goals of the ministers.[3]

They were also very concerned to maintain order in society. The

---

[1] Thomas Cradock, second sermon on Romans 15:5, Cradock Collection,
MdDL.

[2] The quotation is from a sermon by Thomas Chase on Luke 11:35, in the
Vertical File, MdDL.

[3] The ministers in Maryland were not unusual within the Church for
their emphasis on moral teachings. The Latitudinarians have been accused
of reducing religion in the 18th century to a practical but lifeless code
of moral behavior. See, for instance, Sykes, From Sheldon to Secker,
149-150.

clergy thought of society as an organic structure deliberately divided
by God into a hierarchy of orders. A duty of every person was to
recognize their station, keep to it, and to fulfill the obligations due
from each rank to all the others. Persons in superior stations were to
be treated with respect and deference, those in equal stations with kind-
ness and friendship, and social inferiors with liberality. Ministers
cautioned that only when all stations performed their mutual duties was
society in a state of harmony and was the good of the whole promoted.
Arguing that the divisions in society were not unjust but, on the contrary,
suitable and perfectly rational, the clergy endeavored to stamp out envy,
hostility, and anger among those in the less favored classes.[1]

Several ministers felt it necessary to come to the defense of the
privileges of the upper class. A superior class was necessary, they
explained, because the strength and harmony of the whole of society
required "a Super eminence of some executive or ruling Members."[2] Since
the people in this station shouldered a greater share of the burden, they
should be entitled to a greater share of the wealth of society. Clergymen
pointed out that riches did not protect a person from death and misery, and
assured the parishioners that life in the upper stations was not as glorious

---

[1] A few ministers observed with varying degrees of uneasiness that
people did not seem as prone as formerly to stay in their proper ranks.
George Goldie likened the world to an immense inn, in which God had assigned
proper lodgings, but everybody's "whole Employment seems to consist in
looking out for better Accomodations." Sermon on I Chronicles 29:15,
Vertical File, MdDL. Thomas Cradock preached a long sermon outlining the
correct ways of increasing wealth: moving into a superior economic station
was permissible if wealth was procured "as a due recompence for extraordinary diligence or uncommon skill in some work, profession, or employment
serviceable to the Community of which he is a member." Sermon on Proverbs
13:11, Cradock Collection, MdDL.

[2] William Brogden, Freedom and Love, a Sermon preached before the
Ancient and Honourable Society of Free and Accepted Masons in St. Anne's,
Annapolis, 27 December 1749, (Annapolis, 1750).

as one might envision.[1]

A sense that the Church in Maryland was under siege prompted some (and perhaps most ministers on some occasions) to put aside their latitudinarian reluctance to discuss doctrine. The Church as a whole was surrounded by enemies--Catholics, dissenters, deists, atheists, and those loosely termed "enthusiastics"--but the Maryland Church, the clergy felt, was in particular danger. The Catholic menace was far more acute in the colony than it was in Britain or elsewhere because the Catholic population was larger and the Roman priests were permitted an unusual degree of freedom.[2] The ministers worried that their parishioners, whom they considered, on the whole, astonishingly ignorant, undisciplined, and passionate, were easy prey to conniving, ever-present Jesuits. Thanks to the colony's tradition of tolerance, the various Protestant sects also abounded, and hapless Anglicans were constantly being lured away from the safety of the Mother Church. At the time when the extant sermons were written a new foe, the evangelicals, had appeared in Maryland, and the ministers found themselves forced to counter the "Raptures of Enthusiasm."[3] Less of a problem were deism and atheism, for although these movements were potentially very dangerous from an intellectual viewpoint, yet they had few advocates in Maryland.[4]

---

[1] Sermon on Galatians 6:14, attributed to George Goundrill; Sermon on Job 6:7 and Psalms 119:71, attributed to John Gordon; George Goldie, Sermon on I Chronicles 29:15; all in the Verticle File, MdDL.

[2] The proprietors of Maryland had been Catholic until 1715. The proportion of the population who were Catholic was estimated at one out of thirteen by Governor Sharpe in 1758. Horatio Sharpe to Lord Baltimore, December 16, 1758, Arch. Md., IX, 316.

[3] Thomas Cradock, Sermon on Acts 2:38-39, preached Whitsunday 1767, Cradock Collection, MdDL.

[4] In the available sermons, very little mention is made of the dissenters such as the Quakers and the Presbyterians. Other sources make it clear, though, that they were perceived as a threat to Anglicanism. The omission of them in this discussion is a product of the limited material, not an indication that they were ignored at the time.

Catholicism, the political and religious bogeyman of the English for over two hundred years, was always the most fearsome enemy, especially whenever Britain and France were at war. From the pulpits, in publications, and in open debate the Anglicans lambasted the Catholics for the same sins traditionally attributed to them: the villainy and venality of the popes, the scurrility and barbarity of the priests, and the tyranny of the whole church system.[1] Should it be necessary after this recital to say something about Catholic theology, the ministers felt themselves on very firm ground, for they were certain that Catholic doctrine violated reason and was therefore absurd superstition. The same measuring rod which so marvelously vindicated Anglicanism demonstrated the inbecility of Catholicism.

The evangelicals failed the test of reason as well. Reliance on an individual "inner light" seemed to the ministers to suggest the usurpation of the passions over intelligence. The manifestations of enthusiasm ("idle raptures...which transport some whimsical Men by ffits and Starts, as they think, into the third Heaven")[2] were repugnant to their sense of order

---

[1]Several of the published sermons deal with Catholicism. William Brogden, Popish Zeal inconvenient to Mankind, and unsuitable to the Law of Christ (Annapolis, 1755), is one example; another, of which no copy is known to exist, is Hugh Jones, A Protest against Popery, showing the Purity of the Church of England, the Errors of the Church of Rome, and the Invalidity of the most plausible Objections, Proofs, and Arguments of the Roman Catholics (Annapolis, 1745). Cradock and Brogden preached cycles of sermons illuminating the error of Catholic doctrine. Giles Rainsford engaged in public disputations with Jesuits during the 1720s and he apparently specialized in countering Catholic doctrine. Giles Rainsford to Bishop Edmund Gibson, July 22, 1725, in Perry, Collections, IV, 252. Other ministers frequently mention the problems created by local Catholic priests and Rainsford was probably not the only one to engage in the fray outside of his pulpit.

[2] Thomas Cradock, Sermon on Acts 2:28-39, preached Whitsunday, 1767, Cradock Collection, MdDL.

and decorum.[1] If the evangelicals disturbed the clergy by the very
blitheness of their irrationality, the atheists and deists outraged them
by claiming to be themselves far more rational and logical than the
Anglicans. Challenged to defend their beliefs by "downright Science &
Infallible Demonstration,"[2] the ministers who discussed deism and atheism
in their sermons reveal a helpless rage which suggests that they dimly
perceived that rationality could eventually be turned against them.

The small collection of surviving sermons suffices to give only an
intimation of what was preached to the people. Obviously the ministers
covered many more topics than have been noted above, though the similarities
between the extant sermons and contemporaneous ones from Britain indicate
that the major themes of the period are represented in the material available. What is missing is a body of sermons to show what the ministers
taught beyond morality, defensive theology, and social control. Only a
few examples of this type of sermon survive. Ministers used their pulpits
to advocate special causes (such as Thomas Bacon's sermon proposing the
establishment of a Charity School), to urge the legislature to take certain
actions (James Sterling's 1754 plea to vote an adequate war supply), and
even to discuss politics and current events (Jonathan Boucher's series of

---

[1] Gerald J. Goodwin has written on the Anglican clergy's perception
of the evangelicals. See Goodwin, "The Anglican Reaction to the Great
Awakening," HMPEC, XXXV, (1966), 343-356. The impact of the New Light
sects on Maryland has not been adequately dealt with, though Rhys Isaac
("Religion and Authority: Problems of the Anglican Establishment in
Virginia in the Era of the Great Awakening and the Parsons' Cause," WMQ,
3d. Ser., XXX, [1973], 3-36) is producing remarkable studies on the same
topic in Virginia.

[2] Thomas Cradock, Sermon on II Peter 3:4, Cradock Collection, MdDL.

highly partisan sermons during the 1770s).[1] Had more of the topical

sermons survived historians would probably have to reassess their

estimation of the Southern clergy as intellectual and political leaders.

Outside of his pulpit a minister impinged on the lives of the

inhabitants of his parish in several respects. As a member of the vestry,

he joined prominent local men to inquire into cases of suspected moral

lapses. If the vestry reached a verdict of guilty, the minister was charged

with delivering the admonition.[2] As a vestryman, too, the cleric took

part in making decisions which reached into the pockets of every taxpayer

in the parish. The vestry had the right not only to levy an extra ten

per poll every year to cover routine church expenses, but could apply to

the legislature for additional levies to pay for costly projects such as

buying a glebe or building a new church. When construction costs were

high, the parish ecclesiastical dues could exceed by half the given poll

taxes for the clergy.[3]

In a tradition which dates back to the beginning of Christianity, the

ministers were also dispensers of hospitality and charity. They found

these duties expensive and sometimes irksome. How much they helped the

---

[1] Thomas Bacon, Sermon preached at St. Peter's, 14 October 1750, for the benefit of a Charity Working School to be set up in the said Parish, for the Maintenance and Education of Orphans and other poor Children, and Negroes (London, 1751); James Sterling, A Sermon Preached before His Excellency the Governor of Maryland and Both Houses of Assembly, at Annapolis, December 13, 1754 (Annapolis, 1755); Jonathan Boucher, A View of the Causes and Consequences of the American Revolution: In Thirteen Discourses, Preached in North America Between the Years 1763 and 1775 (London, 1797).

[2] Ministers seem to have been the deciding factors in whether a vestry took its inquiry/admonishing duties seriously. Some vestries scarcely bothered to exercise their judicial authority under one minister but displayed impressive diligence under a successor.

[3] After the mid-1720s the assembly authorized huge levies to pay for construction expenses and other church projects.

poor and how routinely they housed and fed travelers can no longer be
determined, though sporadic comments indicate that some ministers spent
a good proportion of their salaries for such activities. In June 1726,
for instance, Christopher Wilkinson commented that he had lodged and
provided for a man and a horse for at least three nights a week since the
previous March.[1] Jacob Henderson argued in 1731 that to cut clerical
salaries would destroy the clergy's ability to help the poor or to
exercise hospitality, and he noted that clergymen interpreted their
charitable duties to extend further than simply feeding and clothing the
needy.[2] The customary association of the clergy with charity probably
prompted Governor Sharpe in 1760 to put them in charge of one of the greatest pre-Revolutionary charity projects, a collection to aid the victims
of a disastrous Boston fire. Anglican ministers collected at least half
of the ₤2,004 raised in Maryland to help the Bostonians.[3]

If the ministers sometimes appeared rather regal, lecturing in the
name of God, deciding parish fiscal matters, gravely pronouncing judgment
on wayward people, they also interacted with parishioners on more equal
terms as landowners and citizens. A clergyman was as likely as any other
person to become involved in property and legal disputes, and there is
nothing to indicate that they received any special favors from the
justices. In addition to preaching to their parishioners some ministers
cudgeled them, sued them, became their creditors or debtors, did business

---

[1] Christopher Wilkinson to Bishop Edmund Gibson, June 15, 1726, in
Perry, Collections, IV, 254.

[2] Henderson, Fifth Letter to Dulany, 11-13.

[3] The final collection figure is from the Maryland Gazette, February
12, 1761. The returns from individual Anglican clergyman may be found, in
a somewhat unorganized fashion, in the Maryland State Papers, Black Books,
Volume X.

with them, libeled them, and had them thrown in jail, and the parishioners
did the same to the clergy. Some of the most respected and revered
clergymen in Maryland spent days or months behind bars, charged with
debt, trespassing, or disobeying the marriage laws by performing ceremonies
without first posting the banns or demanding of the couple a license from
the governor.

Although the Anglican ministers were responsible for the spiritual
welfare of their black as well as their white parishioners, pastoral
interaction between slaves and ministers was apparently minimal. The
clergy did indeed baptize and catechize slaves, perform marriages for
them, and did offer them communion, but slaves touched by these services
were few. For the most part, the blacks in Maryland were beyond the
purview of the ministry. The ignorance of the slaves (particularly that
of the immigrants) frustrated attempts to teach them the catechism
and initiate them into the faith. The reluctance of slaveowners to
permit the ministers to instruct slaves in religious matters was,
however, an even more daunting obstacle. Ministers persistently averred
that they took special pains to convert blacks but were prevented from
meeting with them and teaching them by masters fearful of the consequences
of education. Even the best people, a minister remarked in 1731, said
"they are very sorry, and Lament that they cannot comply" when requested
for permission to instruct slaves. A fellow cleric agreed that parishioners
thought abstractly that religious training for blacks was "a good thing,"
yet "they generally excuse themselves as thinking it to be impracticable."[1]

---

[1] Henry Nichols and James Cox, comments made during a visitation of
the Eastern Shore clergy, June 16, 1731, in the visitation proceedings,
printed in Perry, Collections, IV, 305.

When ministers did interact with slaves in their roles as priests they seem to have been aiming primarily at conversions, transforming the heathens into Christians, and after baptism had little regular contact with newly-made Anglicans. From reports made to Commissary Henderson and Bishop Gibson during the 1720s and 1730s the number of blacks who regularly attended church and those who accepted Communion was unimpressive.[1] The number may have risen later in the century, but it never included more than a small proportion of the black population.

Social Life

Ministers performed roles in society which extended beyond their professional duties. Some of them were teachers, some were civil servants, and others were cultural and intellectual leaders. Many were planters, a few may have been merchants, and a couple were even doctors or lawyers. Those who had both the funds and the inclination were landed or monied gentry who acted the part. Clearly, Anglican ministers had an impact on Maryland society quite apart from their professional activities.

Christian clergymen have customarily served as teachers in societies which lack a widespread public education system. The Anglicans in Maryland were no exception. Although bold plans for a network of free county schools had been drawn up in 1723, only a few of these schools functioned

---

[1] Bishop Gibson asked in his 1723 queries how well the ministers were converting the "infidels." The answers to this question (in Perry, Collections, IV, 191-231) and the minutes of the two visitations held by Henderson in 1731 (ibid., 304-307) constitute about all the evidence regarding minister-slave relations in Maryland.

for any length of time.[1] Most people were educated by private tutors or

in private establishments. A number of ministers--for lack of hard

evidence the figure cannot even be estimated--ran schools, tutored select

students, or served as masters in what free public schools existed.[2] The

schools run by Thomas Cradock and Charles Lake became well known and

respected institutions. Some of the ministers taught because they needed

the extra money, but there were others, such as John Eversfield, one of

the wealthiest clergymen in Maryland, who must have taught for the love of

the work or out of a sense of responsibility. Ministers who did not them-

selves teach sometimes helped the cause of education by serving on school

boards, drumming up support for the founding of new schools, lending out

their libraries, and writing textbooks.[2] The most interesting scheme to

better Maryland's school system was Thomas Bacon's "Charity Working School,"

which operated in Talbot County for a short time during the mid-1750s.[4]

Modeled on the English working schools, the institution was to board,

house, and educate poor children. The children were to be taught to

support themselves, and part of the expenses of the school were to be met

---

[1] The "Act for the Encouragement of Learning, and erecting of Schools
in the several Counties within this Province" (Arch. Md., XXXIV, 740-745)
ordered a school built and endowed with land at public expense in every
county. Anglican masters were to be paid ₺20 and provided with a house.
The act nominated a board of visitors for each county (at least one minister
was on each board) and granted them supervisory powers. Ministers continued
to serve on the boards of the schools which remained in operation, and they
were sometimes also the masters of the schools. Apparently (no full study
of the subject has been done) most of the schools failed in a few decades.

[2] Ten percent of the clergy are known to have served as tutors or
schoolmasters previous to their clerical service in Maryland. The number
of men who actually did so must run substantially higher. The proportion
of ministers who served as educators during their Maryland incumbencies
may run as high as one out of five or six.

[3] Alexander Malcolm, for instance, wrote a Latin grammar. Maryland
Gazette, June 9, 1757.

[4] Bacon began a subscription drive for the school in 1750 and the
building was finished in 1755; it apparently closed within a year or two.
I have not been able to ascertain the exact dates of operation.

by selling the products of their labor. The rest of the cost of maintaining

the school would be paid through private subscription. Bacon collected

sufficient funds to build a residence-schoolhouse for the children (Lord

Baltimore even subscribed a hundred guineas) but for lack of funds the

school closed shortly.[1]

Only three clergymen held public office in Maryland. English law barred

clergymen from serving in Parliament (with the exception of the bishops, of

course) but did not hinder them from becoming magistrates or justices,

and ministers commonly served on the bench. In Maryland, on the other

hand, no minister ever held a judgeship. The clergy were formally excluded

from the legislature in 1692, when the Reverend John Hewitt, a delegate from

Somerset County, was ejected after the assembly determined that his

presence violated English law.[2] After Hewitt only Samuel Skippon, James

Sterling, and Bennet Allen served in any government capacity. Skippon

worked as clerk of the council from 1721 to 1724, while he was the incumbent

of St. Anne's Parish, Annapolis. His position does not seem to have aroused

any animosity, but Sterling and Allen received their commissions through

interest and the appointments were not altogether popular. An English friend

of Sterling's procured him the post of naval collector of Chester, a

sinecure worth £60 a year, in 1742. Complaints to the Commissioners of the

Treasury and the Customs led to an investigation which condemned Sterling's

---

[1] Thomas Bacon, Sermon....for the benefit of a Charity Working School;
Cecilius Calvert to Thomas Bacon, January 5, 1754, Vertical File, MdDL;
Thomas Bacon to Henry Callister, May 13, 1755, Vertical Vile, MdDL: Horatio
Sharpe to Lord Baltimore, May 23, 1760, and April 20, 1761, Arch. Md., IX,
415, 509.

[2] Arch. Md., XIII, 268, 350, 359, 364. In 1696 John Coode, who had
once been an Anglican minister and who had served twenty years in the
assembly, was also ejected after a bitter fight. Arch. Md., XIX, 435-437,
479, 482.

appointment, but he was permitted to retain the post for life.[1] Bennet

Allen became Agent Escheator and Receiver General of Rents in March 1768

after hectoring the governor and flaunting his friendship with the

proprietor. He lost the post seven months later, to the relief of almost

everyone.[2] The government drew on the education and talents of the members

of the clergy in other ways, though. Jonathan Boucher stated in his

memoirs that during the early 1770s Governor Eden permitted him to manage

the assembly ("and hardly a Bill was brought in which I did not either draw

or at least revise") and to write all his speeches and messages.[3] No other

minister ever claimed to be so intimate with the executive of the colony,

but others did on occasion offer help and advice. Thomas Cradock and

Thomas Chase served as government aides during the 1740s when Maryland

was negotiating a land treaty with the Six Nations.[4] Hugh Jones, Alexander

Malcolm, and John Barclay put their talents as mathematicians and surveyors

at the disposal of Lord Baltimore during the boundary disputes with

Pennsylvania during the late 1750s and early 1760s.[5]

Ministers were participants in and even leaders of the increasingly

sophisticated and urbane cultural life of the colony. First-class musicians

such as Thomas Bacon and Alexander Malcolm composed music and wrote

---

[1] Governor Sharpe to William Sharpe, July 8, 1760, Arch. Md., IX, 437;
Remonstrance of William Burch, Charles Parson et al., September 28, 1772,
Treasury Paper, Fisher Transcripts, MS. 360, MdHi.

[2] Maryland Commission Record, 1733-1773, fol. 208, MdA.; Horatio
Sharpe to Hugh Hammersley, October 30, 1768, Arch. Md., XIV, 536.

[3] Jonathan Boucher, Reminiscences, 92-93.

[4] Arch. Md. XXVIII, 293-295, 305, 336.

[5] Horatio Sharpe to Lord Baltimore, July 9, 1758, Arch. Md., IX, 224,
233; Sharpe to Cecilius Calvert, May 11, 1762, Arch. Md., XIV, 54; Cecilius
Calvert to Sharpe, n.d. but spring, 1756, Arch. Md., VI, 373; Sharpe to
Lord Baltimore, June 23, 1761, Arch. Md., IX, 256; see also Richard L.
Morton, "The Reverend Hugh Jones: Lord Baltimore's Mathematician,"
WMQ, 3d. Ser., VII (1950), 107-115.

musicological treatises in addition to performing for appreciative audiences.[1] Bacon's home in Talbot County became a center for music on the Eastern Shore.[2] James Sterling, Jonathan Boucher, and Thomas Cradock were among the ministers who entertained the readers of the Maryland Gazette with essays and poems. Before he came to Maryland in 1737 James Sterling was an established poet and playwright in Great Britain, and he continued to write in the colony.[3] Thomas Bacon, a man of remarkable intellectual and literary abilities, researched the history of the Maryland legislature and in 1766 published The Laws of Maryland. This work, a compilation of the legislation of the colony, was one of the most famous pre-Revolutionary books and is still used today.[4] Benjamin Franklin's friend, Archibald Spencer, amazed the inhabitants in a less scholarly fashion. A medical doctor, Spencer gave public lectures on "experimental philosophy" which featured peculiar phenomena such as electricity.[5]

---

[1] Alexander Hamilton, "History of the Ancient and Honorable Tuesday Club," MS., Johns Hopkins University Library, Baltimore, Maryland; The Tuesday Club Record Book, MS. No. 854, MdHi.

[2] This is evident from the correspondence between Henry Callister and Thomas Bacon, preserved in the Callister Papers, MdDL.

[3] J.A. Leo Lemay's Men of Letters in Colonial Maryland (Knoxville, Tenn., 1972) contains a chapter on Sterling's literary achievements and samples of his work.

[4] There were several scholars besides Bacon among the Maryland ministry. Alexander Malcolm produced works on mathematics and music, and Isaac Campbell completed one volume of a projected four volume study entitled A Rational Enquiry into the Origin, Foundation, Nature and End of Civil Government, shewing it to be a Divine Institution, Legitimately deriving its Authority from the Law of Revelation only, and not from the Law of Nature, as hath heretofore been generally held by Writers, from Time supposed immemorial (MdDL). See James F. and Jean H. Vivian, "The Reverend Isaac Campbell: An Anti-Lockean Whig," HMPEC XXXIX (1970), 71-88.

[5] The Maryland Gazette, September 26, 1750; J.A.L. Lemay, "Franklin's 'Dr. Spence': The Reverend Archibald Spencer," Md. Hist. Mag. LIX (1964), 199-216.

Ministers also became prominent members of the social clubs. These convivial gatherings were centers of wit, music, and entertainment. The first minister known to have become a member of a club was William Brogden, who joined other members of the South River Club from at least 1742 to 1754, while he was the incumbent of All Hallow's Parish in Anne Arundel County.[1] His successor, Archibald Spencer, also became a member of this club. The premier Maryland association, however, was Alexander Hamilton's Tuesday Club, which met biweekly in Annapolis from 1744 to 1756. The members of this exclusive club were some of the most talented and distinguished gentlemen in the province. Daniel Dulany and his sons, Daniel, Walter, and Dennis, were members, as were John Beale Bordley, Stephen Bordley, Robert Gordon, and Daniel of St. Thomas Jenifer. The meetings were relaxed and jovial in mood. The group entertained interesting or important visitors to Annapolis, held humorous debates, acted out skits, listened or played music, and otherwise amused each other. Thomas Bacon, Alexander Malcolm, John Gordon, and Andrew Lendrum were regular members or frequent visitors and consorted with the other men as social equals.[2] The Hominy Club, formed in Annapolis in 1770 to replace the Tuesday Club (which had disbanded when Hamilton died) and conducted on the same mirthful principles, elected Jonathan Boucher president.[3] The

---

[1] The South River Club Minute Book, MS. 771, MdHi. Brogden may have joined the club a few years before 1742, for earlier records of the club have been lost.

[2] The Tuesday Club Record Book, MS. 854, MdHi; Elaine G. Breslaw, "The Chronicle as Satire: Dr. Hamilton's 'History of the Tuesday Club'," Md. Hist. Mag., LXX (1975), 129-148; Breslaw, "Wit, Whimsy, and Politics: The Uses of Satire by the Tuesday Club of Annapolis, 1744 to 1756," WMQ, 3d. Ser., XXXII (1975), 295-306.

[3] Hominy Club Records, Gilmor Papers, MS. 387.1, Volume III, MdHi; Boucher, Reminiscences, 66-67.

ministers who were asked to join these great clubs became the friends and
intimates of some of the colonial elite.[1] Besides the purely social or
professional advantages of membership, though, the clubs offered very
gifted ministers the opportunity to show off and exercise their special
abilities.

The social lives of the ministers naturally varied from man to man,
depending on certain conditions such as the location of the parish, the
repletion of his coffers, his social status, and his disposition. The
incumbent of St. Anne's Parish in Annapolis, who lived in the colony's
center of government and culture, was able to lead a life comparatively
rich in social activities and entertainment. Many ministers loved the
life of the capital, but the parish was a poor one and most moved out,
with regret, to take over more lucrative rural livings. The urban life
of the small tidewater towns, however, attracted several ministers who
could have easily afforded to settle down on large plantations. Both
immigrants and natives complained of the loneliness and dullness of life
in some of the rural parishes, particularly along the frontiers, and
tried to ease their pain with trips to the cities and long visits with
relatives and friends. Some greeted the arrival of books sent to them by
sympathetic acquaintances with cries of delight or offered hospitality
to interesting travelers.[2] The clergy in the country parishes sometimes

---

[1] Robert Eden, the governor, and William Eddis, Charles Carroll of
Carrollton, Samuel Chase, and William Paca were among the members of the
Hominy Club. Not surprisingly, given the membership, the club disbanded
in 1773.

[2] The best description of clerical life in a rural parish is provided
by the letters written during the early 1760s by Alexander Williamson II,
the minister of a parish in Frederick County. Howard Papers, MS. 469,
MdHi. Dr. Alexander Hamilton related in his *Itinerarium* how he was entertained by the Rev. Hugh Deans while traveling. See Bridenbaugh, ed.,
Gentlemen's Progress, 5.

worried that for lack of mental stimulation their wits deteriorated.[1]

In Maryland the clergy were permitted considerable latitude in choosing their leisure time activities. Apparently few parishioners were offended if ministers attended horse races, balls, lotteries, or the theater, and they were not usually censured for drinking (moderately) in private or in the public ordinaries. In 1733 one of the ministers' inventories lists a backgammon table among the household items, and thereafter cards, billiards, cribbage boards, and other play paraphernalia appear with increasing frequency until by the 1760s they are practically omnipresent among the clergy.[2]

The increasing wealth of the ministers enabled an ever-larger proportion of them to live in a style which announced to the world that they were indeed the gentlemen they claimed to be. Their houses became large and gracious, filled with stylish and expensive furnishings. The early clergy made do with a few pieces of rude furniture and a small number of amenities, but their successors lived in comfort in homes filled with mahogany furnishings, books, mirrors, pictures, clocks, silver place settings, damask draperies, and imported china and crystal. Until the 1750s it was rare for a minister to own a more imposing method of transportation than a saddled horse, but after mid-century many and then most incumbent ministers were able to travel in their own chaises, riding

---

[1] See, for instance, Boucher, Reminiscences, 52-53, where Boucher says of his friend, Henry Addison, an Oxford M.A., that "his lot having also fallen in a country where literature was not at all in vogue, he, too, like myself, seemed to have renounced all literary pursuits; and reading little or nothing, was degenerating fast into a mere humdrum country parson. After our acquaintance... we did occasionally shame one another into a somewhat better practice."

[2] Inventory of Leigh Massey, St. Mary's County, d. February 24, 1733, in Inventories, Liber 17, fol. 151, MdA.

chairs, sulkies, and even in their own carriages. While the early ministers proclaimed their gentility in their dress with a wig, a watch, and perhaps silver shoe buckles, their successors wore suits of imported broadcloth, decorated themselves with buttons of silver or gold, and carried finely-tooled canes.

During the course of the establishment period a change seems to have occurred in the self-consciousness of many of the ministers. Although the Maryland clergy were always consciously professional men, servants in an ancient and honorable institution, the men who officiated in the provincial ministry during the last few decades of the colonial era appear to have considered themselves as gentlemen who happened to be priests rather than as priests who were—ipso facto—therefore gentlemen. This change in self-awareness was a luxury permitted by economic well-being. Early ministers, regretting their shabby apparel and their poorly furnished houses, insisted that, notwithstanding appearances, their priesthood elevated them to gentle status. Their successors, habitually dressing, living, and amusing themselves as members of the upper class, regretted canonical rules prohibiting them from carrying swords or fighting duels, and wore their priesthood lightly. For these men, the ministry was perhaps less a vocation than a career, less a calling than an agreeable, suitable occupation.

Epilogue

The establishment of the provincial Anglican Church effectively came
to an end on November 3, 1776, when the Maryland Convention in Annapolis
adopted a Declaration of Rights which annulled the ecclesiastical
financial settlement. Article 13, declaring that "the levying [of] taxes
by the poll is grievous and oppressive," abolished that form of taxation
and substituted one levied relative to personal wealth. Article 33
forbade compulsory support for "any particular place of worship, or any
particular ministry." Although permitted to retain all churches, chapels,
and glebes, the Church was not to be granted any more tax money to buy,
improve, or maintain such properties. The Declaration of Rights did not,
however, entirely rule out the possibility of any future financial support
for the Church. The act bestowed on the legislature descretionary powers
to "lay a general and equal tax for the support of the christian religion,
leaving to each individual the power of appointing the payment over of the
money collected from him, to the support of any particular place of
worship or minister, or for the benefit of the poor." No doubt with the
approbation of most citizens of Maryland, the legislature ignored the
authorization, and in 1810 ultimately decreed that any taxation for the
support of religion was unlawful.[1]

By 1776 the Anglican establishment was already collapsing and the
Declaration of Rights was only the final coup de grâce. The resolution of
the lower house in 1773 that the 1702 Establishment Act was void had

---

[1] The Declaration of Rights of 1776 is reprinted in Constitutional
Revision Study Documents of the Constitutional Convention Commission of
Maryland (Baltimore, 1968), 369-374. Article 13 may be found on p. 370,
Article 33 on p. 372, and the reference to the law of 1810 is on p. 31.

destroyed the clergy's faith in the permanence of their preferred status.
The clerical salaries act of that year was due to expire in 1785, at which
time the clergy knew that the legislature would restructure the financial
settlement of the Church to suit current economic and political conditions.
Governor Eden had not proved himself a bulwark of the faith, and to rely
on the new proprietor, underage and head of a foundering regime, to
protect the Church was clearly folly. In 1773 and again in 1775, Jonathan
Boucher, speaking for many of his colleagues, gloomily predicted that the
establishment would not even survive until the scheduled expiration date
of the salaries act.[1] The formal deposition of the Church came as no
surprise.

Ministers began to abandon their livings in September 1775, and if
the vacancies created by the early emigrants were quickly filled by curates,
pulpits stood empty soon enough. Those clergymen unwilling to violate
their oaths of loyalty to the king (sworn at ordination) by promising
allegiance to the new state, as required by the Security Act of 1777, moved
out of Maryland, retired from their incumbencies, or served until forced
to resign. Other ministers joined the armies as chaplains. The men who
continued to serve in the Maryland ministry were generally hired on a
yearly basis by parish vestries, and depended on private subscriptions for
their income.[2]

In 1783 Connecticut S.P.G. ministers chose Samuel Seabury to go to
England to receive episcopal orders. The English Church refused to

---

[1] Jonathan Boucher to the Rev. M. James, November 16, 1773, and
Boucher to William Smith, May 4, 1775, in "Letters of Jonathan Boucher,"
Md. Hist. Mag., VII (1913), 183, 238.

[2] For a discussion of the fate of the Maryland clergy during the war,
see Sandra Ryan Dresbeck, "The Episcopalian Clergy in Maryland and Virginia,
1765-1805," (Ph.D. diss., University of California, Los Angeles, 1976),
chapters 3-5.

consent to the ceremony, but in November 1784 Seabury was consecrated by bishops of the Scots Episcopal Church. Three years later, having obtained the permission of Parliament, the archbishops of Canterbury and York joined other English prelates in consecrating Samuel Provoost of New York and William White of Pennsylvania. With the consecration of three bishops the American succession was secure, for according to canon law that number was necessary to elevate another man to the episcopate.[1] In a convention held in Philadelphia in 1789, the Protestant Episcopal Church of the United States was formed. Affiliated with the English Church but independently structured and governed, the new church repaired the two major faults of its colonial predecessors: it was not dependent on the state for support, and its members were disciplined from within the organization. The body stood alone, but it had finally been given a head.

---

[1] Cross, Anglican Episcopate, 266-267.

Appendix A

The Church and State in England

The relationship between the Established Church and the state in
England following Henry VIII's break with the Church in Rome in 1534 was
intricate and symbiotic. Neither institution was confined to what we would
now consider its proper sphere of action, for each of them defined its
respective rights and functions so broadly that they overlapped one another.
The Church's raison d'être was theoretically to provide organized oversight
into spiritual and ecclesiastical affairs. In practice, this meant that the
Church believed itself divinely authorized to supervise public morality,
exact tithes for the support of its ministers, and to harass and challenge
unbelievers with all available legal means. From the point of view of the
Church the plain duty of the state was to enact the appropriate statutes,
fight the necessary religious wars, and lend the Church physical force as
necessary. Church and state, the spiritual and the temporal governing
institutions, were the twin pillars which supported the monarchy. The
state did not consider the relative positions of the two institutions in
quite the same light. Religious sanctions were an enormous asset, bolster-
ing the authority of a government, and the Church was simply too important
to leave to the Church. Religion was inseparable from politics, and
politics was the business of the state; the English state, therefore,
considered both religion and the Church under its own rightful jurisdiction.
As long as the Catholic Church was established in England the spiritual
institution remained a very dangerous rival to the state, but its successor
was deliberately constructed as a subordinate body. Henry VIII exemplified

the new church/state relationship by proclaiming himself Supreme Head of the Church in England. Thereafter, all members of the new Church swore personal allegiance to him as their ecclesiastical superior, to whom they owed obedience second only to God.

The control of the state over the Church was always apparent. During the first decades of the English establishment, when both the structure and the theology of the infant Church were being decided, the clergy and theologians proposed the new forms but laymen on the throne, in the council, and in Parliament gave final approval to the legal and liturgical framework of the Church. The laws which established the Church and defined the new faith sometimes implied that they had been divinely inspired but no one claimed that the laws themselves were anything but secular, identical in essence to any other laws passed in the kingdom. There was nothing sacred or unalterable about them, even if they dealt with articles of faith or church doctrine or biblical exegesis. The authority of the ecclesiastical laws derived from the state, not God, and they were to be obeyed not because they reflected God's will (though they happily did) but because the king and Parliament said so.

For over half a century after the establishment both the content of the official religion and the limits of the legal jurisdiction of the Church were unclear. By 1604, however, what became known as the constitution of the Established Church was essentially complete.[1] The fundamental theological position of Anglicanism had been formulated by then, a system of canon law had the consent of king and Parliament, and the Erastian arrangement

---

[1] The final revision of the Thirty-Nine Articles was completed in 1571; Richard Hooker's Of the Laws of Ecclesiastical Polity, which formulated the doctrinal basis of Anglicanism, appeared in 1593; and the canons of the Church were agreed upon in 1603 and published under the Great Seal in 1604.

between Church and state, once so alien, had been legitimized by time.
The constitution remained in force (except during the Civil War) with
moderate changes until the reign of Victoria. Ironically, that very close
identification of Church and state which was the hallmark of the relationship proved the downfall of both; King James I's aphorism "No Bishop, no
King" proved true. In order to endow the Church with unquestionable legal
validity, the later Tudors and the first Stuart permitted Parliament to
legislate the Church into existence. The process took seventy years.
Beginning in 1641, Parliament began to legislate the Church into oblivion --
without the consent of its supreme governor. Within eight years neither the
king nor the Established Church existed in England.

The settlement of 1660 restored the Anglican Church for the most part
to its former position. Parliament, this time fervently Anglican, passed
a series of measures over the next fifteen years which were designed to
compel all persons holding office to take the sacrament according to
Anglican practice, to discomfit non-Anglicans by heaping liabilities on them,
and generally to ensure that the government remained Anglican and that the
Church was protected from dissenter competition. The danger that
a Catholic monarch would successfully subvert the constitution of the Church
was eliminated with the Glorious Revolution. By the last decade of the
seventeenth century the relationship between Church and state seemed so
natural and harmonious that Englishmen congratulated themselves that it was
yet another expression of their particular political genius.

Many clergymen and prelates were less appreciative. Between the Restoration
and the end of the century the state repeatedly and very brusquely demonstrated
the complete subservience of the Church. To ministers who sincerely

believed that the Church was a separate but equal order, the truth was
frightening and humiliating. Between 1686 and 1688 Bishop Henry Compton
was suspended from his office by James II for refusing to remove a
subordinate who disobeyed a royal order (the king set up a special ecclesiastical court to try the prelate), and the archbishop of Canterbury
and six other bishops were sent to the Tower for declining to read James II's
Second Declaration of Indulgence. Most unnerving of all, after the Glorious
Revolution six bishops and about four hundred clergymen were deprived of
their offices for refusing to take an oath of allegiance to William and Mary.[1]
William was not able to deprive the clerics of their ecclesiastical status--
that is, he could not vitiate a consecration or an ordination, but he
did remove what the state had granted in the first place: livings and all
temporal power, including the right to preach in benefices and dioceses.[2]
New bishops were appointed to the "vacant" posts. William's dismissal of
the non-jurors split the Church into two bitter factions. Significantly,
though, the disagreement was not in regard to whether the king per se had
the power to suspend or deprive clergymen (for James II had done so before
William), but whether William was the king by divine right and thus could
exercise this prerogative as supreme governor of the Church.[3]

The non-juror controversy touched off other debates centering on the
nature of the Church's temporal rights and its relationship vis-a-vis the
state. Concerned clergymen began to point out to their brethren that the
Church--particularly during the years following the Restoration--had absent-
mindedly given up, or been induced to give up, privileges which it had held

---

[1] The non-jurors believed that their previous oath of loyalty to James II
prohibited them from swearing allegiance to William and Mary.

[2] Sykes, Church and State, 25-28, 285-290.

[3] Ibid., 288-290.

by divine right, medieval statute, or simply custom. Academic lamentations
for lost dignities changed into active efforts to rectify the inequality
between Church and state when contention focused on the issue of convocations
in 1697. Convocations, which dated back at least to the thirteenth century,
were the Church's counterpart to Parliament. They were assemblies of
representatives of the ministry, organized into a lower house for ordinary
clergy and an upper house for prelates. The archbishop of Canterbury
and the archbishop of York each presided over a separate concurrent
convocation. The Church's internal quarrel over the power of convocations
began in 1697 when Francis Atterbury, a clergyman under Canterbury's
jurisdiction, published his explosive pamphlet Letter to a Convocation Man.
Pointing out that convocation had met only once since the Restoration,
Atterbury argued that convocation and Parliament were equal bodies with
separate spheres of power, that convocation should have the exclusive
right to legislate ecclesiastical matters, and that Parliament should
be restricted solely to lay affairs. He demanded that convocation be permitted
to meet as frequently as Parliament. Atterbury believed that the clergy
in convocation should have the right to debate freely and to draft canons
on any religious subject they felt necessary. His vision of a parity
between convocation and Parliament was, to judge by the size of his following,
extremely alluring to many clergymen who were uneasy with Anglican
Erastianism. However, as his opponents were quick to point out,
Atterbury's cause was a quarter of a century too late. In the Act of
Submission of the Clergy in 1534, convocation meetings were forbidden without
a royal writ, and the Church was prohibited from discussing or enacting any
legislation whatever without a license from the Crown. The Long Parliament

passed a resolution forbidding the clergy to convene or make canons which affected clergy or laymen without its consent, and although part of this ordinance was withdrawn after the Civil War, Parliament in 1662 reserved its right to debate the actions of convocation. The independence and important of convocation were permanently destroyed in 1664, when Archbishop Gilbert Sheldon, by private agreement with Lord Chancellor Clarendon, agreed that the clergy would relinquish their ancient privilege of voting taxes on their own body. While the clergy had retained this right, the Crown had been obliged to call convocations periodically, but afterwards neither Charles II nor James II thought clerical meetings necessary. Neither of them licensed another convocation. William III summoned one in 1689, but when the clergy did not discuss the specific issues he advised, it was suspended, and another was not licensed until 1700. For seventeen years after that meeting a convocation almost always met in conjunction with Parliament--probably as a concession to Atterbury's party and Queen Anne's High Church loyalties--but little business was concluded because the upper house and the lower house of the Canterbury convocation became embroiled in a fruitless but acrimonious argument concerning their respective rights. (The York convocation was unicameral and dormant during this period.) The 1717 Canterbury convocation was suspended by royal writ, and with two short-lived exceptions, suspension followed suspension and the clergy did not meet together again until the nineteenth century.[1]

The convocation and non-juror controversies demonstrate not only the subordination of the Anglican Church to the state during the period when the Maryland Church was being established, but also the frustration and

---

[1] For a brief discussion of the history of important convocations in England, see John Henry Blunt, The Book of Church Law (London, 1899), 13-18; for the convocation controversy, see Sykes, Church and State, 297-314; Sykes, From Sheldon to Secker, 36-65; and George Every, The High Church Party 1688-1718 (London, 1956), 75-91.

indignation this unbalanced relationship aroused in many clergymen. In the

pamphlets and books which poured forth at this time another idea was

expressed which also bears on the history of the colonial Church.[1] The

clergy of the Anglican Church were deeply convinced that by virtue of

their orders they were fundamentally separate from the rest of mankind.

They had an ingrained sense that their office marked them off from other

people, and they resented the casualness with which some of the laity

treated them. In its structure and doctrine, the Anglican Church was the

most nearly Catholic of any of the Protestant churches, and never more so than

in its conception of the role of the priest. In Anglicanism, priests were

central to the sacraments because they were the chief vessels through which

God dispensed grace to the people.[2] They were as necessary for the

completion of the rites as wine was for communion. Moreover, they acted

as teachers of morality and faith, extraordinary teachers consecrated to

God for life. Derivatively, no devout clergyman could have conceived of

the Church, the corporate body of priests, as a mere administrative adjunct

to the government. The Church was holy: God decreed both its duties and

its episcopal structure, and since it operated (theoretically, at least)

under his authority and not by license of the state, it was a sovereign

institution.

The size and ordered composition of the Church fostered the clergy's

sense of independence. About 15,000 men were arranged into a strict

hierarchy of position, wealth, and power.[3] At the apex of the structure

---

[1] Sykes quotes from the literature at length in Church and State, 284-313.

[2] For a discussion of the role of the priest in Anglicanism, see John F.H. New, Anglican and Puritan: The Basis of Their Opposition 1558-1640 (Stanford, California, 1964), 70-76.

[3] Francis Godwin James, "Clerical Incomes in Eighteenth Century England," HMPEC, XVIII (1949), 312.

were the archbishops of Canterbury and York, who were the superiors of
the bishops and clergy in their halves of the kingdom. Archepiscopal power
was not solely ecclesiastical. Canterbury held a seat in the Privy Council,
which gave him access to the king and made him a figure of political
importance. Both archbishops held seats in the House of Lords, as did
the twenty-four bishops who occupied the next tier of authority within the
Church. Appointed by the Crown, the bishops headed or supervised a vast
system of ecclesiastical courts, with jurisdiction over all testamentary and
probate cases, the regulation of the clergy, a wide variety of moral
offenses, and violations of church doctrine, codes, and sacraments. In
addition, the bishops were responsible for examining and ordaining candidates
for orders, prosecuting recalcitrant ministers and punishing them when
guilty with admonition, deprivation, or excommunication.[1] They presented
ministers to livings when the livings were in the bishops' gift, and
approved the presentation of ministers to livings controlled by another
agency such as the Crown, a corporation, or a lay patron.

The political position of the prelates, the ecclesiastical courts, and
the internal regulating mechanism of the Church gave the institution a
deceptive appearance of power and autonomy that many were happy to accept
at face value. As late as 1736, Bishop William Warburton considered the
Church sufficiently independent to pronounce the relationship between Church
and state an "alliance." Yet he must have known that bishops were carefully
selected by politicians for their political views as well as their
saintliness.[2] The temporal courts could use a writ of prohibition to bar any

---

[1] Wilson, ed., Constitutions and Canons, Canons XXXI, XXXV, CXXII.

[2] William Warburton, The Alliance Between Church and State (London, 1736)

ecclesiastical court proceedings, and the government could both pressure
bishops into accepting specific candidates into orders and coerce them
to remove ministers.

The Church in Maryland was established during the height of the non-
juror and convocation controversies, when the old cherished ideals of the
Church's independence and its partnership with the state were still dear
but growing unbelievable. In England at least the state was a known
entity, and the relationship of the Church to the state was familiar and
accepted as natural by almost everyone except dissenters and some
discontented clerics. In Maryland, though, the Church shortly found out
that a different state could, with perfect equanimity, accept Erastianism
as its due and proceed to refashion the temporal Church as it saw fit.

Appendix B

Ministers Officiating In Maryland, 1692 - 1775*

Year	Number		Year	Number
1692	7		1735	35
1693	6		1736	34
1694	8		1737	35
1695	9		1738	36
1696	10		1739	40
1697	12		1740	37
1698	20		1741	35
1699	15		1742	41
1700	18		1743	38
1701	21		1744	41
1702	18		1745	42
1703	21		1746	40
1704	20		1747	36
1705	19		1748	38
1706	19		1749	40
1707	16		1750	41
1708	20		1751	40
1709	20		1752	40
1710	19		1753	42
1711	22		1754	39
1712	25		1755	41
1713	28		1756	41
1714	24		1757	43
1715	24		1758	42
1716	24		1759	42
1717	24		1760	42
1718	26		1761	44
1719	25		1762	45
1720	25		1763	43
1721	28		1764	40
1722	28		1765	41
1723	25		1766	46
1724	28		1767	49
1725	27		1768	50
1726	32		1769	55
1727	31		1770	56
1728	34		1771	55
1729	33		1772	55
1730	34		1773	53
1731	35		1774	52
1732	37		1775	52
1733	37			
1734	37			

* All ministers who served in Maryland over two months of any given year are included in these annual figures.

Appendix C

Ministers Accused of Irregular Conduct

Date of Accusation(s)	Minister Charged	Accusation	Weight of Evidence	Result
1692	John Lillingston	one episode of excessive drinking	inconclusive	acquitted by council
1698	Nicholas Moreau	"unfit for employment"	insubstantial	
1698	James Clayland	"scandalous and not Qualify'd"	insubstantial	
1698	George Tubman	bigamy/fornication	guilty of fornication and breach of promise	suspended
1702-1704	Joseph Holt	adultery, drunkenness, fighting	probably guilty of all charges	deprived
1714-1732	William Tibbs	negligence, drinking, swearing, etc.	probably guilty of most charges	suspended from North Carolina parish
1717	William Wye	forgery, theft	conclusive	left Maryland
1718	Thomas Baylie	drunkenness, quarreling, swearing	quite conclusive	
1718	Henry Hall	one period of excessive drinking	inconclusive	
1720	Thomas Howell	general irregular conduct	conclusive	admonished
1720s	James Williamson	general negligence, immorality	substantial	reformed
1720s	Thomas Phillips	murder, fornication, negligence, etc.	for murder, inconclusive; was probably guilty of other charges	
1724	John Donaldson	drinking, general irregular conduct	inconclusive	
1724	William Maconchie	drinking, general irregular conduct	inconclusive	
1720s	Thomas Thomson	general irregular conduct	probably guilty	
1730s	Theodore Eudras Edzard	general irregular conduct	probably guilty	
1730-1731	John Urmston	drunkenness, negligence	conclusive	deprived
1735	Richard Chase	freethinking, lack of learning	inconclusive	
1730s, 1740s	Nathaniel Morrell	drunkenness, negligence	conclusive	
1740s	Archibald Spencer	deism	inconclusive	
1740s	Hamilton Bell 1	fornication	seems conclusive	occurred before ordination

Date of Accusation(s)	Minister Charged	Accusation	Weight of Evidence	Result
1749-1750	Thomas Johnston	drinking, lack of learning	inconclusive	never inducted
1752-1753	Matthias Harris	forgery, fraud	conclusive	denied induction for many years
1740s-1760s	Nathaniel Whittaker	general unfitness	conclusive	
1750s-1760s	Thomas Chase	excessive litigiousness, fighting	conclusive	
1750s	Walter Chalmers	drinking	inconclusive	
1750s	George Cooke	murder	inconclusive	
1760s	Francis Lauder	adultery	was innocent	
1760s	William McClenaghan	schismatic	conclusive	
1760(?)	Alexander Williamson II	sexual improprieties	was innocent	
1766	James Cosgreve	drunkenness, unfitness	charges probably true	never inducted
1768	Neil McCallum	drunkenness, negligence	fairly conclusive	resigned
1768	Andrew Lendrum	adultery, drinking	probably incorrect identification for adultery charge; other uncertain	
1768	Richard Brown	murder	probably guilty	inquest inconclusive
1760s	Bennet Allen	fornication, negligence, drinking	probably not guilty of specific charge of fornication	